ENGLISH
FOR EVERYONE

INGLÉS PARA
EL DÍA A DÍA

AUDIO GRATUITO
www.dkefe.com

ENGLISH
FOR EVERYONE

INGLÉS PARA EL DÍA A DÍA

Edición del proyecto Amanda Eisenthal
Edición de arte sénior Gilda Pacitti
Edición Andrea Mills, Laura Sandford, Rona Skene, James Smart
Edición sénior Estados Unidos Kayla Dugger
Corrección Estados Unidos Sharon Lucas
Edición ejecutiva Estados Unidos Lori Cates Hand
Diseño Karen Constanti, Ali Scrivens, Anna Scully
Ilustración Gus Scott
Edición ejecutiva Carine Tracanelli
Edición ejecutiva de arte Anna Hall
Diseño de cubierta Juhi Sheth
Diseño de maquetación Deepak Mittal
Coordinación de cubiertas sénior Priyanka Sharma Saddi
Dirección de desarrollo de diseño de cubiertas Sophia MTT
Edición de producción sénior Andy Hilliard
Control de producción sénior Meskerem Berhane
Dirección editorial Andrew Macintyre
Dirección general, DK Learning Hilary Fine

De la edición en español:
Servicios editoriales Tinta Simpàtica
Traducción Ismael Belda
Coordinación de proyecto Helena Peña
Dirección editorial Elsa Vicente

Publicado en Estados Unidos en 2024 por DK Publishing,
1745 Broadway, 20th Floor, New York, NY 10019
Parte de Penguin Random House LLC

ISBN: 978-0-5938-4801-2

Los libros de DK pueden adquirirse con un descuento especial
para ventas promocionales, regalo, patrocinios o uso educativo.
Para más detalles, contactar con: DK Publishing Special Markets,
1745 Broadway, 20th Floor, New York, NY 10019
SpecialSales@dk.com

Impreso y encuadernado en Eslovaquia

www.dkespañol.com

Este libro se ha impreso con papel
certificado por el Forest Stewardship
Council™ como parte del compromiso
de DK por un futuro sostenible.
Más información: **www.dk.com/uk/
information/sustainability**

Contenidos

DE VACACIONES

SALUD Y MEDICINA

MEDIOS Y COMUNICACIÓN

Cómo usar este libro

Con *English for Everyone: Inglés práctico para el día a día* podrás aprender, comprender y practicar expresiones del inglés estadounidense que te serán útiles en una gran variedad de situaciones cotidianas. La mayor parte de las unidades del libro consisten en módulos de conversación, con diálogos ilustrados que ponen las expresiones en su contexto y con ejercicios prácticos. Escucha el audio en la web, repite las palabras y expresiones en voz alta y haz los ejercicios para reforzar lo que has aprendido. Encontrarás las respuestas de los ejercicios al final del libro.

Número de unidad El libro se organiza en unidades temáticas.

Módulos de conversación Las conversaciones se organizan en módulos que cubren distintas situaciones.

Ejercicios prácticos La mayor parte de las unidades incluyen ejercicios de escuchar y hablar.

Número de ejercicio Cada ejercicio se identifica con un número propio. Así te será fácil encontrar su audio.

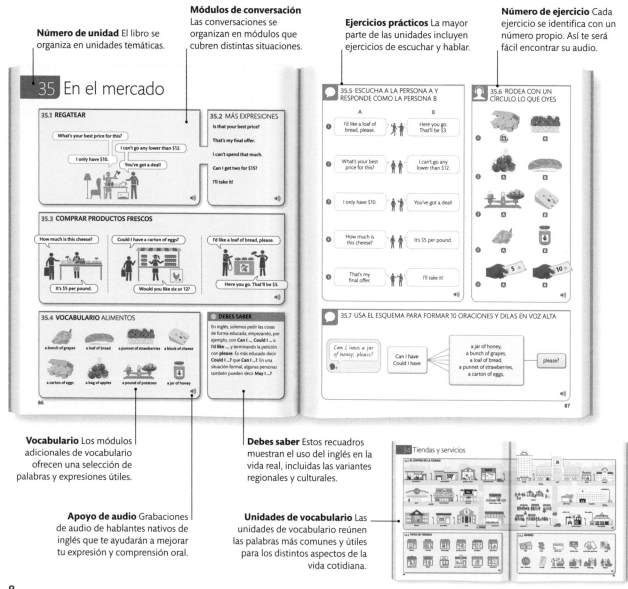

Vocabulario Los módulos adicionales de vocabulario ofrecen una selección de palabras y expresiones útiles.

Apoyo de audio Grabaciones de audio de hablantes nativos de inglés que te ayudarán a mejorar tu expresión y comprensión oral.

Debes saber Estos recuadros muestran el uso del inglés en la vida real, incluidas las variantes regionales y culturales.

Unidades de vocabulario Las unidades de vocabulario reúnen las palabras más comunes y útiles para los distintos aspectos de la vida cotidiana.

Ejercicios prácticos

Los módulos de conversación van seguidos de ejercicios de comprensión y expresión oral. Hazlos para comprobar que comprendes los diálogos, memorizar las nuevas expresiones y mejorar tu fluidez oral. Tienes las respuestas al final del libro.

Ejercicio de escucha Este símbolo indica que debes escuchar una pista de audio para responder a las preguntas del ejercicio.

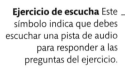

35.6 RODEA CON UN CÍRCULO LO QUE OYES

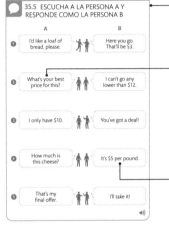

35.5 ESCUCHA A LA PERSONA A Y RESPONDE COMO LA PERSONA B

Ejercicio de comprensión y expresión oral Consiste en escuchar los diálogos y repetirlos.

Escucha a la persona A Escucha la primera parte de la conversación en la pista de audio.

Responde como persona B En respuesta a la persona A, lee en voz alta el texto de la persona B. Tapa los diálogos para ponerte a prueba.

Ejercicio de expresión oral Este símbolo indica que debes decir las respuestas en voz alta.

95.7 DI LAS ORACIONES EN VOZ ALTA, LLENANDO LOS ESPACIOS EN BLANCO CON LAS PALABRAS DEL PANEL

Rellena los espacios Busca en el panel la palabra que falta y di la frase completa en voz alta.

Audio

Este libro ofrece abundantes recursos de audio de apoyo. Todas las palabras y expresiones de los módulos de conversación y vocabulario están grabadas y pueden reproducirse, ponerse en pausa y repetirse tantas veces como se desee.

AUDIO DE APOYO Este símbolo indica que dispones de material de audio adicional de apoyo a un módulo o ejercicio.

EJERCICIOS DE ESCUCHA Este símbolo indica que debes escuchar una pista de audio para responder a las preguntas del ejercicio.

AUDIO GRATUITO www.dkefe.com

Para acceder al audio, entra en la web y elige la opción de **inglés estadounidense**.

Respuestas

La mayoría de los ejercicios incluyen respuestas para que compruebes si has comprendido y recordado las frases y expresiones aprendidas.

Respuestas Al final del libro encontrarás las respuestas de los ejercicios.

Números de ejercicio Estos números corresponden a los de los módulos de los distintos ejercicios.

Audio Este símbolo te indica que también puedes escuchar las respuestas.

Saludos

1.1 SALUDOS INFORMALES

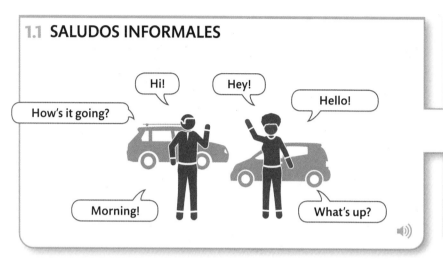

1.2 MÁS EXPRESIONES

Hello there!

Evening, all!

Hey, everyone!

Long time no see!

It's been a while!

1.3 SALUDOS FORMALES

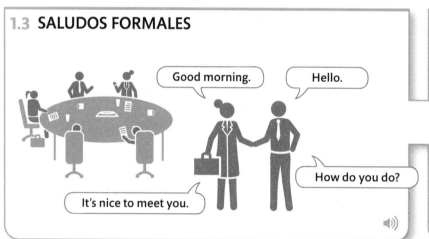

1.4 MÁS EXPRESIONES

Good afternoon.

Good evening.

It's a pleasure to meet you.

It's nice to meet you all.

It's great to meet face to face!

1.5 INTERCAMBIAR SALUDOS

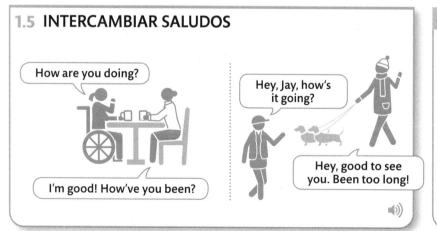

DEBES SABER

En inglés informal, oirás a menudo los saludos en su forma abreviada, como en **How've you been?**, que suena más natural que la forma larga, **How have you been?** También es frecuente omitir **It's** antes de expresiones como **Great to see you**, **Nice to meet you** y **Been too long!**

1.6 ESCUCHA A LA PERSONA A Y RESPONDE COMO LA PERSONA B

A   **B**

1 How are you doing? → I'm good! How've you been?

2 Hey, Jay, how's it going? → Hey, good to see you. Been too long!

3 Morning! → What's up?

4 Good morning. → Hello.

5 It's nice to meet you. → How do you do?

1.7 ESCUCHA Y NUMERA LAS ORACIONES EN EL ORDEN EN QUE LAS OYES

A Morning! ☐

B Evening, all! ☐

C It's nice to meet you all. ☐

D Long time no see! ☐

E How do you do? ☐

F It's been a while! ☐

G Hello there! ☐ 1

H It's a pleasure to meet you. ☐

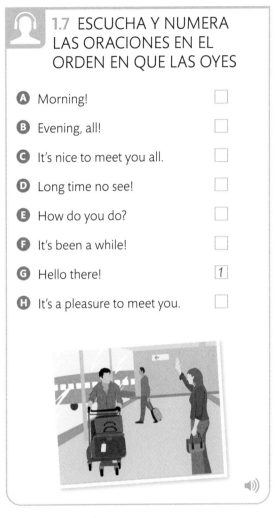

1.8 DI LAS ORACIONES EN VOZ ALTA, LLENANDO LOS ESPACIOS EN BLANCO CON LAS PALABRAS DEL PANEL

doing	afternoon	time	meet	Hey	going	Good	do

1 How do you _____ ?

2 _____ evening.

3 It's nice to _____ you.

4 Good _____ .

5 Hey, Jay, how's it _____ ?

6 _____ , everyone!

7 How are you _____ ?

8 Long _____ no see!

11

02 Presentaciones

2.1 PRESENTARSE UNO MISMO DE MANERA INFORMAL

Hey, I'm Tao.

How's it going? I'm Joe.

Hi, my name's Karim.

I'm Eva. Great to meet you.

You, too!

I don't think we've met. I'm Sofia.

I'm Jasmine, a friend of Jack's.

So nice to meet you.

2.2 PRESENTARSE UNO MISMO DE MANERA FORMAL

Hello, I'm Daniyal Ali.

It's a pleasure to meet you, Mr. Ali.

Good morning! My name's Levi.

Pleased to meet you. I'm Maria.

Wonderful to meet you, Maria.

We have a new employee! Would you like to introduce yourself?

Of course. I'm Samantha, but you can call me Sam.

2.3 PRESENTAR A OTRAS PERSONAS

Aisha, I'd like to introduce you to Karl.

Joe, have you met Ingrid?

I don't think so. Great to meet you!

You, too!

2.4 MÁS EXPRESIONES

This is my friend, Jacob.

Can I introduce my colleague, Kit?

Do you know Sarah, my partner?

I'd like you to meet my son, Carlos.

Have you both met?

2.5 ESCUCHA A LA PERSONA A Y RESPONDE COMO LA PERSONA B

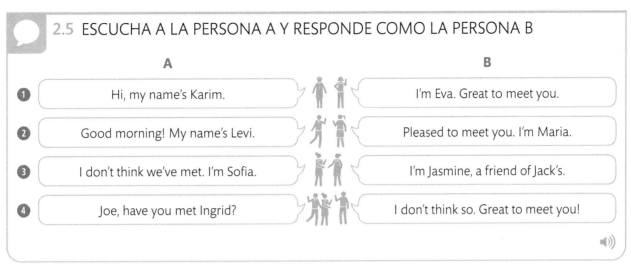

	A		B
❶	Hi, my name's Karim.		I'm Eva. Great to meet you.
❷	Good morning! My name's Levi.		Pleased to meet you. I'm Maria.
❸	I don't think we've met. I'm Sofia.		I'm Jasmine, a friend of Jack's.
❹	Joe, have you met Ingrid?		I don't think so. Great to meet you!

2.6 USA EL ESQUEMA PARA FORMAR NUEVE ORACIONES Y DILAS EN VOZ ALTA

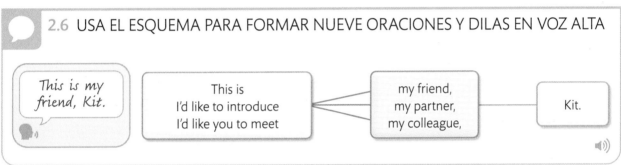

This is my friend, Kit.

| This is / I'd like to introduce / I'd like you to meet | my friend, / my partner, / my colleague, | Kit. |

2.7 RESPONDE EN VOZ ALTA AL AUDIO, LLENANDO LOS ESPACIOS EN BLANCO CON LAS PALABRAS DEL PANEL

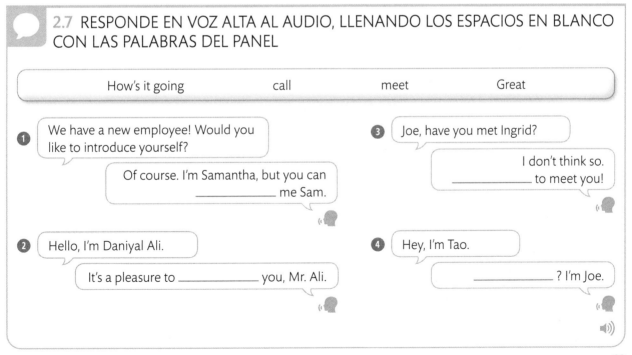

> How's it going   call   meet   Great

❶ We have a new employee! Would you like to introduce yourself?

Of course. I'm Samantha, but you can _____ me Sam.

❷ Hello, I'm Daniyal Ali.

It's a pleasure to _____ you, Mr. Ali.

❸ Joe, have you met Ingrid?

I don't think so. _____ to meet you!

❹ Hey, I'm Tao.

_____? I'm Joe.

03 Palabras de apoyo

3.1 AL COMENZAR UNA ORACIÓN

All right, let's get started!

Okay, I'll weigh the sugar and you whisk the eggs.

So do you like these pants?

Well, I love the color, but I think they're a bit too short.

3.2 EN MEDIO DE UNA ORACIÓN

What did you think of the play?

I **kind of** liked it, but it was a bit long.

How's the new puppy?

He's, **like**, really cute but super naughty!

You must be disappointed with the result.

Yeah, but, **you know**, the team did their best.

3.3 AL FINAL DE UNA ORACIÓN

How was your pasta?

It was okay, **I guess**.

I hate rush hour! I'm thinking of moving to the countryside.

That's not a bad idea, **actually**.

Are you coming to Sam's party tonight?

I'm a bit too tired, **to be honest**.

3.4 TAG QUESTIONS

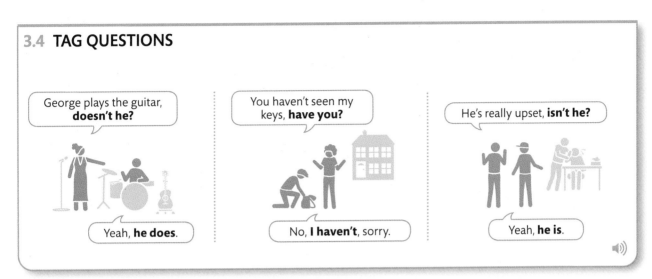

George plays the guitar, **doesn't he?**

Yeah, **he does**.

You haven't seen my keys, **have you?**

No, **I haven't**, sorry.

He's really upset, **isn't he?**

Yeah, **he is**.

3.5 MUESTRA QUE ESCUCHAS

So we've just been to Paris.

Really?

Yes, we saw all the sights.

Uh huh ...

We went up the Eiffel Tower ...

Okay ...

... but it poured rain!

Oh no!

Then we saw the Mona Lisa ...

Wow!

... and caught a show at the Moulin Rouge.

Sounds cool!

3.6 ESCUCHA A LA PERSONA A Y RESPONDE COMO LA PERSONA B

	A	B
1	All right, let's get started!	Okay, I'll weigh the sugar and you whisk the eggs.
2	What did you think of the play?	I kind of liked it, but it was a bit long.
3	You must be disappointed with the result.	Yeah, but, you know, the team did their best.
4	Are you coming to Sam's party tonight?	I'm a bit too tired, to be honest.
5	You haven't seen my keys, have you?	No, I haven't, sorry.

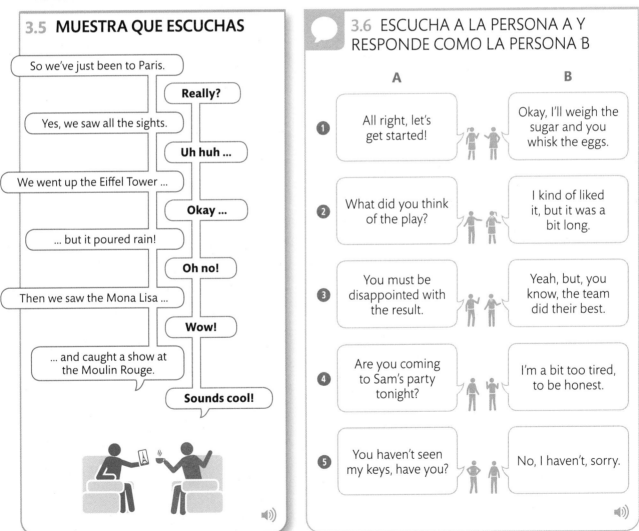

15

04 Decir que no entiendes

4.1 MANERAS DE DECIR QUE NO ENTIENDES

Sorry, I'm not following you.

Sorry, I don't understand. My English isn't great.

I'm not quite sure what you mean.

4.2 DECIR QUE NO PUEDES OÍR A ALGUIEN

Excuse me?

Sorry?

What did you say?

What was that?

Pardon?

What?

Sorry, I didn't hear that.

Sorry, I didn't catch that.

4.3 PEDIRLE A ALGUIEN QUE REPITA ALGO

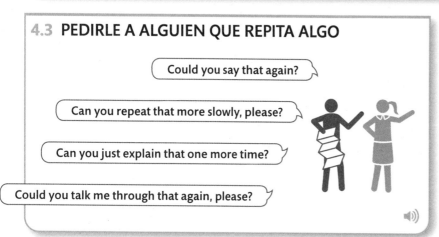

Could you say that again?

Can you repeat that more slowly, please?

Can you just explain that one more time?

Could you talk me through that again, please?

🌐 DEBES SABER

Decir **What?** es una forma sencilla de pedirle a alguien que repita lo que ha dicho, pero puede sonar algo brusco, así que es mejor emplearlo solo cuando se habla con los amigos. **Excuse me?** o **Sorry, I didn't catch that** son alternativas más educadas si se habla con alguien a quien no se conoce bien.

16

4.4 ESCUCHA Y NUMERA LAS ORACIONES EN EL ORDEN EN QUE LAS OYES

A Sorry, I didn't hear that. ☐

B Sorry? ☐

C Excuse me? 1

D Sorry, I'm not following you. ☐

E What was that? ☐

F Pardon? ☐

G What? ☐

H What did you say? ☐

4.5 CONECTA LAS ORACIONES Y DILAS EN VOZ ALTA

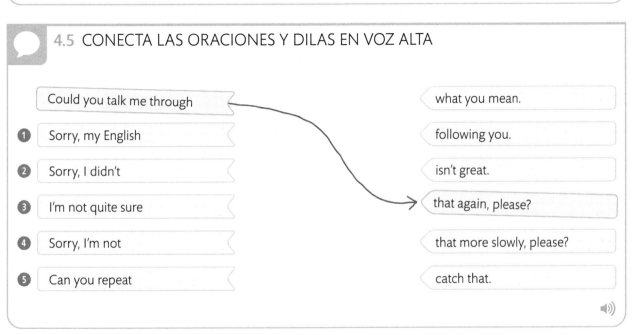

Could you talk me through

1 Sorry, my English

2 Sorry, I didn't

3 I'm not quite sure

4 Sorry, I'm not

5 Can you repeat

what you mean.

following you.

isn't great.

that again, please?

that more slowly, please?

catch that.

4.6 USA EL ESQUEMA PARA FORMAR 12 ORACIONES Y DILAS EN VOZ ALTA

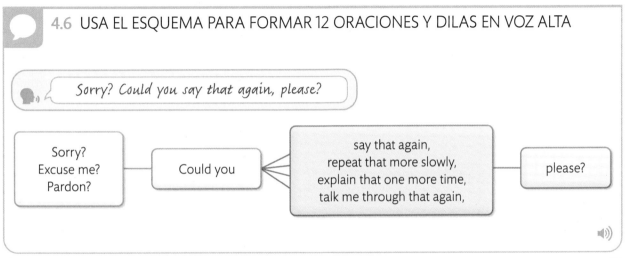

Sorry? Could you say that again, please?

Sorry?
Excuse me?
Pardon?

Could you

say that again,
repeat that more slowly,
explain that one more time,
talk me through that again,

please?

17

05 Opiniones y preferencias

5.1 DECIR QUE ALGO TE GUSTA

I really like these boots. What do you think?

I absolutely love them!

This soup is great, isn't it?

Yeah, it's pretty good!

Are you going hiking again?

Yes, I'm really into it right now!

5.2 DECIR QUE ALGO NO TE GUSTA

Interested in going out for sushi tonight?

Hmm ... I'm not much of a sushi fan.

We're heading to the skate park—wanna come?

No, I'm good. Skateboarding isn't really my thing.

Are you into horror movies?

No way! I can't stand them.

5.3 MÁS EXPRESIONES

I'm a big fan!

It's so my thing!

I've always loved it.

I'm just not really into it.

I'm not that excited about it.

I couldn't think of anything worse!

DEBES SABER

Se puede decir **No way!** para oponerse a algo. Si alguien pregunta **Do you like oysters?** puedes responder **No way! They're gross!** Esta expresión también puede utilizarse para expresar sorpresa: **No way! I can't believe he said that!**

5.4 ESCUCHA A LA PERSONA A Y RESPONDE COMO LA PERSONA B

A   **B**

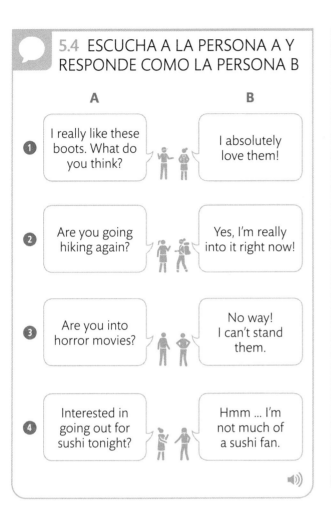

1. I really like these boots. What do you think? — I absolutely love them!

2. Are you going hiking again? — Yes, I'm really into it right now!

3. Are you into horror movies? — No way! I can't stand them.

4. Interested in going out for sushi tonight? — Hmm ... I'm not much of a sushi fan.

5.5 DI LAS ORACIONES EN VOZ ALTA, LLENANDO LOS ESPACIOS CON LAS PALABRAS DEL PANEL

think	fan	great	into
always	love	thing	pretty

1. Yes, I'm really _____ it right now!

2. I absolutely _____ them!

3. I've _____ loved it.

4. I'm a big _____ !

5. Yeah, it's _____ good!

6. It's so my _____ !

7. This soup is _____ , isn't it?

8. What do you _____ ?

5.6 CONECTA LAS ORACIONES Y DILAS EN VOZ ALTA

I'm just not really   →   into it.

1. I'm not much of   a sushi fan.

2. Skateboarding isn't really   my thing.

3. No way! I can't   anything worse!

4. I couldn't think of   stand them.

5.7 DAR TU OPINIÓN DE MANERA FORMAL

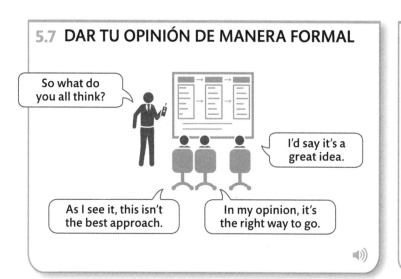

So what do you all think?

I'd say it's a great idea.

As I see it, this isn't the best approach.

In my opinion, it's the right way to go.

5.8 MÁS EXPRESIONES

What's your view?

What's your opinion on this?

How do you feel about it?

I feel like ...

As far as I'm concerned ...

5.9 EXPRESAR PREFERENCIAS

What do you want? Pizza or tacos?

I'd prefer tacos to pizza.

I don't mind tacos, but I'd prefer pizza.

I'd much rather have tacos.

I'd rather have tacos, too.

I'd definitely go for pizza.

5.10 EXPRESAR INDIFERENCIA

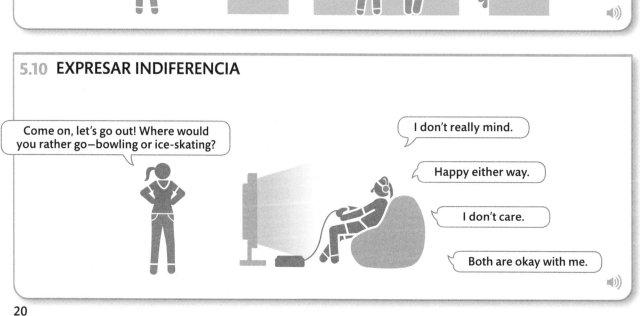

Come on, let's go out! Where would you rather go—bowling or ice-skating?

I don't really mind.

Happy either way.

I don't care.

Both are okay with me.

5.11 ESCUCHA A LA PERSONA A Y RESPONDE COMO LA PERSONA B

	A	B
1	So what do you all think?	I'd say it's a great idea.
2	How do you feel about it?	As I see it, this isn't the best approach.
3	What do you want? Pizza or tacos?	I don't mind tacos, but I'd prefer pizza.
4	I'd much rather have tacos.	I'd rather have tacos, too.
5	Where would you rather go—bowling or ice-skating?	I don't really mind. Happy either way.

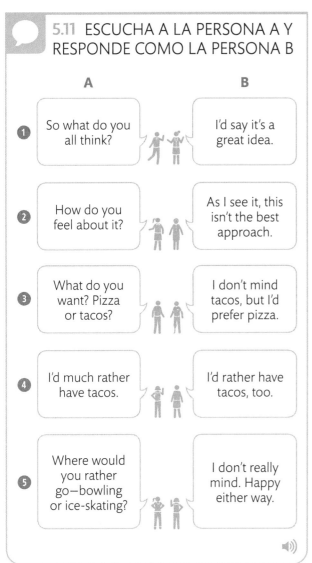

5.12 ESCUCHA Y NUMERA LAS ORACIONES EN EL ORDEN EN QUE LAS OYES

- Ⓐ What's your opinion on this? ☐
- Ⓑ I'd say it's a great idea. ☐
- Ⓒ I don't really mind. ☐
- Ⓓ What's your view? ☐ 1
- Ⓔ I'd definitely go for pizza. ☐
- Ⓕ How do you feel about it? ☐
- Ⓖ In my opinion, it's the right way to go. ☐
- Ⓗ As far as I'm concerned … ☐
- Ⓘ I don't care. Both are okay with me. ☐
- Ⓙ As I see it, this isn't the best approach. ☐

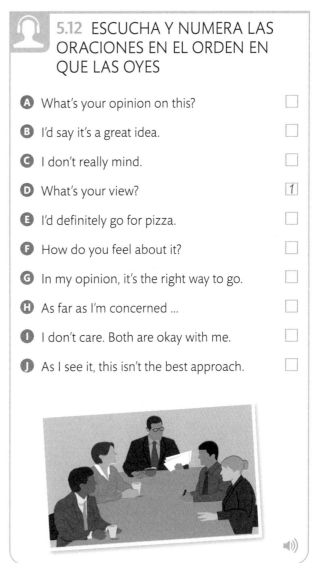

5.13 USA EL ESQUEMA PARA FORMAR OCHO ORACIONES Y DILAS EN VOZ ALTA

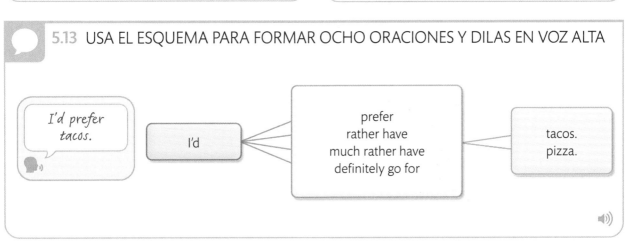

I'd prefer tacos.

I'd	prefer / rather have / much rather have / definitely go for	tacos. / pizza.

06 Estar de acuerdo y discrepar

6.1 ESTAR DE ACUERDO CON ALGO

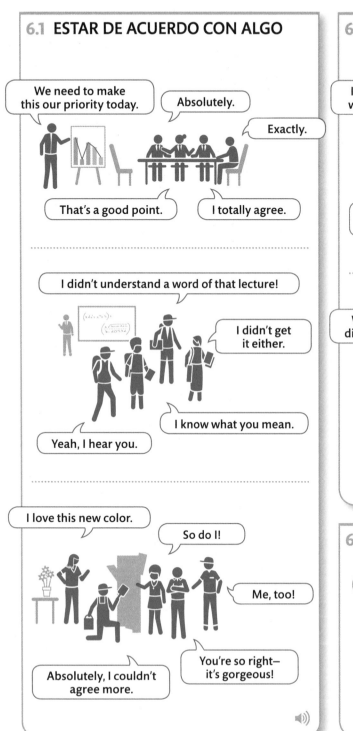

6.2 DISCREPAR DE ALGO

6.3 ACEPTAR EL DESACUERDO

6.4 ESCUCHA A LA PERSONA A Y RESPONDE COMO LA PERSONA B

A		B
1 We need to make this our priority today.		I totally agree.
2 I didn't understand a word of that lecture!		I know what you mean.
3 I thought this book was really inspiring.		Nah, it didn't do it for me.
4 Well, I think she did the right thing.		Do you? I'm not so sure ...

6.5 USA EL ESQUEMA PARA FORMAR 12 ORACIONES Y DILAS EN VOZ ALTA

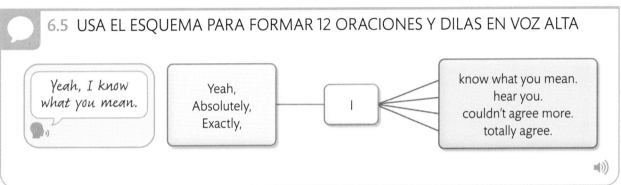

Yeah, I know what you mean.

Yeah,
Absolutely,
Exactly,

I

know what you mean.
hear you.
couldn't agree more.
totally agree.

6.6 CONECTA LAS ORACIONES Y DILAS EN VOZ ALTA

I'm not convinced,   agree more.

1 Absolutely, I couldn't   to disagree on this!

2 I don't think   what you mean.

3 I know   to be honest ...

4 We might have to agree   with you on this one.

5 Sorry, I'm not   so either.

23

07 Hacer sugerencias

7.1 HACER PLANES

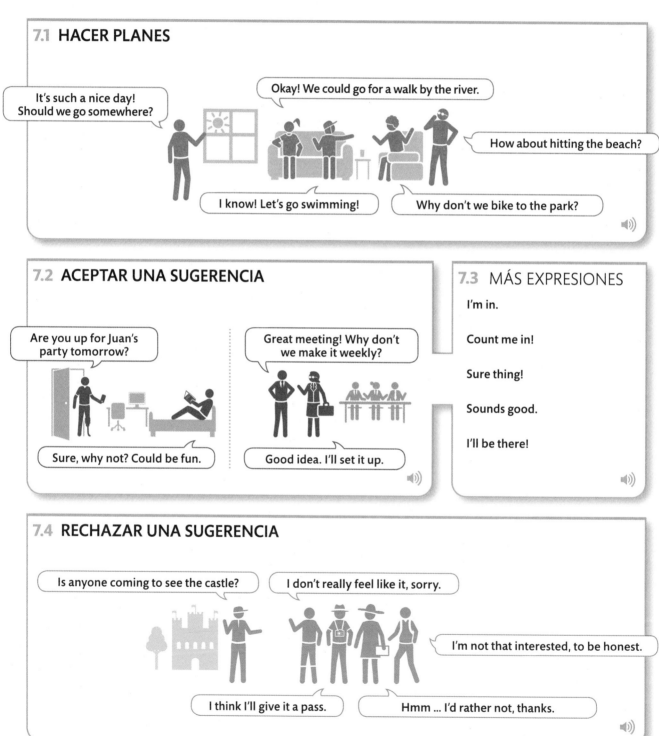

It's such a nice day! Should we go somewhere?

Okay! We could go for a walk by the river.

How about hitting the beach?

I know! Let's go swimming!

Why don't we bike to the park?

7.2 ACEPTAR UNA SUGERENCIA

Are you up for Juan's party tomorrow?

Great meeting! Why don't we make it weekly?

Sure, why not? Could be fun.

Good idea. I'll set it up.

7.3 MÁS EXPRESIONES

I'm in.

Count me in!

Sure thing!

Sounds good.

I'll be there!

7.4 RECHAZAR UNA SUGERENCIA

Is anyone coming to see the castle?

I don't really feel like it, sorry.

I'm not that interested, to be honest.

I think I'll give it a pass.

Hmm ... I'd rather not, thanks.

7.5 ESCUCHA A LA PERSONA A Y RESPONDE COMO LA PERSONA B

A

B

1.
- It's such a nice day! Should we go somewhere?
- Okay! We could go for a walk by the river.

2.
- Are you up for Juan's party tomorrow?
- Sure, why not? Could be fun.

3.
- Great meeting! Why don't we make it weekly?
- Good idea. I'll set it up.

4.
- Is anyone coming to see the castle?
- I'm not that interested, to be honest.

5.
- Why don't we bike to the park?
- I know! Let's go swimming.

7.6 DI LAS ORACIONES EN VOZ ALTA, LLENANDO LOS ESPACIOS CON LAS PALABRAS DEL PANEL

feel	think	Why	interested
Sounds	Count	Let's	Sure

1. _____ don't we bike to the park?

2. I _____ I'll give it a pass.

3. _____ me in!

4. I know! _____ go swimming!

5. _____ thing!

6. I'm not that _____ , to be honest.

7. _____ good.

8. I don't really _____ like it, sorry.

7.7 USA EL ESQUEMA PARA FORMAR NUEVE ORACIONES Y DILAS EN VOZ ALTA

Is anyone going to Juan's party tomorrow?

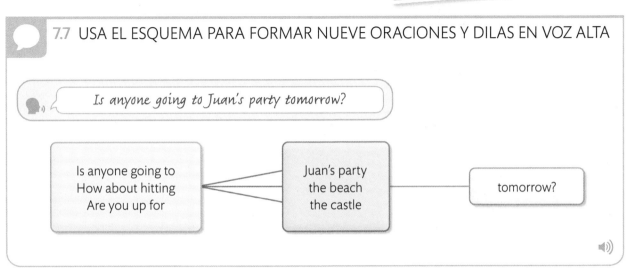

| Is anyone going to / How about hitting / Are you up for | Juan's party / the beach / the castle | tomorrow? |

8.1 FORMAS DE DAR LAS GRACIAS

8.3 ESCUCHA A LA PERSONA A Y RESPONDE COMO LA PERSONA B

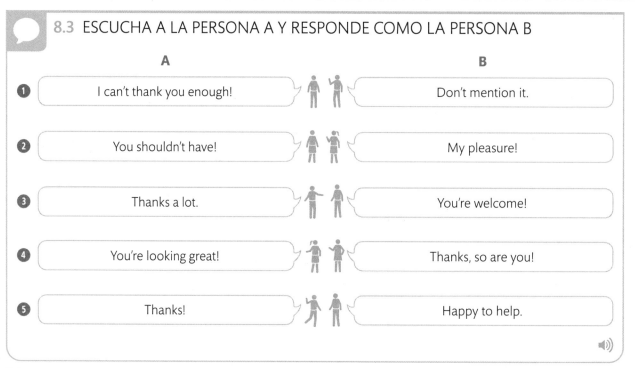

A	B
❶ I can't thank you enough!	Don't mention it.
❷ You shouldn't have!	My pleasure!
❸ Thanks a lot.	You're welcome!
❹ You're looking great!	Thanks, so are you!
❺ Thanks!	Happy to help.

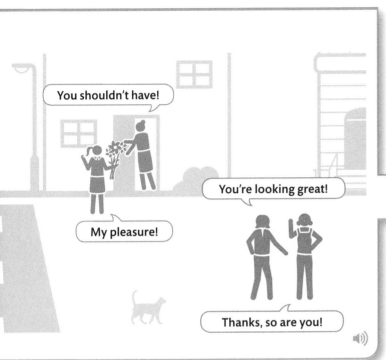

You shouldn't have!

My pleasure!

You're looking great!

Thanks, so are you!

8.2 MÁS EXPRESIONES

Thanks a million!

Thank you, I really appreciate it.

That's so kind!

I owe you one!

Thanks for having me over!

Have a nice day.

Anytime!

No worries!

8.4 ESCUCHA Y NUMERA LAS ORACIONES EN EL ORDEN EN QUE LAS OYES

A Have a nice day. ☐

B Anytime! ☐

C No problem. [1]

D You shouldn't have! ☐

E Thanks a million! ☐

F No worries! ☐

G I owe you one! ☐

H That's so kind! ☐

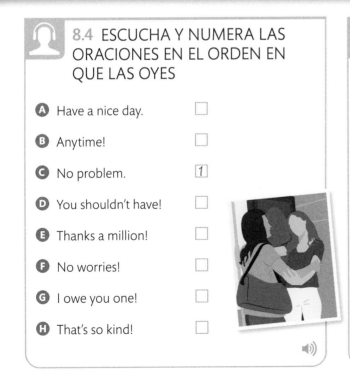

8.5 DI LAS ORACIONES EN VOZ ALTA, LLENANDO LOS ESPACIOS CON LAS PALABRAS DEL PANEL

enough	pleasure	much
	appreciate	mention

1 Don't _____ it.

2 Thank you so _____ !

3 My _____ !

4 I can't thank you _____ !

5 Thank you, I really _____ it.

27

09 Pedir disculpas

9.1 PEDIR Y ACEPTAR DISCULPAS

Oops! Sorry!

No worries!

I'm really sorry I forgot your birthday!

No big deal!

Oh no, I stained your top! Sorry!

It's okay. It'll come out in the wash.

9.2 MÁS EXPRESIONES

My bad!

I'm sorry to bother you.

I owe you an apology.

I feel awful.

That's okay, it was nothing.

No problem, I'm happy to help.

You don't have to apologize!

Thank you, that means a lot.

9.3 EXPRESAR SIMPATÍA

I was sorry to hear you've been in the hospital.

Thank you. I'm feeling much better now.

I'm sorry for your loss.

Thanks, I appreciate you saying that.

🌐 DEBES SABER

Sorry tiene muchos usos. En inglés estadounidense, a veces se dice **sorry** en lugar de **excuse me**. Puedes decir **sorry** para pedirle a alguien que se mueva en un lugar lleno de gente o para disculparte por chocar con él. En inglés estadounidense también se utiliza **sorry** para pedir a alguien que repita lo que acaba de decir: **Sorry? I didn't quite catch that...**

9.4 ESCUCHA A LA PERSONA A Y RESPONDE COMO LA PERSONA B

	A		B
❶	Oops! Sorry!		No worries!
❷	Oh no, I stained your top! Sorry!		It's okay. It'll come out in the wash.
❸	I'm really sorry I forgot your birthday!		No big deal!
❹	My bad!		That's okay, it was nothing.
❺	I'm sorry for your loss.		Thanks, I appreciate you saying that.

🔊

9.5 ESCUCHA Y NUMERA LAS ORACIONES EN EL ORDEN EN QUE LAS OYES

Ⓐ I'm sorry for your loss. ☐

Ⓑ I owe you an apology. ☐

Ⓒ I was sorry to hear you've been in the hospital. ☐ 1

Ⓓ I feel awful. ☐

Ⓔ Thank you. I'm feeling much better now. ☐

Ⓕ No problem, I'm happy to help. ☐

Ⓖ I'm sorry to bother you. ☐

Ⓗ You don't have to apologize! ☐

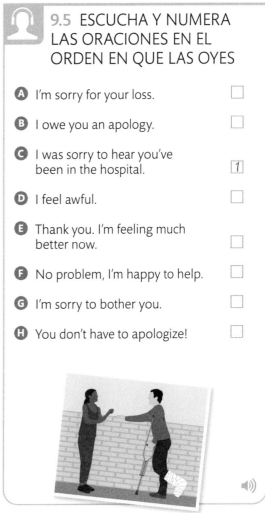

🔊

9.6 CONECTA LAS ORACIONES Y DILAS EN VOZ ALTA

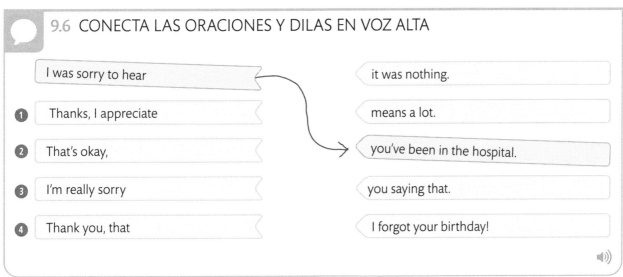

	I was sorry to hear		it was nothing.
❶	Thanks, I appreciate		means a lot.
❷	That's okay,		you've been in the hospital.
❸	I'm really sorry		you saying that.
❹	Thank you, that		I forgot your birthday!

🔊

10 Despedirse

10.1 DESPEDIDAS INFORMALES

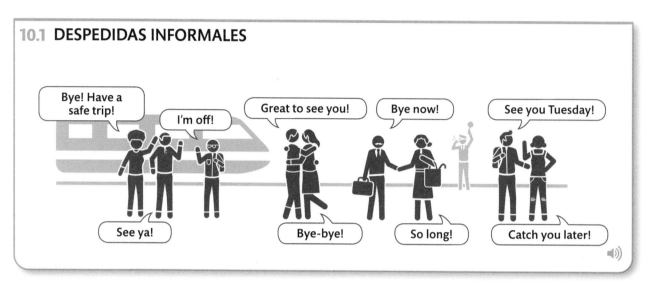

Bye! Have a safe trip!

I'm off!

Great to see you!

Bye now!

See you Tuesday!

See ya!

Bye-bye!

So long!

Catch you later!

10.2 DESPEDIDAS FORMALES

Goodbye.

Look forward to seeing you again soon.

It was a pleasure meeting you.

All the best.

Speak to you soon.

Good talking with you.

Thank you for your time.

10.3 HACER PLANES PARA EL FUTURO

Got to run! See you at the next game?

Great to catch up!

Yes, let's do it again soon!

Definitely. Catch you then!

⊕ DEBES SABER

A la hora de decir adiós, el inglés tiene muchas variantes regionales y culturales. **I should head out** se utiliza a menudo en el Medio Oeste, mientras que **Later!** o **I'm out!** son comunes entre los hablantes más jóvenes.

10.4 ESCUCHA Y NUMERA LAS ORACIONES EN EL ORDEN EN QUE LAS OYES

A Goodbye. ☐

B See you Tuesday! 1

C Speak to you soon. ☐

D See ya! ☐

E All the best. ☐

F I'm off! ☐

G Catch you later! ☐

H Bye now! ☐

🔊

10.5 CONECTA LAS ORACIONES Y DILAS EN VOZ ALTA

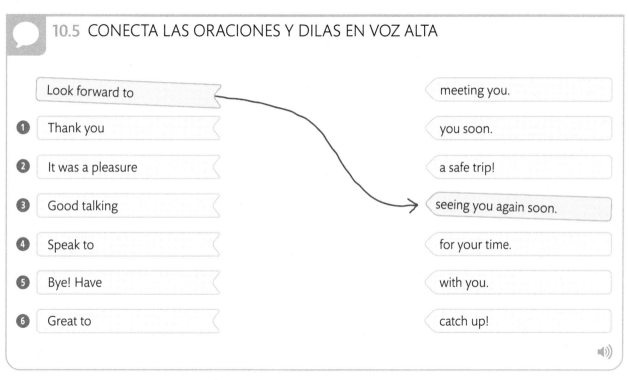

Look forward to	meeting you.
1 Thank you	you soon.
2 It was a pleasure	a safe trip!
3 Good talking	seeing you again soon.
4 Speak to	for your time.
5 Bye! Have	with you.
6 Great to	catch up!

🔊

10.6 USA EL ESQUEMA PARA FORMAR NUEVE ORACIONES Y DILAS EN VOZ ALTA

It was a pleasure meeting you.

It was → a pleasure / great / good → meeting you. / to see you. / talking with you.

🔊

31

11 Fechas, horas y meteorología

11.1 HABLAR DE LAS FECHAS

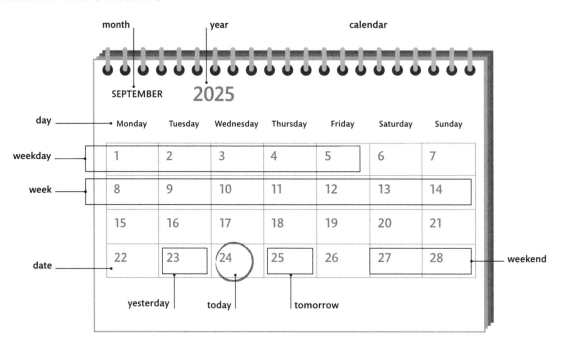

month   year   calendar

SEPTEMBER 2025

day

	Monday	Tuesday	Wednesday	Thursday	Friday	Saturday	Sunday
weekday	1	2	3	4	5	6	7
week	8	9	10	11	12	13	14
	15	16	17	18	19	20	21
date	22	23	24	25	26	27	28

weekend

yesterday   today   tomorrow

11.2 DECIR LA HORA

one o'clock / 1 p.m.	five after one	ten after one	quarter after one	twenty after one	twenty-five after one

one thirty / half (past) one	twenty-five to two	twenty to two	quarter to two	ten to two	five to two

second	minute	half hour	hour

What time does it start?

6 p.m.

🔊

1st	2nd	3rd	4th	5th	6th
first	second	third	fourth	fifth	sixth

7th	8th	9th	10th	20th	21st
seventh	eighth	ninth	tenth	twentieth	twenty-first

 once a week   twice a week   three times a week   every day   every week   every month

1900	1901	1910	2000	2001	2033
nineteen hundred	nineteen oh-one	nineteen ten	two thousand	two thousand and one	twenty thirty-three

11.3 DESCRIBIR EL TIEMPO

 warm

 sunny

 boiling

 freezing

 icy

 snowy

 misty

 windy

 cloudy

 overcast

 pouring

 foggy

11.4 CLIMA EXTREMO

 storm   flood

 heat wave   drought

 hurricane

 blizzard

12 Organizar el tiempo

12.1 HORAS

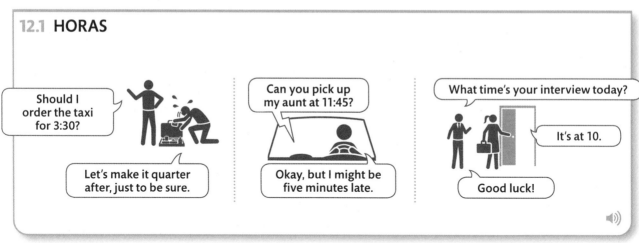

12.2 DÍAS

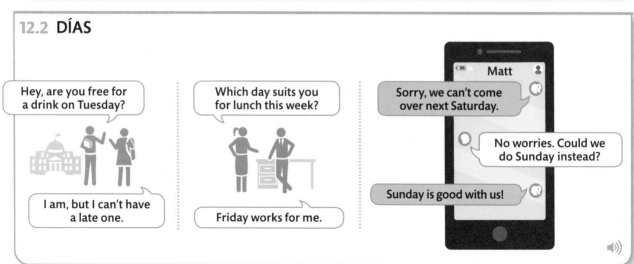

12.3 CITAS

🌐 DEBES SABER

El inglés estadounidense utiliza palabras distintas para hablar de fechas por escrito u oralmente. Por escrito suele expresar una fecha como un número cardinal seguido de un mes (por ejemplo, **May 31**), pero al hablar expresaría esta fecha como **May 31st** o **the 31st of May**.

12.4 ESCUCHA EL AUDIO Y CONECTA LA RESPUESTA CORRECTA

Can you pick up my aunt at 11:45?

1 Sorry, we can't come over next Saturday.

2 Should I order the taxi for 3:30?

3 Which day suits you for lunch this week?

4 What time's your interview today?

Could we do Sunday instead?

Let's make it quarter after, just to be sure.

It's at 10.

Okay, but I might be five minutes late.

Friday works for me.

12.5 ESCUCHA A LA PERSONA A Y RESPONDE COMO LA PERSONA B

A   **B**

1 Hey, are you free for a drink on Tuesday? — I am, but I can't have a late one.

2 Which day suits you for lunch this week? — Friday works for me.

3 So when's the big day? — We've set the date for May 31st of next year!

4 What time's your interview today? — It's at 10.

12.6 DI LAS ORACIONES EN VOZ ALTA, LLENANDO LOS ESPACIOS CON LAS PALABRAS DEL PANEL

works   on Tuesday   next   good
      May 31st   free   suits

1 Which day _____ you for lunch this week?

2 Friday _____ for me.

3 Sunday is _____ with us!

4 Hey, are you free for a drink _____ ?

5 Sorry, we can't come over _____ Saturday.

6 Keep it _____ !

7 We've set the date for _____ of next year!

13 Hablar de la meteorología

13.1 DESCRIBIR LA METEOROLOGÍA

What's the weather like out there?

It's boiling! Over 90 degrees every day.

How was the weather on your vacation?

A bit mixed—the usual sunshine and showers!

It's a little chilly today, isn't it?

Yes, the weather's turned, hasn't it?

13.2 MÁS EXPRESIONES

What's the temperature like?

It's freezing outside!

It's really windy!

Lovely weather, isn't it?

It's very overcast out there.

It's absolutely pouring!

13.3 PREVISIÓN METEOROLÓGICA

Here's the forecast for tomorrow.

It will be mainly cloudy ...

... with a few sunny spells ...

... and a slight chance of showers ...

... with temperatures a little below normal.

13.4 MÁS EXPRESIONES

Today, we'll see scattered showers.

Mist and fog will form later.

There'll be plenty of warm sunshine.

Snow is expected.

Temperatures are above average for this time of year.

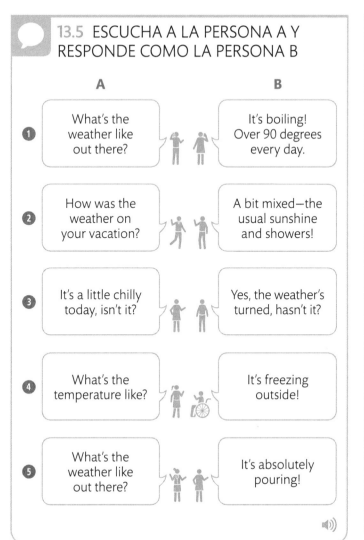

13.5 ESCUCHA A LA PERSONA A Y RESPONDE COMO LA PERSONA B

A

1 What's the weather like out there?

2 How was the weather on your vacation?

3 It's a little chilly today, isn't it?

4 What's the temperature like?

5 What's the weather like out there?

B

It's boiling! Over 90 degrees every day.

A bit mixed—the usual sunshine and showers!

Yes, the weather's turned, hasn't it?

It's freezing outside!

It's absolutely pouring!

13.6 ESCUCHA Y NUMERA LAS IMÁGENES EN EL ORDEN EN QUE SE DESCRIBEN

A ☐

B 1

C ☐

D ☐

E ☐

F ☐

G ☐

H ☐

13.7 USA EL ESQUEMA PARA FORMAR 10 ORACIONES Y DILAS EN VOZ ALTA

It's really windy today, isn't it?

It's

really windy
freezing
boiling
a little chilly
lovely weather

today, isn't it?
out there!

14 Familia y relaciones

14.1 MI FAMILIA

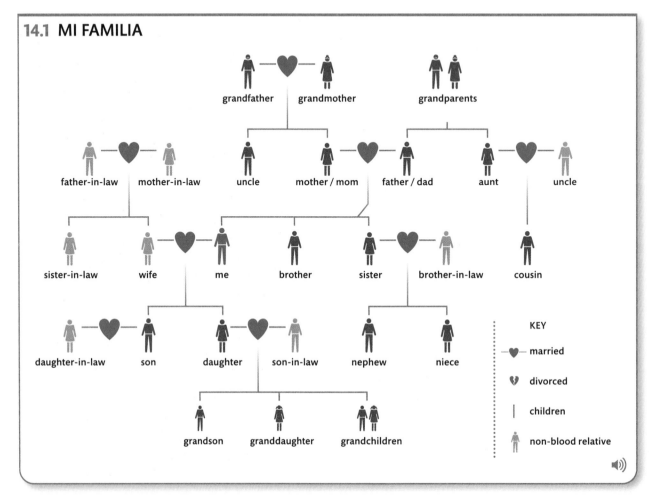

KEY
- ♥ married
- 💔 divorced
- | children
- non-blood relative

14.2 FAMILIAS RECONSTITUIDAS

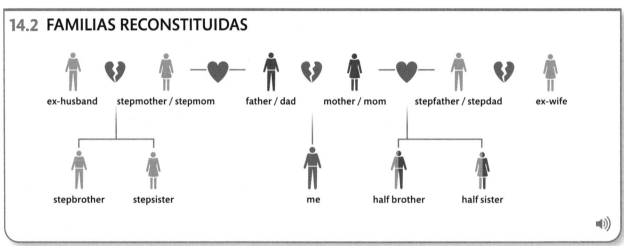

14.3 RELACIONES

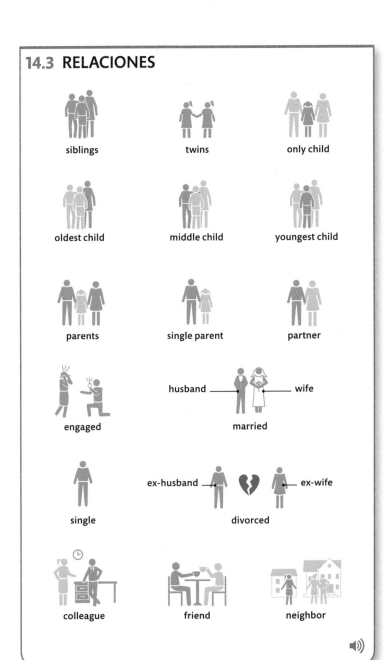

siblings

twins

only child

oldest child

middle child

youngest child

parents

single parent

partner

engaged

husband — wife

married

single

ex-husband — ex-wife

divorced

colleague

friend

neighbor

14.4 HITOS DE LA VIDA

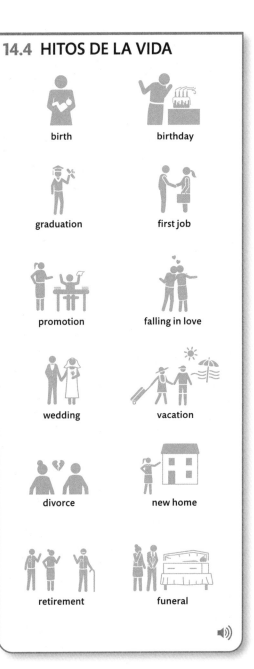

birth

birthday

graduation

first job

promotion

falling in love

wedding

vacation

divorce

new home

retirement

funeral

14.5 CRECER

baby

toddler

girl   boy

children

teenagers

woman   man

adults

senior citizens

15 Hablar sobre la familia

15.1 FAMILIARES CERCANOS

Do you have any brothers or sisters, Tarik?

Yes, I have a brother and two stepsisters.

I'm the youngest.

Are you close to your family, Chloe?

Yeah, I speak to my parents almost every day.

But I don't see my sister much. She moved to India.

So do you have any kids?

Yes, two daughters. How about you?

I have a toddler, and baby number two on the way!

🌐 DEBES SABER

Para referirse a algunos miembros de la familia se utilizan distintos nombres. **Mom** o **Mommy** y **Dad** o **Daddy** son comunes en Estados Unidos, mientras que en algunas regiones les pueden llamar **Mama** o **Ma** y **Papa**, **Pop** o **Pa**. **Grandma** y **Grandpa** son nombres comunes para llamar a los abuelos.

15.2 OTROS FAMILIARES

Don't forget we're visiting Grandma today.

Auntie Dot will be there, too.

Oh, and cousin Henry!

How many grandchildren do you have?

Two grandsons and a granddaughter. I adore them!

15.3 MÁS EXPRESIONES

I'm the oldest.

I'm the middle child.

I'm an only child.

I have two younger sisters.

We grew up in Springfield.

15.4 ESCUCHA Y NUMERA LAS IMÁGENES EN EL ORDEN DE LAS DESCRIPCIONES

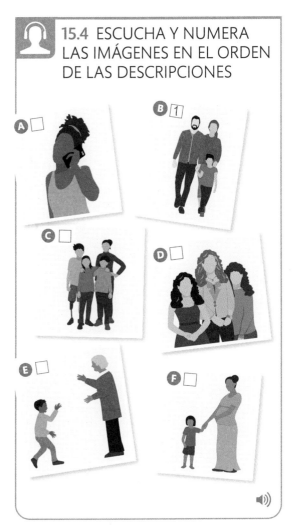

15.5 ESCUCHA A LA PERSONA A Y RESPONDE COMO LA PERSONA B

15.6 CONECTA LAS ORACIONES Y DILAS EN VOZ ALTA

I'm the → middle child.

1 Yes, I have a — brother and two stepsisters.

2 I'm an — only child.

3 I have two — younger sisters.

4 We grew up — in Springfield.

16 Acontecimientos de la vida

16.1 CELEBRACIONES

Happy birthday!

What presents did you get?

I hear congratulations are in order?

Yes, I got the promotion!

Here's to the newlyweds!

Thanks, everyone!

16.2 HECHOS IMPORTANTES

Congrats on the birth of your baby boy!

Isn't he beautiful!

Well done!

Happy graduation!

We're really proud of you!

Welcome to my new home!

Your very own place at last!

16.3 OTROS ACONTECIMIENTOS

Happy anniversary! Here's to another 30 years!

Oh, they're gorgeous! Thank you!

All the best for your retirement.

I'll miss you all!

I'm so sorry for your loss.

Let me know if there's anything I can do.

16.4 ESCUCHA A LA PERSONA A Y RESPONDE COMO LA PERSONA B

A		B
1 I hear congratulations are in order?		Yes, I got the promotion!
2 Happy anniversary! Here's to another 30 years!		Oh, they're gorgeous! Thank you!
3 All the best for your retirement.		I'll miss you all!
4 Here's to the newlyweds!		Thanks, everyone!

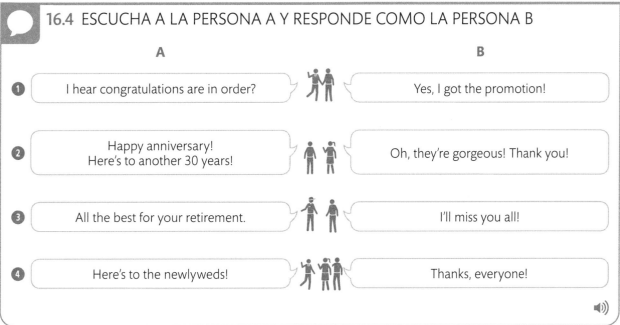

16.5 ESCUCHA Y NUMERA LAS ORACIONES EN EL ORDEN EN QUE LAS OYES

A What presents did you get? ☐

B Isn't he beautiful! ☐

C I'm so sorry for your loss. ☐

D Thanks, everyone! ☐

E We're really proud of you! ☐

F Congrats on the birth of your baby boy! 1

G Let me know if there's anything I can do. ☐

H Here's to the newlyweds! ☐

I Yes, I got the promotion! ☐

J Welcome to my new home! ☐

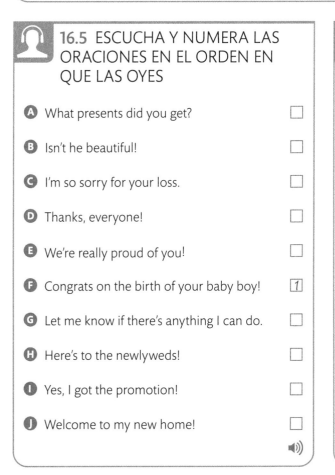

16.6 DI LAS ORACIONES EN VOZ ALTA, LLENANDO LOS ESPACIOS CON LAS PALABRAS DEL PANEL

> proud   miss   done
>
> Happy   best   congratulations

1 _____ birthday!

2 I hear _____ are in order?

3 We're really _____ of you!

4 All the _____ for your retirement.

5 Well _____ !

6 I'll _____ you all!

17 Relacionarse con los demás

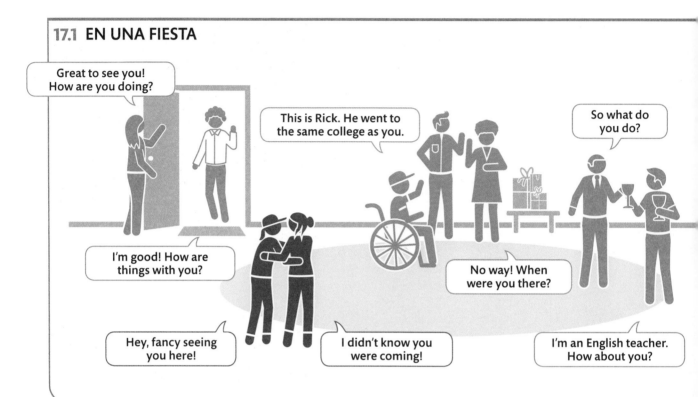

17.3 ESCUCHA EL AUDIO Y CONECTA LA RESPUESTA CORRECTA

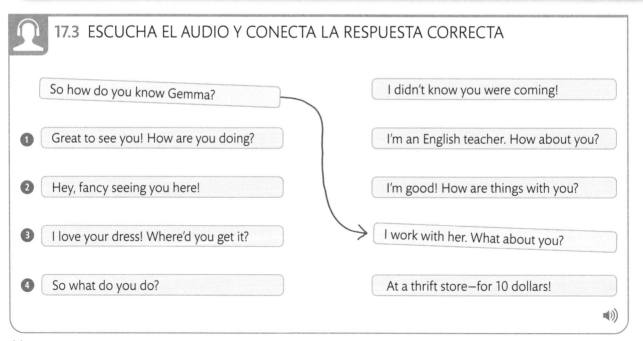

17.2 MÁS EXPRESIONES

How have you been?

How's it going?

What have you been up to?

Not bad. How are you?

I'm really well!

We used to work together.

Long time no see!

You look great!

Thanks so much for coming!

17.4 ESCUCHA A LA PERSONA A Y RESPONDE COMO LA PERSONA B

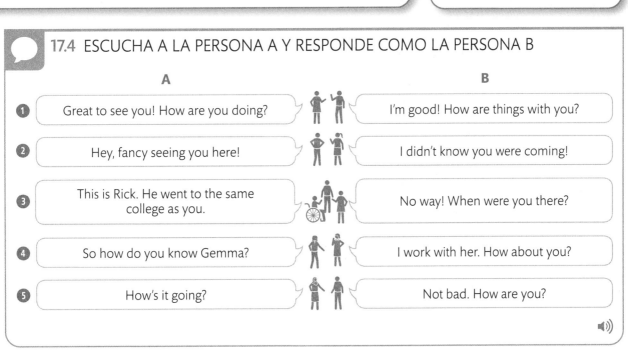

	A		B
1	Great to see you! How are you doing?		I'm good! How are things with you?
2	Hey, fancy seeing you here!		I didn't know you were coming!
3	This is Rick. He went to the same college as you.		No way! When were you there?
4	So how do you know Gemma?		I work with her. How about you?
5	How's it going?		Not bad. How are you?

18 Citas y romance

18.1 PEDIRLE UNA CITA A ALGUIEN

I was wondering if you'd like to go out this Saturday?

I'd love to!
Pick me up at 7?

Interested in going for coffee next week?

Yeah, I'd like that.
Next Friday, maybe?

We should meet up sometime.

Sure, sounds good.

Saturday afternoon?

Cool, I'll message you.

18.2 OTRAS OPCIONES

Sounds great!

That would be really nice.

Sure, let's meet up.

I was hoping you'd ask me.

You took your time!

I thought you'd never ask!

18.3 RECHAZAR UNA CITA

I'd love to take you out tonight.

That's really kind, but I already have plans.

Another night, maybe?

Thanks, but I'm not dating right now.

18.4 OTRAS OPCIONES

I'm not looking for a relationship, sorry.

I just like you as a friend.

Thanks, but I'm actually already seeing someone.

It was nice to meet you, but I'm not really feeling a connection.

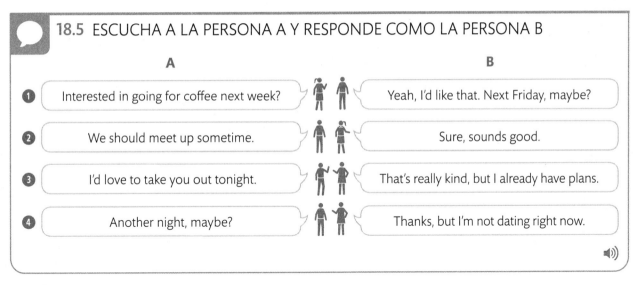

18.5 ESCUCHA A LA PERSONA A Y RESPONDE COMO LA PERSONA B

A	B
1 Interested in going for coffee next week?	Yeah, I'd like that. Next Friday, maybe?
2 We should meet up sometime.	Sure, sounds good.
3 I'd love to take you out tonight.	That's really kind, but I already have plans.
4 Another night, maybe?	Thanks, but I'm not dating right now.

18.6 USA EL ESQUEMA PARA FORMAR 12 ORACIONES Y DILAS EN VOZ ALTA

Interested in going for coffee this Saturday?

Interested in going / I was wondering if you'd like to go	for coffee / out	this Saturday? / next Friday? / sometime?

18.7 CONECTA LAS ORACIONES Y DILAS EN VOZ ALTA

I'm not looking	you'd ask me.
1 I was hoping	as a friend.
2 You took	for a relationship, sorry.
3 That would be	your time!
4 I just like you	really nice.

18.8 EN LA PRIMERA CITA

Hey! Nice to see you.

You, too. You look great.

Thanks, so do you. Should we get a coffee first?

Sounds good!

I can't lie, I'm a little nervous.

So am I. I haven't been on a date for ages!

Me neither!

Have you been on the app a while?

What kind of things are you into?

How long have you been single?

Are you looking for something serious?

18.9 TERMINAR UNA CITA

Thanks so much for tonight. I had a really great time.

Same here. Let's do it again soon.

Yeah, definitely. I'll message you.

That was great. Do you wanna meet up again?

Maybe. I'll call you.

How are you getting home?

I'm just booking a ride.

18.10 MÁS EXPRESIONES

Thanks for a fun night.

It was nice to hang out with you.

Can I call you?

I'd really like to see you again.

I'd better head off. Early start tomorrow!

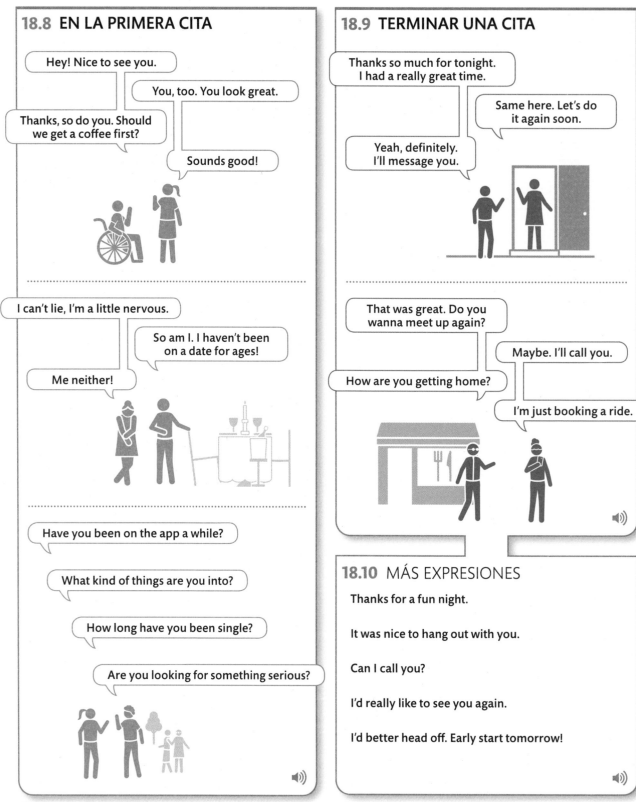

18.11 ESCUCHA A LA PERSONA A Y RESPONDE COMO LA PERSONA B

	A		B
❶	Hey! Nice to see you.	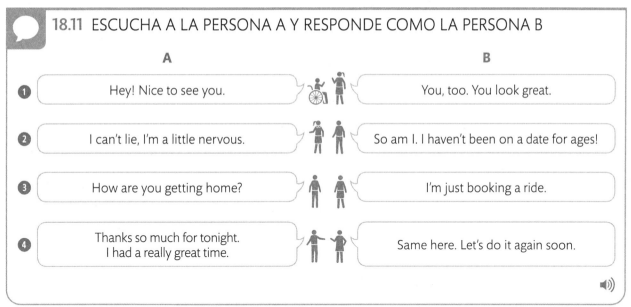	You, too. You look great.
❷	I can't lie, I'm a little nervous.		So am I. I haven't been on a date for ages!
❸	How are you getting home?		I'm just booking a ride.
❹	Thanks so much for tonight. I had a really great time.		Same here. Let's do it again soon.

18.12 ESCUCHA Y NUMERA LAS ORACIONES EN EL ORDEN EN QUE LAS OYES

Ⓐ Can I call you? ☐

Ⓑ Thanks, so do you. Should we get a coffee first? ☐1

Ⓒ Are you looking for something serious? ☐

Ⓓ Thanks for a fun night. ☐

Ⓔ Have you been on the app a while? ☐

Ⓕ Yeah, definitely. I'll message you. ☐

Ⓖ That was great. Do you wanna meet up again? ☐

Ⓗ I can't lie, I'm a little nervous. ☐

Ⓘ Maybe. I'll call you. ☐

Ⓙ How long have you been single? ☐

18.13 DI LAS ORACIONES EN VOZ ALTA, LLENANDO LOS ESPACIOS CON LAS PALABRAS DEL PANEL

> single   again   into
> booking   head   hang

❶ It was nice to _____ out with you.

❷ What kind of things are you _____ ?

❸ I'd really like to see you _____ .

❹ I'd better _____ off. Early start tomorrow!

❺ How long have you been _____ ?

❻ I'm just _____ a ride.

19 Mostrar apoyo

19.1 DAR ÁNIMOS

I'm so stressed. My exams are in two weeks!

Hang in there, sweetheart. I know you can do it!

We're never going to finish on time.

Come on, we've got this!

I don't know whether to try out for the team.

Go on, it's worth a shot!

Yeah, you're a great player!

19.2 OFRECER APOYO

I know things are tough, but we're here for you.

Thanks, guys, you're the best!

You can talk to me anytime. My door's always open.

Thank you, I really appreciate it.

It's good to have you back! Anything you need, just ask.

That's really sweet. I will!

19.3 MÁS EXPRESIONES

Let me know if I can do anything.

I know this hasn't been easy.

We've got your back.

You've been a lot of help.

That means a lot.

I'm very grateful.

19.4 ESCUCHA Y NUMERA LAS ORACIONES EN EL ORDEN EN QUE LAS OYES

A We've got your back. ☐

B Thank you, I really appreciate it. ☐ 1

C I know things are tough, but we're here for you. ☐

D You can talk to me anytime. My door's always open. ☐

E That means a lot. ☐

F I'm very grateful. ☐

G Go on, it's worth a shot! ☐

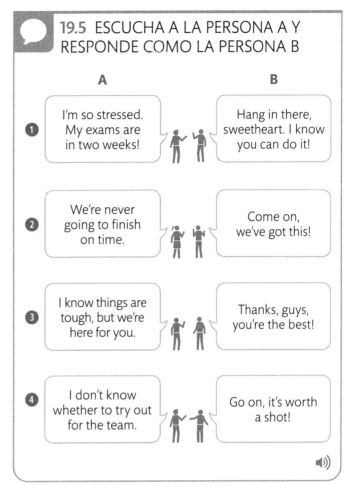

19.5 ESCUCHA A LA PERSONA A Y RESPONDE COMO LA PERSONA B

A   **B**

1 I'm so stressed. My exams are in two weeks! → Hang in there, sweetheart. I know you can do it!

2 We're never going to finish on time. → Come on, we've got this!

3 I know things are tough, but we're here for you. → Thanks, guys, you're the best!

4 I don't know whether to try out for the team. → Go on, it's worth a shot!

19.6 DI LAS ORACIONES EN VOZ ALTA, LLENANDO LOS ESPACIOS EN BLANCO CON LAS PALABRAS DEL PANEL

sweet	tough	help	appreciate
easy	ask	grateful	anything

1 Anything you need, just _____ .

2 Let me know if I can do _____ .

3 I know things are _____ , but we're here for you.

4 You've been a lot of _____ .

5 That's really _____ . I will!

6 I'm very _____ .

7 I know this hasn't been _____ .

8 Thank you, I really _____ it.

20.1 CAFÉS, INFUSIONES Y REFRESCOS

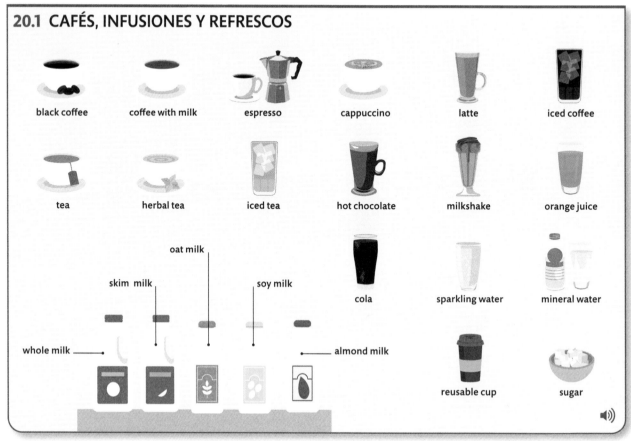

black coffee

coffee with milk

espresso

cappuccino

latte

iced coffee

tea

herbal tea

iced tea

hot chocolate

milkshake

orange juice

oat milk

skim milk

soy milk

cola

sparkling water

mineral water

whole milk

almond milk

reusable cup

sugar

20.2 VERBOS

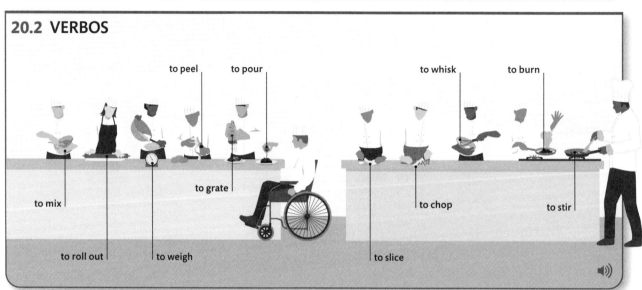

to peel

to pour

to whisk

to burn

to mix

to grate

to chop

to stir

to roll out

to weigh

to slice

20.3 MENAJE DE COCINA

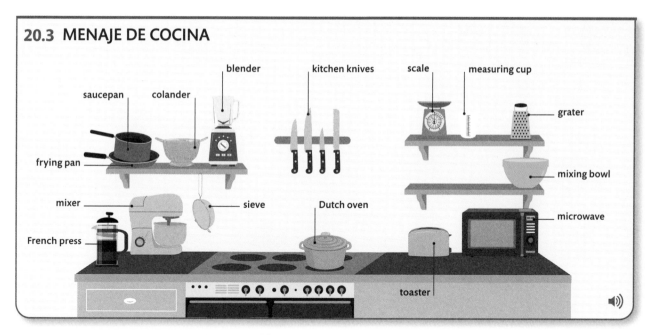

blender

kitchen knives

scale

measuring cup

saucepan

colander

grater

frying pan

mixing bowl

mixer

sieve

Dutch oven

microwave

French press

toaster

20.4 PREPARACIÓN DE ALIMENTOS

fried

stir-fried

deep-fried

poached

boiled

stewed

roasted

baked

grilled

marinated

steamed

smoked

20.5 COMER FUERA

appetizer

entrée

side order

dessert

to book a table

to order

check

to split the check

gluten-free

vegan

vegetarian

dairy-free

21 Cafeterías

21.1 EN LA CAFETERÍA

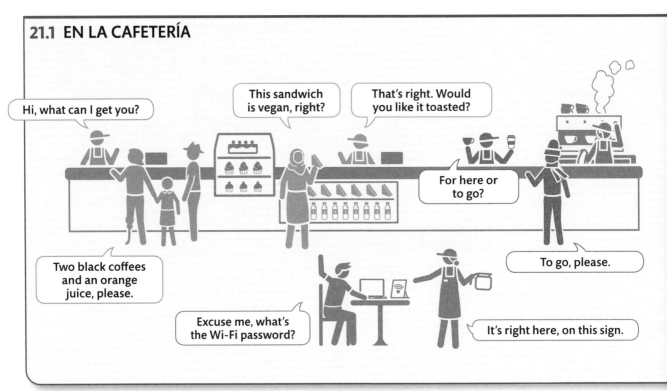

Hi, what can I get you?

This sandwich is vegan, right?

That's right. Would you like it toasted?

For here or to go?

Two black coffees and an orange juice, please.

To go, please.

Excuse me, what's the Wi-Fi password?

It's right here, on this sign.

21.2 MÁS EXPRESIONES

An iced coffee to go, please.

Could I have a skinny latte?

I brought my own cup.

Any milk or sugar?

Do you have a loyalty card?

Regular or large?

Take a seat and I'll bring your drinks over to you.

21.3 ESCUCHA Y RODEA CON UN CÍRCULO EL OBJETO QUE OYES

1 Ⓐ B

2 A R

3 A B

4 A B

5 A B

6 A B

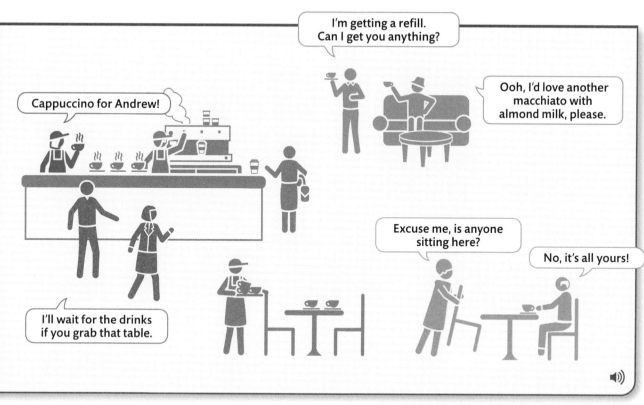

21.4 ESCUCHA A LA PERSONA A Y RESPONDE COMO LA PERSONA B

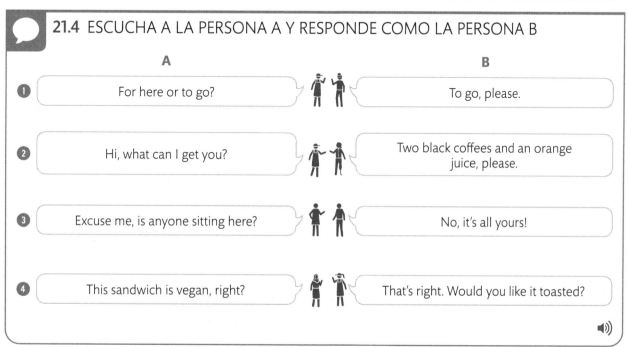

	A		B
❶	For here or to go?		To go, please.
❷	Hi, what can I get you?		Two black coffees and an orange juice, please.
❸	Excuse me, is anyone sitting here?		No, it's all yours!
❹	This sandwich is vegan, right?		That's right. Would you like it toasted?

22 Comida para llevar y a domicilio

22.1 COMPRAR COMIDA PARA LLEVAR

Want to get curry takeout tonight?

Good idea. I'll pick it up on my way home.

Two burgers to go, please.

Do you want fries with that?

I'm here to pick up my order.

Can I take your name, please?

22.2 PEDIR COMIDA A DOMICILIO

We have no food. Let's get pizza!

Okay, I'll order it on the app.

Could you check if you deliver to this address?

Of course. What's your zip code?

Our fried chicken order still hasn't arrived.

Sorry about that. Let me check what's happening.

22.3 VOCABULARIO COMIDA PARA LLEVAR

curry	noodles	pizza
sushi	tacos	kebab
burgers	fried chicken	fries
nachos	takeout	delivery

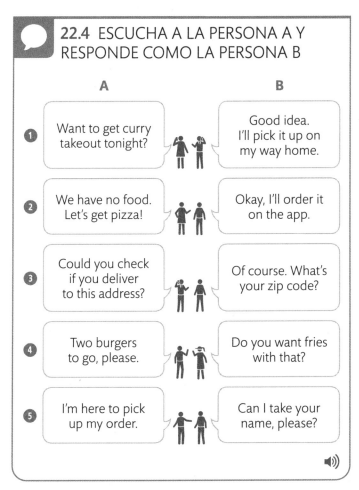

22.4 ESCUCHA A LA PERSONA A Y RESPONDE COMO LA PERSONA B

A **B**

1. Want to get curry takeout tonight? — Good idea. I'll pick it up on my way home.

2. We have no food. Let's get pizza! — Okay, I'll order it on the app.

3. Could you check if you deliver to this address? — Of course. What's your zip code?

4. Two burgers to go, please. — Do you want fries with that?

5. I'm here to pick up my order. — Can I take your name, please?

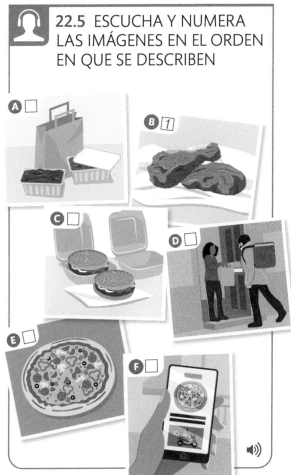

22.5 ESCUCHA Y NUMERA LAS IMÁGENES EN EL ORDEN EN QUE SE DESCRIBEN

A ☐
B 1
C ☐
D ☐
E ☐
F ☐

22.6 DI LAS ORACIONES EN VOZ ALTA, LLENANDO LOS ESPACIOS EN BLANCO CON LAS PALABRAS DEL PANEL

| want | go | arrived | pick |
| order | check | takeout | Let's |

1. Want to get curry _____ tonight?

2. Two burgers to _____ , please.

3. I'll _____ it up on my way home.

4. Okay, I'll _____ it on the app.

5. We have no food. _____ get pizza!

6. Our fried chicken order still hasn't _____ .

7. Let me _____ what's happening.

8. Do you _____ fries with that?

23 Bares y pubs

23.1 PEDIR BEBIDAS

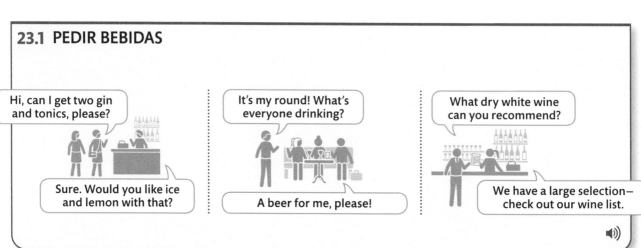

Hi, can I get two gin and tonics, please?

Sure. Would you like ice and lemon with that?

It's my round! What's everyone drinking?

A beer for me, please!

What dry white wine can you recommend?

We have a large selection—check out our wine list.

23.2 MÁS PREGUNTAS

What beers do you have on tap?

What soft drinks are there?

Do you have a bar menu?

Do we pay at the bar?

Do you serve mocktails?

What time do you stop serving?

23.3 ÚLTIMOS PEDIDOS

Last call! We close in 10 minutes.

Can we have the same again, please?

🌐 DEBES SABER

En inglés estadounidense, **Can I get ... ?** es una forma cada vez más común de pedir cosas en tiendas, cafeterías o restaurantes.

23.4 VOCABULARIO BEBIDAS

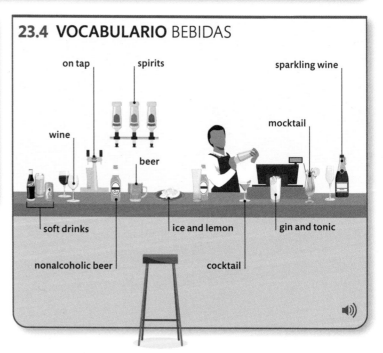

on tap

spirits

sparkling wine

wine

mocktail

beer

soft drinks

ice and lemon

gin and tonic

nonalcoholic beer

cocktail

23.5 ESCUCHA A LA PERSONA A Y RESPONDE COMO LA PERSONA B

A

B

1. Last call! We close in 10 minutes.

   Can we have the same again, please?

2. It's my round! What's everyone drinking?

   A beer for me, please!

3. What dry white wine can you recommend?

   We have a large selection—check out our wine list.

4. Hi, can I get two gin and tonics, please?

   Sure. Would you like ice and lemon with that?

23.6 ESCUCHA Y NUMERA LAS ORACIONES EN EL ORDEN EN QUE LAS OYES

A. Do you have a bar menu? ☐

B. What time do you stop serving? ☐

C. Hi, can I get two gin and tonics, please? ☐

D. It's my round! What's everyone drinking? 1

E. Can we have the same again, please? ☐

F. We have a large selection—check out our wine list. ☐

G. What beers do you have on tap? ☐

H. Do we pay at the bar? ☐

23.7 DI LAS ORACIONES EN VOZ ALTA, REEMPLAZANDO LAS IMÁGENES CON PALABRAS

1. Can I get a 🍺, please?

2. Do you serve 🍹 🍹 ?

3. A glass of 🍷 for me, please!

4. What 🍸 🍸 can you recommend?

5. What 🥤 🧃 are there?

24.1 RESERVAR UNA MESA

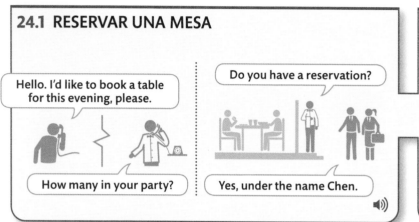

Hello. I'd like to book a table for this evening, please.

Do you have a reservation?

How many in your party?

Yes, under the name Chen.

24.2 MÁS EXPRESIONES

Do you take group bookings?

Is it possible to sit on the terrace?

Is there parking nearby?

I'd like to book a table for four, please.

24.3 PEDIR LA COMIDA

Are you ready to order?

I'll have the fish, please.

I think I'll go for the salad, too.

I'd like the salad, please.

Could I have the steak?

24.4 MÁS EXPRESIONES

Does anyone have any allergies?

Yes, I'm allergic to nuts.

I'll bring you the wine list.

Could you bring us another fork, please?

24.5 VOCABULARIO LA MESA DEL RESTAURANTE

wine list · menu · table number · wine glass · pitcher of water · dessert spoon · white wine · black pepper · ice bucket · salt · side plate · bread basket · napkin · fork · plate · knife · soup spoon

24.6 ESCUCHA A LA PERSONA A Y RESPONDE COMO LA PERSONA B

A		B
1 Do you have a reservation?		Yes, under the name Chen.
2 I'd like to book a table for this evening, please.		How many in your party?
3 Are you ready to order?		I'll have the fish, please.
4 Does anyone have any allergies?		Yes, I'm allergic to nuts.

24.7 ESCUCHA Y NUMERA LAS IMÁGENES EN EL ORDEN EN QUE SE DESCRIBEN

A ☐   **B** ☐   **C** 1   **D** ☐   **E** ☐   **F** ☐

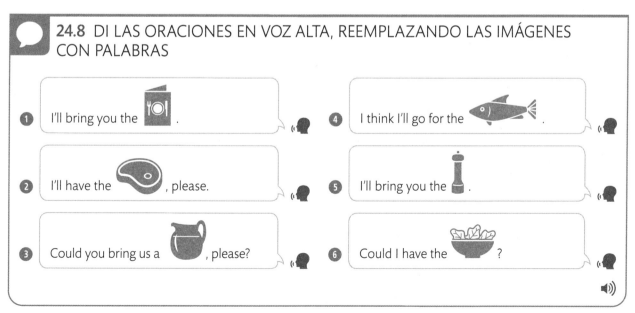

24.8 DI LAS ORACIONES EN VOZ ALTA, REEMPLAZANDO LAS IMÁGENES CON PALABRAS

1 I'll bring you the ⬚ .

2 I'll have the ⬚ , please.

3 Could you bring us a ⬚ , please?

4 I think I'll go for the ⬚ .

5 I'll bring you the ⬚ .

6 Could I have the ⬚ ?

24.9 HABLAR DE LA COMIDA

How's your soup?

Really tasty. How's yours?

It's really good. Want to try some?

Your chicken looks delicious.

It's a bit too salty, actually.

How's your steak?

Nothing special, to be honest. I should've ordered the salad!

24.10 QUEJAS SOBRE LA COMIDA

Excuse me,

... this pasta is a bit cold.

... I didn't order red wine. I ordered white.

... this glass is dirty.

24.11 PAGAR LA CUENTA

Would you like to see the dessert menu?

Not for me, thanks. I'm done!

Just the check, please.

Should we split the check?

No, I'll get this. It's your birthday, after all!

24.12 MÁS EXPRESIONES

How would you like to pay?	Let's each pay half.
Can we pay in cash?	Let's split it three ways.
Would you like a receipt?	It's on me!

24.13 ESCUCHA Y RODEA CON UN CÍRCULO EL OBJETO QUE OYES

① Ⓐ B

② A B

③ A B

④ A B

24.14 RESPONDE EN VOZ ALTA AL AUDIO, LLENANDO LOS ESPACIOS CON LAS PALABRAS DEL PANEL

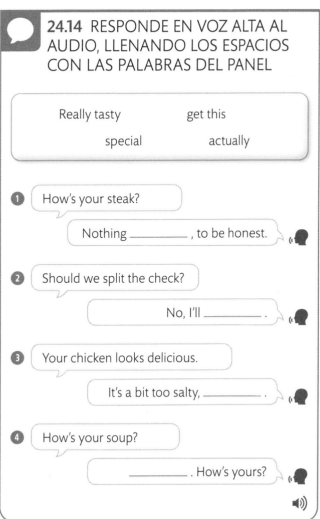

Really tasty   get this
       special   actually

① How's your steak?

Nothing _____ , to be honest.

② Should we split the check?

No, I'll _____ .

③ Your chicken looks delicious.

It's a bit too salty, _____ .

④ How's your soup?

_____ . How's yours?

24.15 USA EL ESQUEMA PARA FORMAR OCHO ORACIONES Y DILAS EN VOZ ALTA

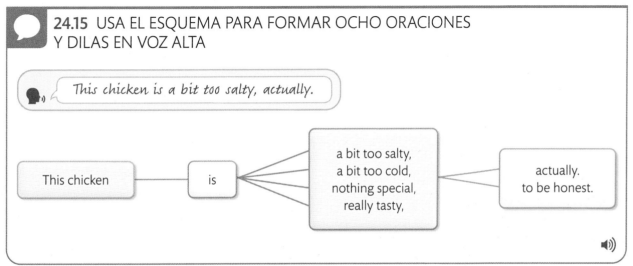

This chicken is a bit too salty, actually.

| This chicken | is | a bit too salty,
a bit too cold,
nothing special,
really tasty, | actually.
to be honest. |

25 Cocinar y comer

25.1 SEGUIR UNA RECETA

What are you making?

I'm trying a new recipe for brownies. Wanna help?

Sure, love to! I'll start weighing the flour.

How long does the bread need in the oven?

It says to check it after 30 minutes.

Okay, I'll set the timer!

So what do we do next?

Let's see ... Peel and slice the apples.

25.3 MÉTODOS PARA COCINAR

How are you cooking the broccoli?

I'm steaming it to keep the flavor.

I've brought the soup to a boil. What next?

Turn it down and simmer for 20 minutes.

Want eggs for breakfast? Poached or scrambled?

Poached for me.

I'll have scrambled!

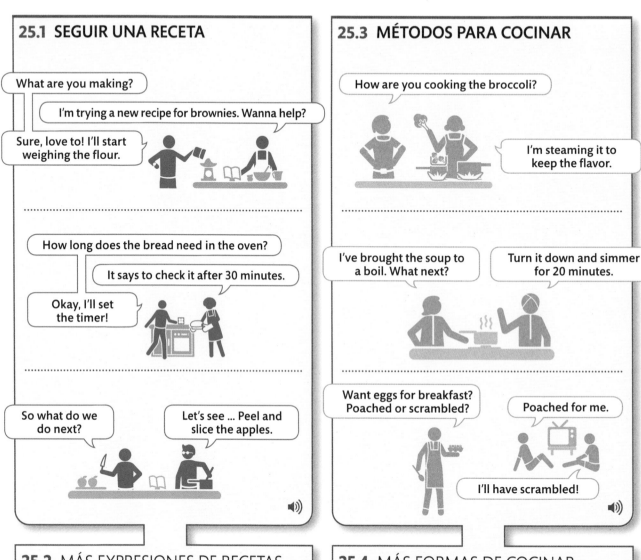

25.2 MÁS EXPRESIONES DE RECETAS

Chop the butter into cubes.

Mix the ingredients together.

Stir the cheese into the sauce.

Preheat the oven to 475°F (250°C).

25.4 MÁS FORMAS DE COCINAR

Fry the onions for five minutes.

Should I grill or fry the fish?

I'm roasting a chicken for lunch.

I've baked you a birthday cake!

25.5 ESCUCHA Y NUMERA LAS IMÁGENES EN EL ORDEN EN QUE SE DESCRIBEN

Ⓐ ☐   Ⓑ ☐   Ⓒ 1   Ⓓ ☐   Ⓔ ☐   Ⓕ ☐

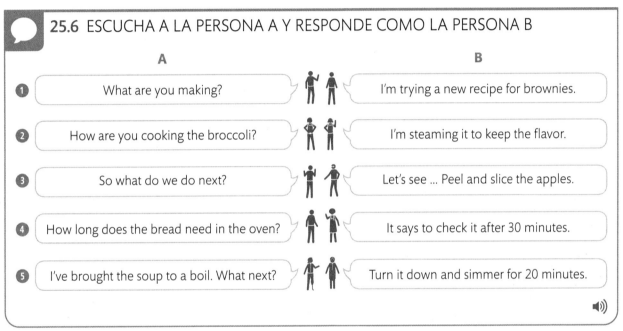

25.6 ESCUCHA A LA PERSONA A Y RESPONDE COMO LA PERSONA B

A	B
1 What are you making?	I'm trying a new recipe for brownies.
2 How are you cooking the broccoli?	I'm steaming it to keep the flavor.
3 So what do we do next?	Let's see ... Peel and slice the apples.
4 How long does the bread need in the oven?	It says to check it after 30 minutes.
5 I've brought the soup to a boil. What next?	Turn it down and simmer for 20 minutes.

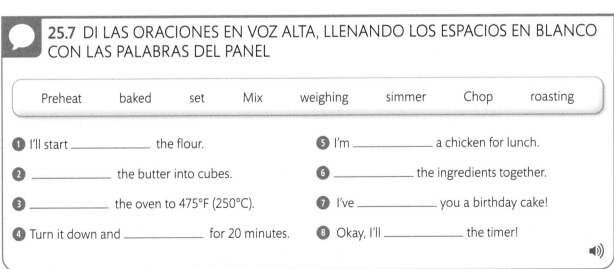

25.7 DI LAS ORACIONES EN VOZ ALTA, LLENANDO LOS ESPACIOS EN BLANCO CON LAS PALABRAS DEL PANEL

Preheat   baked   set   Mix   weighing   simmer   Chop   roasting

① I'll start _____ the flour.

② _____ the butter into cubes.

③ _____ the oven to 475°F (250°C).

④ Turn it down and _____ for 20 minutes.

⑤ I'm _____ a chicken for lunch.

⑥ _____ the ingredients together.

⑦ I've _____ you a birthday cake!

⑧ Okay, I'll _____ the timer!

25.8 COCINANDO JUNTOS

Who's cooking tonight?

It's my turn. I'm doing veggie lasagna.

Great! I love the way you make it.

Should I make some garlic bread to go with it?

25.9 DISFRUTAR DE LA COMIDA

This is so delicious.

It tastes amazing!

It's really tasty.

This is absolutely fantastic!

That was yummy.

25.10 COMER AL AIRE LIBRE

Can I get anyone a drink?

Ooh, what have you got?

Food's ready! Grab a plate.

Can I have one of those hot dogs?

I think I'll start with a mushroom kebab.

I'd love a bit of everything!

25.11 COCINAR PARA LOS AMIGOS

Thanks for having us over. Something smells good!

I've made a Thai green curry. Hope you like it!

25.12 PARA TENER EN CUENTA

Is there anything you don't eat?

I don't eat pork.

I can't have things that contain gluten.

I'm vegetarian / vegan / pescatarian.

I'm allergic to shellfish.

I don't really like peppers.

A Food's ready! Grab a plate. ☐

B This is so delicious. ☐

C Who's cooking tonight? ☐ 1

D Can I get anyone a drink? ☐

E I've made a Thai green curry. ☐

F Is there anything you don't eat? ☐

G I can't have things that contain gluten. ☐

H Ooh, what have you got? ☐

🔊

25.14 CONECTA LAS ORACIONES Y DILAS EN VOZ ALTA

Can I have		having us over.
1 I think I'll start		a bit of everything!
2 I'd love		one of those hot dogs?
3 I'm allergic		garlic bread to go with it?
4 Should I make some		to shellfish.
5 Thanks for		smells good!
6 Something		with a mushroom kebab.

🔊

25.15 USA EL ESQUEMA PARA FORMAR 12 ORACIONES Y DILAS EN VOZ ALTA

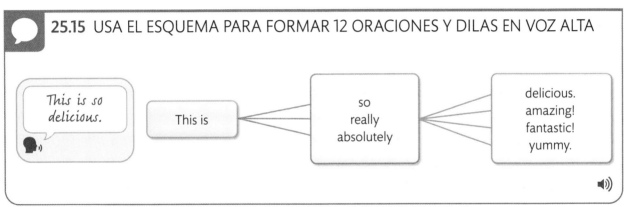

This is so delicious.

This is → so / really / absolutely → delicious. / amazing! / fantastic! / yummy.

🔊

26 Tiempo libre y aficiones

26.1 AL AIRE LIBRE

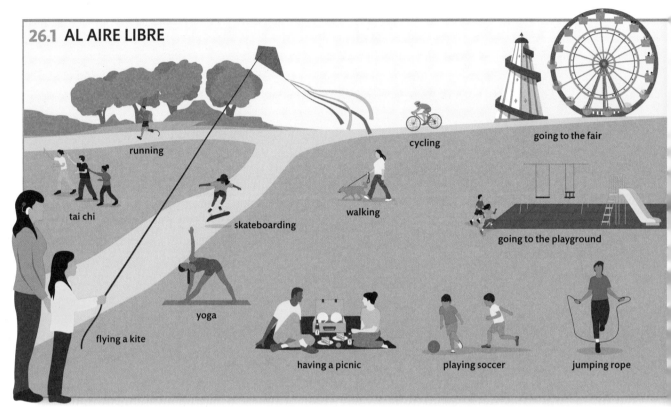

running

cycling

going to the fair

tai chi

walking

going to the playground

skateboarding

yoga

flying a kite

having a picnic

playing soccer

jumping rope

26.2 JUEGOS

darts

board game

jigsaw puzzle

cards

gaming

dominoes

chess

chess pieces

chessboard

26.3 AFICIONES CREATIVAS

painting

drawing

crafting

knitting

sewing

photography

pottery

baking

gardening

snowboarding

mountain biking

climbing

skiing

sailing

quad biking

fishing

hiking

swimming

orienteering

foraging

camping

horseback riding

bird-watching

26.4 ENTRETENIMIENTO

theater

movie theater

nightclub

ballet

concert

festival

band

orchestra

choir

26.5 GÉNEROS MUSICALES

pop

rock

country

hip-hop

dance

bhangra

jazz

classical

opera

27 En el cine

27.1 COMPRAR LOS BOLETOS

What time is the next screening?

It's at 2 p.m. We're just in time!

Three tickets for the 2 p.m. screening, please.

27.2 OTRAS PREGUNTAS

How long is the movie?

Which screen is it showing at?

Is there time to get popcorn?

Is the next screening sold out?

Can we have seats at the back?

27.3 PEDIR INFORMACIÓN

Is the movie okay for kids under 10?

It's PG, so it's fine for all ages!

Can I get to Screen 2 this way?

Yes, just follow the ramps.

Is this the subtitled screening?

You need to go to Screen 5, down the hall.

27.4 HABLAR DE LA PELÍCULA

How good was that?

Those action scenes really blew me away!

The 3D glasses made it so realistic!

That was way too long!

The acting was terrible.

I wasn't happy about the ending.

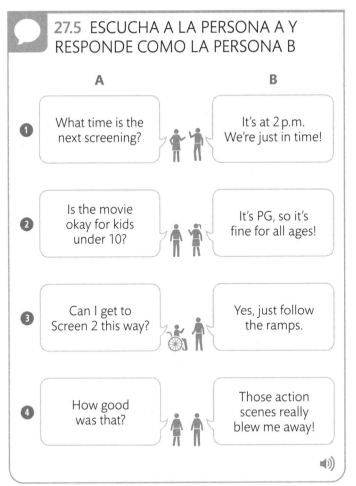

27.5 ESCUCHA A LA PERSONA A Y RESPONDE COMO LA PERSONA B

A	B
1 What time is the next screening?	It's at 2 p.m. We're just in time!
2 Is the movie okay for kids under 10?	It's PG, so it's fine for all ages!
3 Can I get to Screen 2 this way?	Yes, just follow the ramps.
4 How good was that?	Those action scenes really blew me away!

27.6 ESCUCHA Y NUMERA LAS IMÁGENES EN EL ORDEN EN QUE SE DESCRIBEN

A ☐ SCREEN 5

B ☐1

C ☐

D ☐ ?

E ☐

F ☐ "Will we ever see

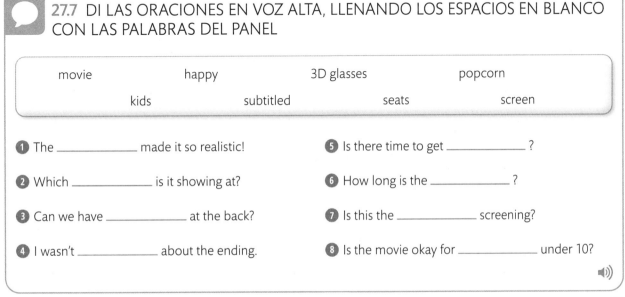

27.7 DI LAS ORACIONES EN VOZ ALTA, LLENANDO LOS ESPACIOS EN BLANCO CON LAS PALABRAS DEL PANEL

movie	happy	3D glasses	popcorn
kids	subtitled	seats	screen

1 The _____ made it so realistic!

2 Which _____ is it showing at?

3 Can we have _____ at the back?

4 I wasn't _____ about the ending.

5 Is there time to get _____ ?

6 How long is the _____ ?

7 Is this the _____ screening?

8 Is the movie okay for _____ under 10?

28 En el teatro

28.1 EN LA TAQUILLA

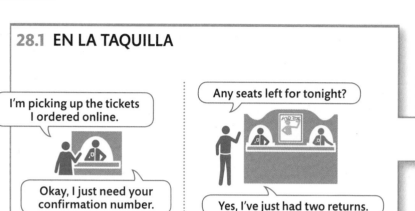

I'm picking up the tickets I ordered online.

Okay, I just need your confirmation number.

Any seats left for tonight?

Yes, I've just had two returns.

28.2 MÁS EXPRESIONES

When is opening night?

I've booked seats in the front row.

Is tonight's performance sold out?

Is there an intermission?

Where is the cloakroom?

28.3 ANTES DE LA FUNCIÓN

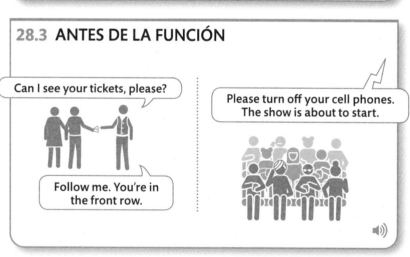

Can I see your tickets, please?

Follow me. You're in the front row.

Please turn off your cell phones. The show is about to start.

28.4 EN EL INTERMEDIO

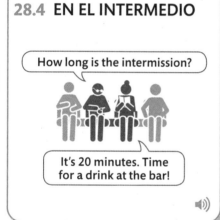

How long is the intermission?

It's 20 minutes. Time for a drink at the bar!

28.5 VOCABULARIO DENTRO DEL TEATRO

seat

performer

box

front row

audience

curtain

prop

set

stage

back row

28.6 ESCUCHA Y RODEA CON UN CÍRCULO EL OBJETO QUE OYES

1. (A) B
2. A B
3. A B
4. A B
5. A B
6. A B

28.7 CONECTA LAS ORACIONES Y DILAS EN VOZ ALTA

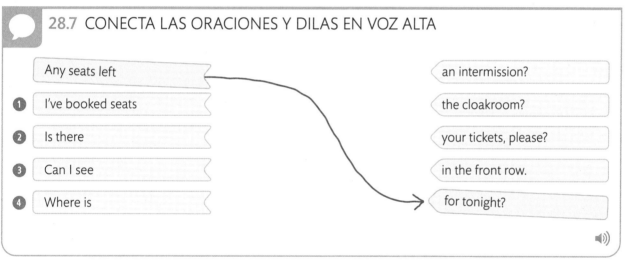

Any seats left —————————————→ for tonight?

1. I've booked seats — an intermission?
2. Is there — the cloakroom?
3. Can I see — your tickets, please?
4. Where is — in the front row.

28.8 USA EL ESQUEMA PARA FORMAR CINCO ORACIONES Y DILAS EN VOZ ALTA

Follow me. You're in the front row.

Follow me. You're
I've booked seats — in — the front row.
the back row.
Box 5.

29 Conciertos y festivales

29.1 EN UN CONCIERTO

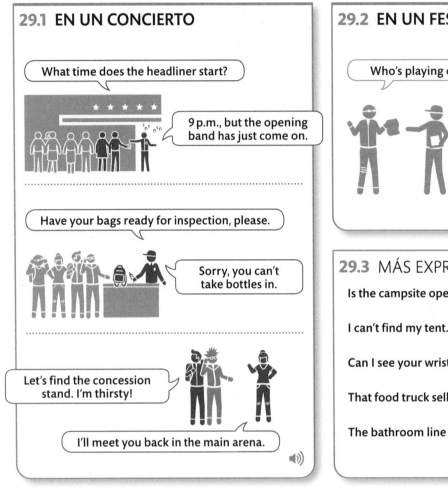

What time does the headliner start?

9 p.m., but the opening band has just come on.

Have your bags ready for inspection, please.

Sorry, you can't take bottles in.

Let's find the concession stand. I'm thirsty!

I'll meet you back in the main arena.

29.2 EN UN FESTIVAL AL AIRE LIBRE

Who's playing on the main stage tonight?

Here's the lineup for the whole weekend. Enjoy!

29.3 MÁS EXPRESIONES

Is the campsite open yet?

I can't find my tent.

Can I see your wristband, please?

That food truck sells great burgers.

The bathroom line is too long!

29.4 EN UN CONCIERTO DE MÚSICA CLÁSICA

There's a free classical concert at the park tonight.

Do we have to reserve tickets?

No, we can just turn up.

That was really impressive!

What an amazing performance!

Encore! Encore!

29.5 ESCUCHA Y NUMERA LAS IMÁGENES EN EL ORDEN EN QUE SE DESCRIBEN

A
B
C
D
E 1
F
G
H

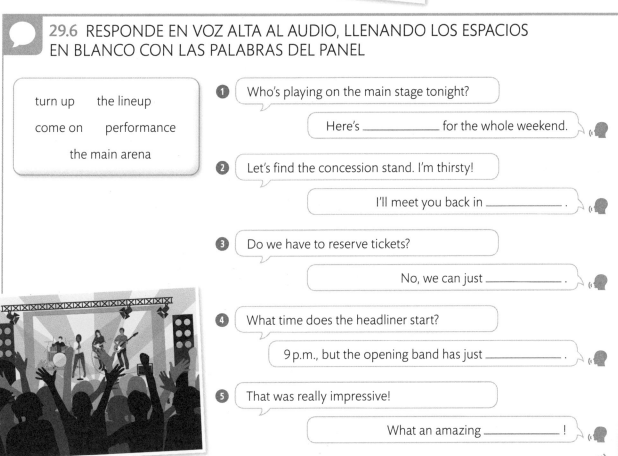

29.6 RESPONDE EN VOZ ALTA AL AUDIO, LLENANDO LOS ESPACIOS EN BLANCO CON LAS PALABRAS DEL PANEL

turn up   the lineup
come on   performance
        the main arena

1 Who's playing on the main stage tonight?

Here's _____ for the whole weekend.

2 Let's find the concession stand. I'm thirsty!

I'll meet you back in _____ .

3 Do we have to reserve tickets?

No, we can just _____ .

4 What time does the headliner start?

9 p.m., but the opening band has just _____ .

5 That was really impressive!

What an amazing _____ !

30 En el gimnasio

30.1 HACERSE SOCIO

How much does it cost to join?

Here's our list of membership options.

Can I have a tour?

Yes, I'll show you around now.

So what do you think?

It all looks great. Sign me up!

30.2 OTRAS PREGUNTAS

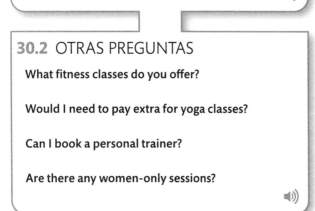

What fitness classes do you offer?

Would I need to pay extra for yoga classes?

Can I book a personal trainer?

Are there any women-only sessions?

30.3 ASISTIR A UNA CLASE

Have you been to this fitness class before?

Yes, a few times. It's super fun!

Hi, I'm here for the spin class.

Great. Grab a free bike and join in!

30.4 VOCABULARIO EN EL GIMNASIO

personal trainer

to work out

weight training

spin class

yoga

Pilates

fitness class

HIIT

dance class

30.5 ESCUCHA A LA PERSONA A Y RESPONDE COMO LA PERSONA B

A   **B**

1 How much does it cost to join?  Here's our list of membership options.

2 Have you been to this fitness class before? Yes, a few times. It's super fun!

3 Can I have a tour? Yes, I'll show you around now.

4 So what do you think? It all looks great. Sign me up!

5 Hi, I'm here for the spin class. Great. Grab a free bike and join in!

🔊

30.6 ESCUCHA Y NUMERA LAS ORACIONES EN EL ORDEN EN QUE LAS OYES

A Can I have a tour? ☐

B It all looks great. Sign me up! ☐

C Can I book a personal trainer? 1

D Here's our list of membership options. ☐

E What fitness classes do you offer? ☐

F How much does it cost to join? ☐

G Are there any women-only sessions? ☐

H Would I need to pay extra for yoga classes? ☐

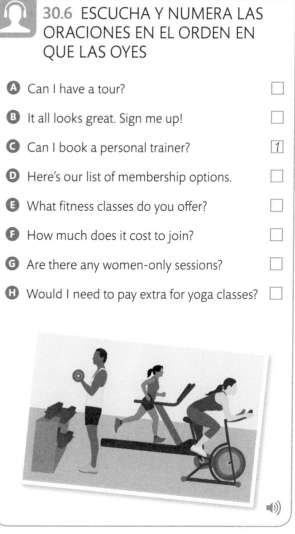

🔊

30.7 USA EL ESQUEMA PARA FORMAR CINCO ORACIONES Y DILAS EN VOZ ALTA

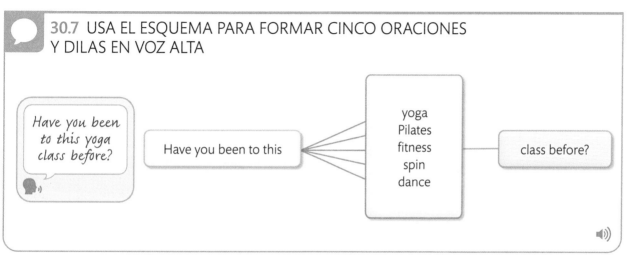

Have you been to this yoga class before?

Have you been to this

yoga
Pilates
fitness
spin
dance

class before?

🔊

31 Actividades deportivas

31.1 DEPORTES DE EQUIPO

31.2 EN EL CLUB DEPORTIVO

31.3 VOCABULARIO DEPORTES

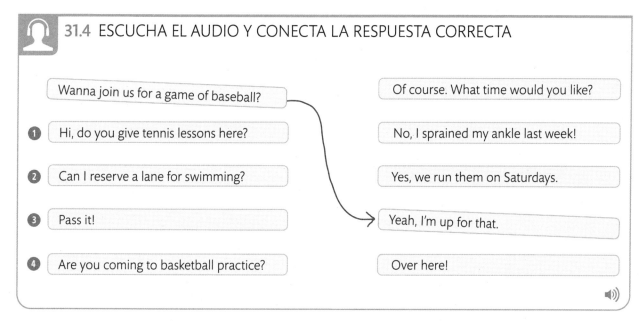

31.4 ESCUCHA EL AUDIO Y CONECTA LA RESPUESTA CORRECTA

Wanna join us for a game of baseball?

Of course. What time would you like?

1 Hi, do you give tennis lessons here?

No, I sprained my ankle last week!

2 Can I reserve a lane for swimming?

Yes, we run them on Saturdays.

3 Pass it!

Yeah, I'm up for that.

4 Are you coming to basketball practice?

Over here!

31.5 ESCUCHA A LA PERSONA A Y RESPONDE COMO LA PERSONA B

A | **B**

1 Can I reserve a lane for swimming? | Of course. What time would you like?

2 Are you coming to basketball practice? | No, I sprained my ankle last week!

3 You look lost. Do you need any help? | I'm looking for the badminton court.

4 Wanna join us for a game of baseball? | Yeah, I'm up for that.

31.6 DI LAS ORACIONES EN VOZ ALTA, REEMPLAZANDO LAS IMÁGENES CON PALABRAS

1 Wanna join us for a game of ?

2 Are you coming to practice?

3 Do you give lessons here?

4 I'd like to book a lesson, please.

5 We run practice on Mondays.

32.1 COMPRAR BOLETOS

32.2 OTRAS PREGUNTAS

Is the event sold out?

Can I buy a season ticket?

Is there a student discount?

Do you have seats for disabled spectators?

32.3 VER DEPORTES

32.4 ESCUCHA A LA PERSONA A Y RESPONDE COMO LA PERSONA B

A	B
1 Want to go to the golf tournament?	Yes! When do tickets go on sale?
2 Are you showing the soccer game here?	Yes, we are. Tonight at 8.
3 Any seats left for the tennis final today?	Yes, there are a few. You're just in time!
4 Are you watching track and field?	You bet! It starts in half an hour.
5 Come on, guys!	You can do it!

32.5 ESCUCHA Y NUMERA LAS IMÁGENES EN EL ORDEN EN QUE SE DESCRIBEN

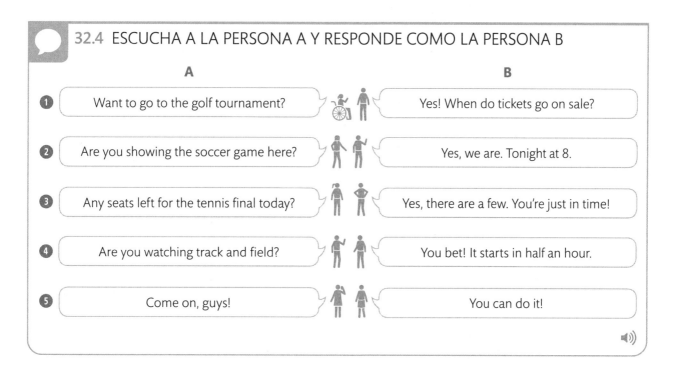

32.6 USA EL ESQUEMA PARA FORMAR OCHO ORACIONES Y DILAS EN VOZ ALTA

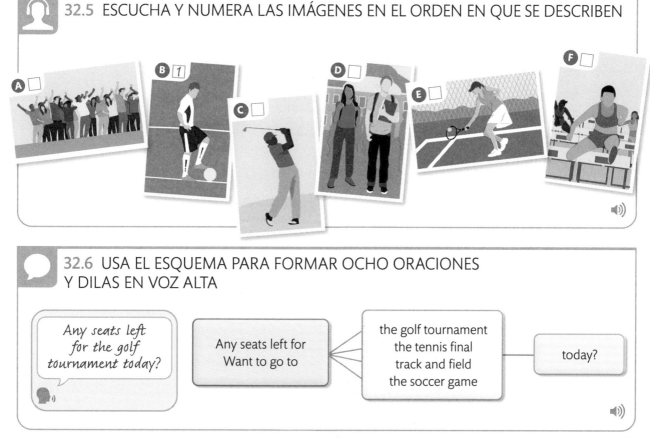

Any seats left for the golf tournament today?

| Any seats left for / Want to go to | the golf tournament / the tennis final / track and field / the soccer game | today? |

81

33 Aficiones

33.1 COMENZAR UNA NUEVA AFICIÓN

Guess what? I've just started doing karate!

No way! Good for you!

Check this out ... I'm giving knitting a try!

Wow! Maybe I'll try it, too!

I've taken up pottery recently.

That sounds fun— I might join you.

33.2 PREGUNTAR POR LAS AFICIONES DE LOS DEMÁS

Do you have any hobbies?

Yeah, I play tennis and I'm learning the guitar.

So what do you normally do in your free time?

I usually go swimming on weekends. How about you?

What do you do outside of work?

Gaming, mostly. And I'm writing a blog.

33.3 HABLAR SOBRE NUESTRAS AFICIONES

So how long have you all been playing?

The piano? Since I was 11.

I've been playing the sax for 10 years!

How about you?

I only started learning the bass guitar three years ago.

33.4 ESCUCHA Y RODEA CON UN CÍRCULO EL OBJETO QUE OYES

33.5 DI LAS ORACIONES EN VOZ ALTA, REEMPLAZANDO LAS IMÁGENES CON PALABRAS

33.6 USA EL ESQUEMA PARA FORMAR OCHO ORACIONES Y DILAS EN VOZ ALTA

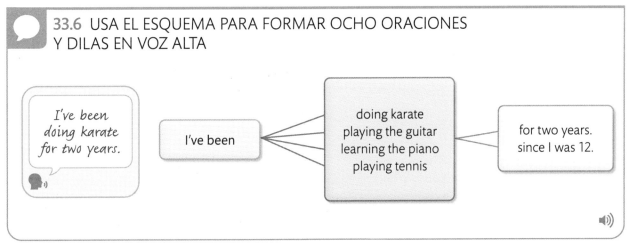

34 Tiendas y servicios

34.1 EL CENTRO DE LA CIUDAD

gas station   supermarket   garden center   hardware store

gym   movie theater   theater   coffee shop / café

library   post office   bank   restaurant

(SPACE MOVIE 3   PUPPET STORY)

34.2 TIPOS DE TIENDAS

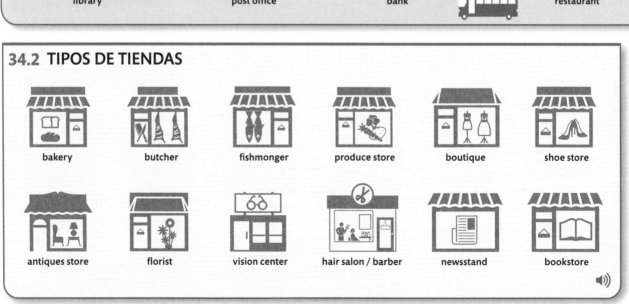

bakery   butcher   fishmonger   produce store   boutique   shoe store

antiques store   florist   vision center   hair salon / barber   newsstand   bookstore

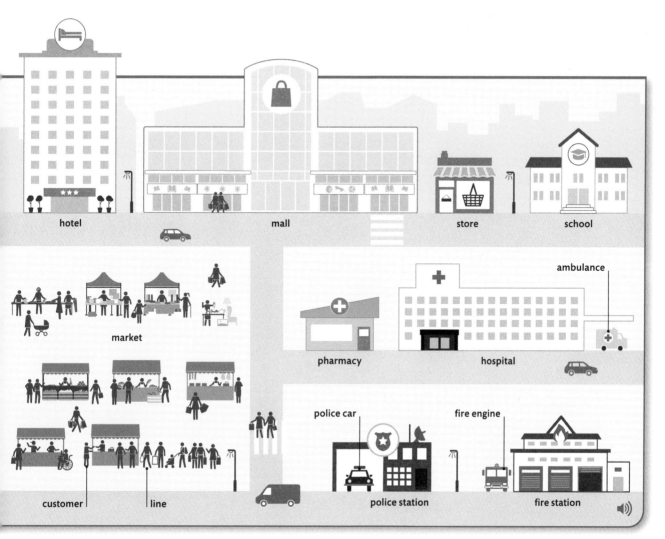

hotel

mall

store

school

ambulance

market

pharmacy

hospital

police car

fire engine

customer

line

police station

fire station

34.3 DINERO

bills

coins

debit card

loyalty card

contactless payment

ATM

sale / reduced

receipt

pay (for something)

return goods

exchange

refund

35 En el mercado

35.1 REGATEAR

What's your best price for this?

I can't go any lower than $12.

I only have $10.

You've got a deal!

35.2 MÁS EXPRESIONES

Is that your best price?

That's my final offer.

I can't spend that much.

Can I get two for $15?

I'll take it!

35.3 COMPRAR PRODUCTOS FRESCOS

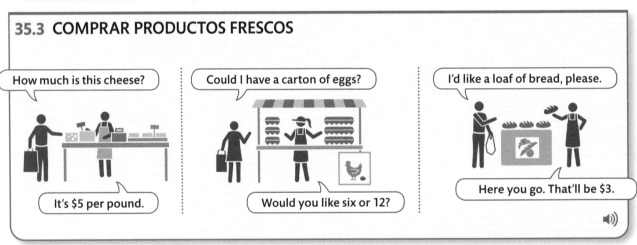

How much is this cheese?

Could I have a carton of eggs?

I'd like a loaf of bread, please.

It's $5 per pound.

Would you like six or 12?

Here you go. That'll be $3.

35.4 VOCABULARIO ALIMENTOS

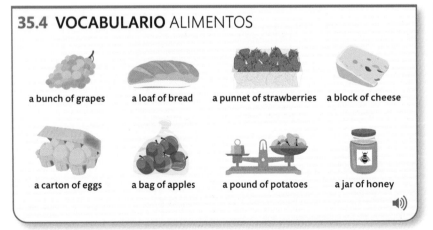

a bunch of grapes

a loaf of bread

a punnet of strawberries

a block of cheese

a carton of eggs

a bag of apples

a pound of potatoes

a jar of honey

⊕ DEBES SABER

En inglés, solemos pedir las cosas de forma educada, empezando, por ejemplo, con **Can I ...**, **Could I ...** o **I'd like ...**, y terminando la petición con **please**. Es más educado decir **Could I ...?** que **Can I ...?**. En una situación formal, algunas personas también pueden decir **May I ...?**

35.5 ESCUCHA A LA PERSONA A Y RESPONDE COMO LA PERSONA B

A	B
1 I'd like a loaf of bread, please.	Here you go. That'll be $3.
2 What's your best price for this?	I can't go any lower than $12.
3 I only have $10.	You've got a deal!
4 How much is this cheese?	It's $5 per pound.
5 That's my final offer.	I'll take it!

35.6 RODEA CON UN CÍRCULO LO QUE OYES

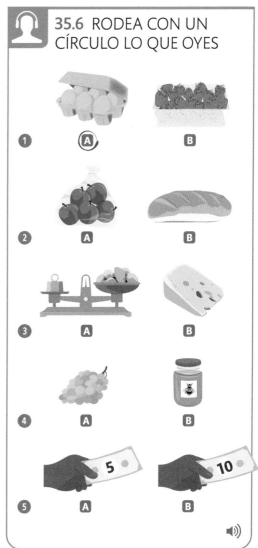

1. Ⓐ   B
2. A   B
3. A   B
4. A   B
5. A   B

35.7 USA EL ESQUEMA PARA FORMAR 10 ORACIONES Y DILAS EN VOZ ALTA

Can I have a jar of honey, please?

| Can I have / Could I have | a jar of honey, a bunch of grapes, a loaf of bread, a punnet of strawberries, a carton of eggs, | please? |

36 En el supermercado

36.1 HACER PREGUNTAS

36.2 ESCUCHA Y NUMERA LAS ORACIONES EN EL ORDEN EN QUE LAS OYES

A You'll find it in aisle 10. ☐

B I can't find the pet food. ☐

C Can I help you? ☑ 1

D How many slices of ham? ☐

E Do you have oat milk here? ☐

F I'd like eight, please. ☐

🔊

36.3 ESCUCHA Y RODEA CON UN CÍRCULO EL OBJETO QUE OYES

① A Ⓑ   ② A B   ③ A B

④ A B   ⑤ A B   ⑥ A B

🔊

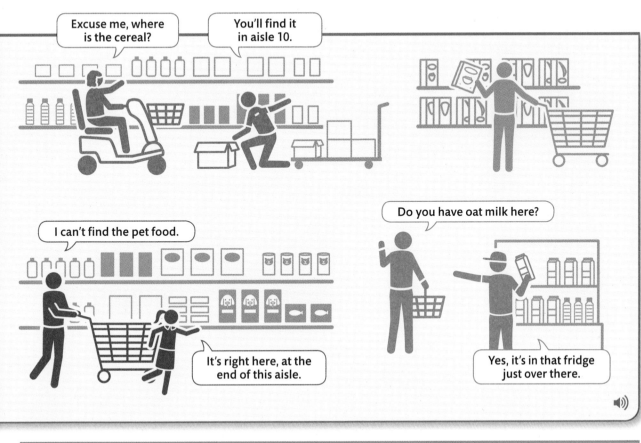

36.4 ESCUCHA A LA PERSONA A Y RESPONDE COMO LA PERSONA B

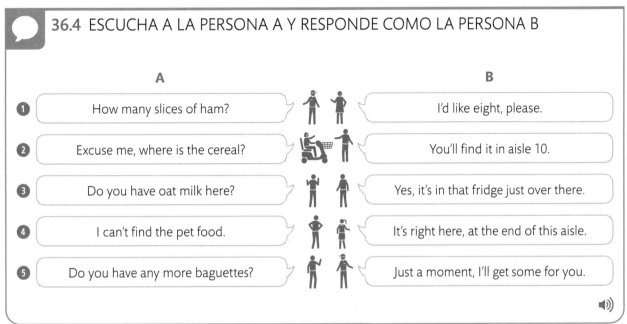

	A		B
①	How many slices of ham?		I'd like eight, please.
②	Excuse me, where is the cereal?		You'll find it in aisle 10.
③	Do you have oat milk here?		Yes, it's in that fridge just over there.
④	I can't find the pet food.		It's right here, at the end of this aisle.
⑤	Do you have any more baguettes?		Just a moment, I'll get some for you.

36.5 EN LA CAJA

Do you need a bag?

No, I've brought my own, thanks.

That's $45.20. Do you have a loyalty card?

Yes, just a second ...

That's all gone through. Would you like a receipt?

No, that's fine, thanks.

36.7 USAR LA CAJA DE AUTOSERVICIO

Excuse me, this milk carton is leaking.

No problem. I'll go and get another one.

This barcode won't scan.

Here, I'll give it a try.

Please tap or insert your card into the payment device.

36.8 VOCABULARIO SECCIONES

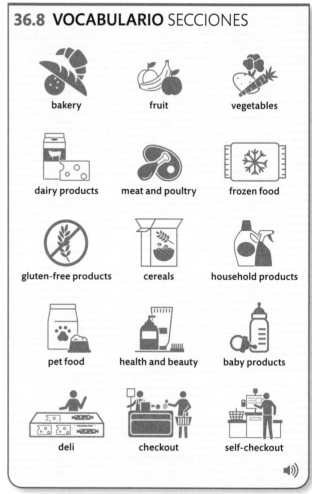

bakery

fruit

vegetables

dairy products

meat and poultry

frozen food

gluten-free products

cereals

household products

pet food

health and beauty

baby products

deli

checkout

self-checkout

Would you like to use the self-checkout?

No, thanks. I'm happy to wait.

36.6 MÁS EXPRESIONES

Do you take cash?

How much is it for a bag?

Could I have a receipt, please?

Could you scan my loyalty card, please?

I don't have my loyalty card with me.

Can I use these coupons?

36.9 ESCUCHA Y NUMERA LAS ORACIONES EN EL ORDEN EN QUE LAS OYES

A Do you need a bag? ☐

B This barcode won't scan. ☐

C Would you like to use the self-checkout? 1

D No, thanks. I'm happy to wait. ☐

E That's $45.20. Do you have a loyalty card? ☐

F Can I use these coupons? ☐

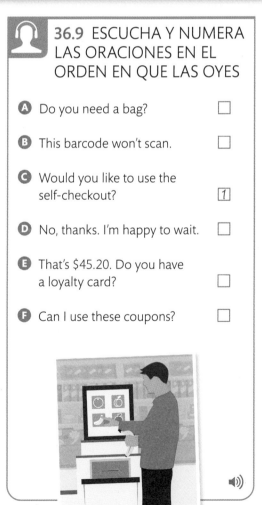

36.10 DI EN VOZ ALTA, REEMPLAZANDO LAS IMÁGENES CON PALABRAS

1 Excuse me, where's the ❄ aisle?

2 Would you like to use the 🖥 ?

3 Where can I find the 🐾 ?

4 Do you have 🍼 here?

5 I can't find the 🍌🍎 and 🥕 .

37 En el centro de jardinería

37.1 COMPRAR PLANTAS

Hello, how can I help?

We need some advice on starting a vegetable garden.

What kind of houseplants are you looking for?

I don't really mind, but my apartment doesn't get much light.

37.2 CUIDADO DE LAS PLANTAS

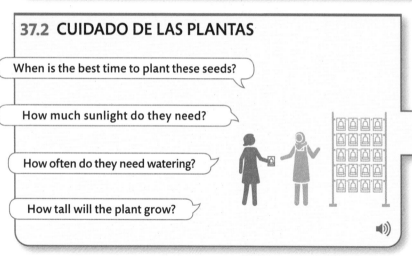

When is the best time to plant these seeds?

How much sunlight do they need?

How often do they need watering?

How tall will the plant grow?

37.3 MÁS PREGUNTAS

How often should I feed it?

Does it need much looking after?

Will it survive the winter?

What's a good compost to use?

How do I get rid of weeds?

37.4 VOCABULARIO JARDINERÍA

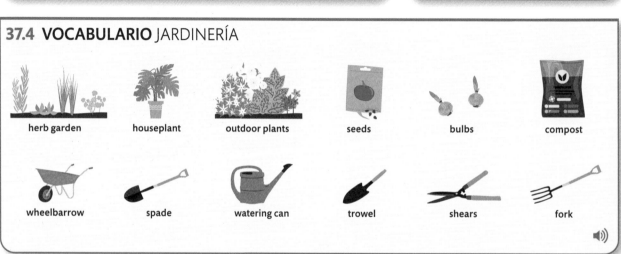

herb garden	houseplant	outdoor plants	seeds	bulbs	compost
wheelbarrow	spade	watering can	trowel	shears	fork

37.5 ESCUCHA Y NUMERA LAS IMÁGENES EN EL ORDEN EN QUE SE DESCRIBEN

Ⓐ ☐   Ⓑ ☑ 1

Ⓒ ☐   Ⓓ ☐

Ⓔ ☐   Ⓕ ☐

🔊

37.6 DI LAS ORACIONES EN VOZ ALTA, LLENANDO LOS ESPACIOS EN BLANCO CON LAS PALABRAS DEL PANEL

seeds	feed	sunlight
weeds	survive	looking

❶ Will it _____ the winter?

❷ When is the best time to plant these _____ ?

❸ How much _____ do they need?

❹ Does it need much _____ after?

❺ How often should I _____ it?

❻ How do I get rid of _____ ?

🔊

37.7 CONECTA LAS ORACIONES Y DILAS EN VOZ ALTA

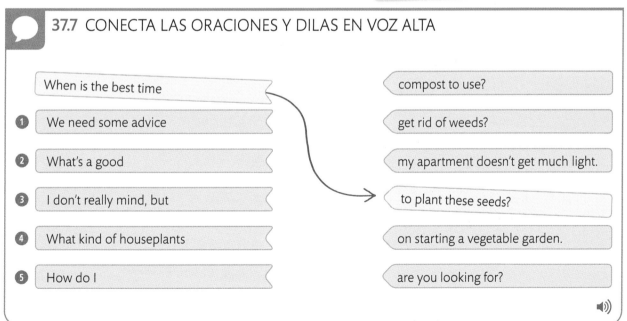

When is the best time   compost to use?

❶ We need some advice   get rid of weeds?

❷ What's a good   my apartment doesn't get much light.

❸ I don't really mind, but   to plant these seeds?

❹ What kind of houseplants   on starting a vegetable garden.

❺ How do I   are you looking for?

🔊

38 En la tienda de manualidades

38.1 PEDIR CONSEJO

What would you recommend for sanding a table?

What do I need for tiling my bathroom?

What's best for plastering walls?

What do you have for filling a crack?

38.2 MÁS EXPRESIONES

I'd like to remodel my bedroom.

I need to hang a picture.

What should I use for painting my kitchen?

I'd like some advice about plastering.

38.3 COMPRAR HERRAMIENTAS

Can you show me to the tool section?

I'm looking for a hammer and nails.

Where can I find a saw?

Who can I ask about drills?

38.4 MÁS EXPRESIONES

Will I need ID to buy this saw?

Where are the screws?

What kind of screwdrivers do you sell?

Do you have any cordless power tools?

38.5 VOCABULARIO HERRAMIENTAS Y REFORMAS

| hammer | nail | screwdriver | screw | saw | drill |

| to paint | to plaster | to sand | to tile | to fill | to hang |

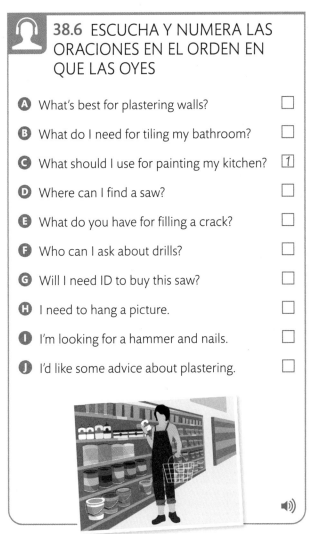

38.6 ESCUCHA Y NUMERA LAS ORACIONES EN EL ORDEN EN QUE LAS OYES

A What's best for plastering walls? ☐

B What do I need for tiling my bathroom? ☐

C What should I use for painting my kitchen? ☑ 1

D Where can I find a saw? ☐

E What do you have for filling a crack? ☐

F Who can I ask about drills? ☐

G Will I need ID to buy this saw? ☐

H I need to hang a picture. ☐

I I'm looking for a hammer and nails. ☐

J I'd like some advice about plastering. ☐

38.7 DI LAS ORACIONES EN VOZ ALTA, REEMPLAZANDO LAS IMÁGENES CON PALABRAS

1 I'm looking for a ⟋ .

2 Where can I find a 🔨 ?

3 Do you have any 🪛 ?

4 Who can I ask about 🪚 ?

5 What kind of 📍 do you sell?

6 Where are the 🔩 ?

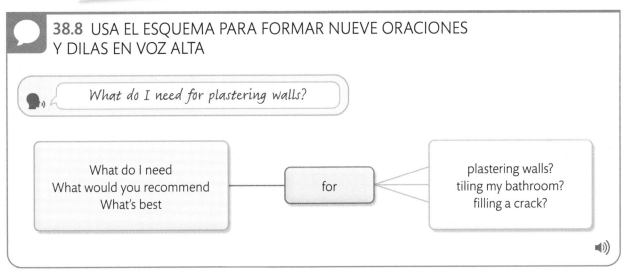

38.8 USA EL ESQUEMA PARA FORMAR NUEVE ORACIONES Y DILAS EN VOZ ALTA

What do I need for plastering walls?

What do I need		plastering walls?
What would you recommend	for	tiling my bathroom?
What's best		filling a crack?

39 Comprar ropa y zapatos

39.1 EN LA TIENDA DE ROPA

Do you have this shirt in a larger size?

Let me go check.

Can I try these dresses on, please?

Yes, you can take up to four items in.

These pants feel too big.

I'll go and get you the next size down.

39.2 EN LA ZAPATERÍA

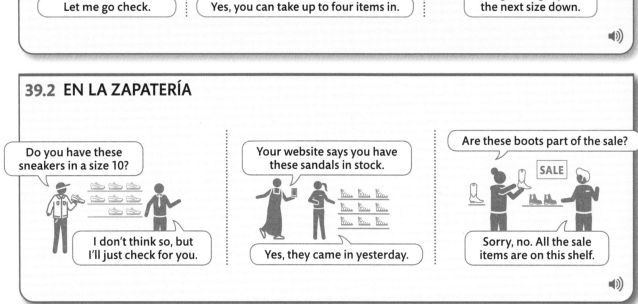

Do you have these sneakers in a size 10?

I don't think so, but I'll just check for you.

Your website says you have these sandals in stock.

Yes, they came in yesterday.

Are these boots part of the sale?

SALE

Sorry, no. All the sale items are on this shelf.

39.3 VOCABULARIO ROPA Y ZAPATOS

pants   skirt   dress   jacket   coat   shorts   suit

sweater   shirt   T-shirt   sandals   sneakers   boots   socks

39.4 ESCUCHA Y NUMERA LAS IMÁGENES EN EL ORDEN EN QUE SE DESCRIBEN

39.5 ESCUCHA A LA PERSONA A Y RESPONDE COMO LA PERSONA B

39.6 USA EL ESQUEMA PARA FORMAR 12 ORACIONES Y DILAS EN VOZ ALTA

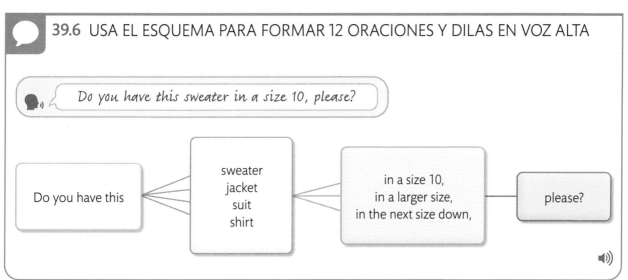

40 Devolver productos

40.1 EXPLICAR EL PROBLEMA

Where can I return this bag? I bought the wrong color.

Our returns desk is on the second floor.

I need to return these pants.

Can I ask what the problem is?

They're too big.

RETURNS

40.2 MÁS EXPRESIONES

I bought the wrong size.

The lamp isn't working properly.

The shoes are too tight.

The dress doesn't fit right.

The vase is broken.

40.3 REEMBOLSOS Y CAMBIOS

I have to return this, but I lost my receipt.

Without a receipt, we can only offer an exchange, I'm afraid.

I'm returning this hat. I just don't like it!

Do you have a receipt?

No, it was a gift.

Don't worry, I'll give you store credit.

I bought this online. Can I get a refund?

Yes, I just need your order number.

40.4 ESCUCHA A LA PERSONA A Y RESPONDE COMO LA PERSONA B

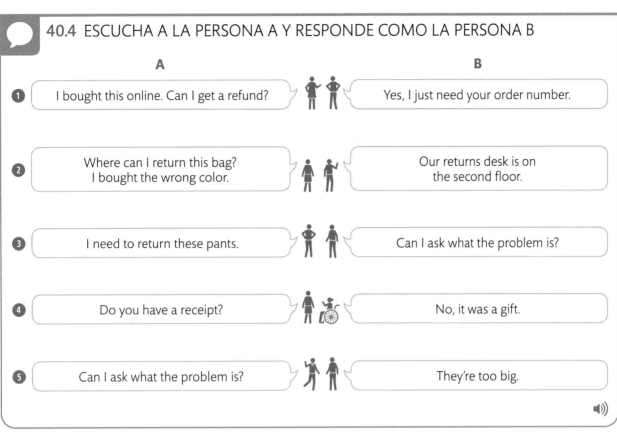

A	B
1 I bought this online. Can I get a refund?	Yes, I just need your order number.
2 Where can I return this bag? I bought the wrong color.	Our returns desk is on the second floor.
3 I need to return these pants.	Can I ask what the problem is?
4 Do you have a receipt?	No, it was a gift.
5 Can I ask what the problem is?	They're too big.

40.5 DI LAS ORACIONES EN VOZ ALTA, REEMPLAZANDO LAS IMÁGENES CON PALABRAS

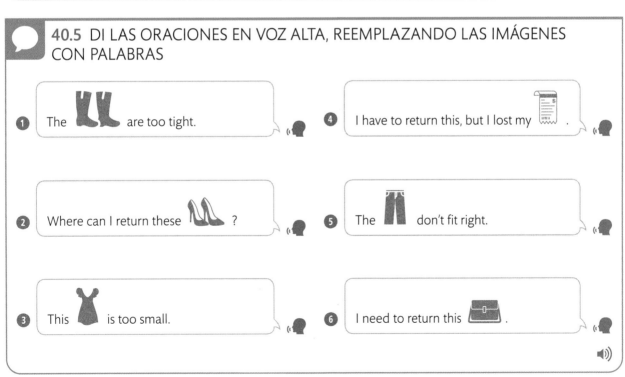

1 The [boots] are too tight.

2 Where can I return these [heels]?

3 This [dress] is too small.

4 I have to return this, but I lost my [receipt].

5 The [pants] don't fit right.

6 I need to return this [bag].

41 Cabello, belleza y cuidados

41.1 PEDIR CITA

Would you like to make an appointment?

Yes, please. Can you do Thursday at 3 p.m.?

Sorry, we're fully booked on Thursday.

How about Friday morning?

Friday is fine. Is 9:30 okay?

41.2 MÁS PREGUNTAS

Would you like a wash and cut?

Have you been to this salon before?

Who normally does your hair?

Can you come in on Monday?

Is Saturday afternoon any good?

What's the earliest you could fit me in?

Would you like to make another appointment?

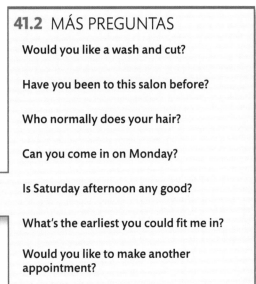

41.3 EN LA PELUQUERÍA

I just need a quick trim. Can you fit me in?

Could you wait 20 minutes? There's one person ahead of you.

Not too much off the top, please.

Sure. No problem.

41.4 VOCABULARIO CABELLO Y BELLEZA

hairdresser

barber

beautician

beard trim

cut

blow-dry

highlights

bangs

facial

manicure

pedicure

waxing

41.5 ESCUCHA A LA PERSONA A Y RESPONDE COMO LA PERSONA B

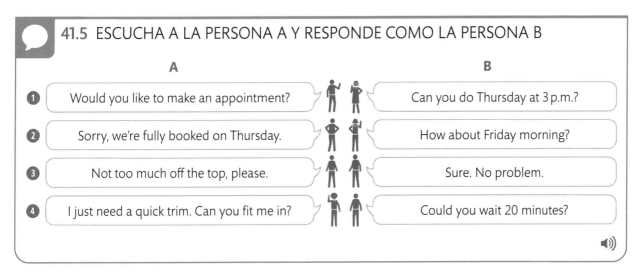

	A	B
1	Would you like to make an appointment?	Can you do Thursday at 3 p.m.?
2	Sorry, we're fully booked on Thursday.	How about Friday morning?
3	Not too much off the top, please.	Sure. No problem.
4	I just need a quick trim. Can you fit me in?	Could you wait 20 minutes?

41.6 CONECTA LAS ORACIONES Y DILAS EN VOZ ALTA

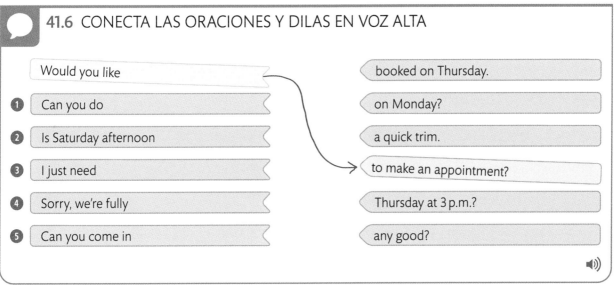

Would you like — to make an appointment?

1. Can you do — Thursday at 3 p.m.?
2. Is Saturday afternoon — any good?
3. I just need — a quick trim.
4. Sorry, we're fully — booked on Thursday.
5. Can you come in — on Monday?

booked on Thursday.
on Monday?
a quick trim.
to make an appointment?
Thursday at 3 p.m.?
any good?

41.7 USA EL ESQUEMA PARA FORMAR OCHO ORACIONES Y DILAS EN VOZ ALTA

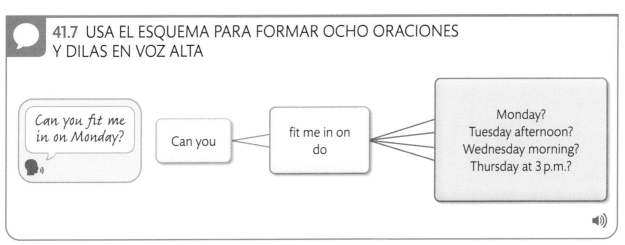

Can you fit me in on Monday?

Can you → fit me in on / do → Monday? / Tuesday afternoon? / Wednesday morning? / Thursday at 3 p.m.?

41.8 PREGUNTAS AL PELUQUERO

So what are we doing today?

Just my usual, I think.

I feel like a change, but I don't know what to go for.

Have a look through these styles to get some ideas.

I was thinking of something like this ...

I think a shorter style would really suit you.

41.9 MÁS EXPRESIONES

What color would be best for me?

Could you cut it a bit shorter at the sides?

Leave it longer on top, please.

Could you cut the bangs a bit more?

I'll have some gel on it, please.

Do you think I should go for highlights?

41.10 BELLEZA Y CUIDADOS

I'd like a manicure, please.

Okay. Have a look at these colors and take your pick.

I booked a back wax for 4 p.m.

Could I take your name, please?

So you're having the aromatherapy facial today?

Yes, that's right.

41.11 ESCUCHA Y NUMERA LAS ORACIONES EN EL ORDEN EN QUE LAS OYES

A I'd like a manicure, please. ☐

B What color would be best for me? [1]

C Do you think I should go for highlights? ☐

D Could you cut it a bit shorter at the sides? ☐

E Leave it longer on top, please. ☐

F Could you cut the bangs a bit more? ☐

G So you're having the aromatherapy facial today? ☐

H I feel like a change, but I don't know what to go for. ☐

I I'll have some gel on it, please. ☐

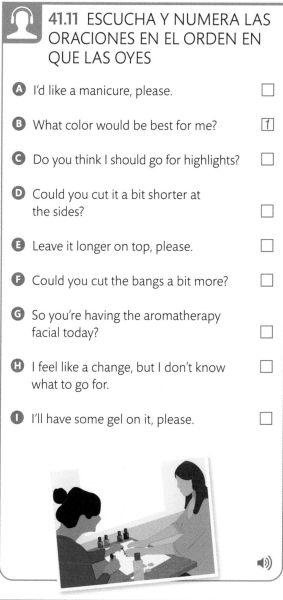

41.12 DI LAS ORACIONES EN VOZ ALTA, LLENANDO LOS ESPACIOS CON LAS PALABRAS DEL PANEL

a bit more	suit you	go for	best
my usual	gel	on top	

1 I feel like a change, but I don't know what to _____ .

2 Just _____ , I think.

3 I'll have some _____ on it, please.

4 What color would be _____ for me?

5 Could you cut the bangs _____ ?

6 I think a shorter style would really _____ .

7 Leave it longer _____ , please.

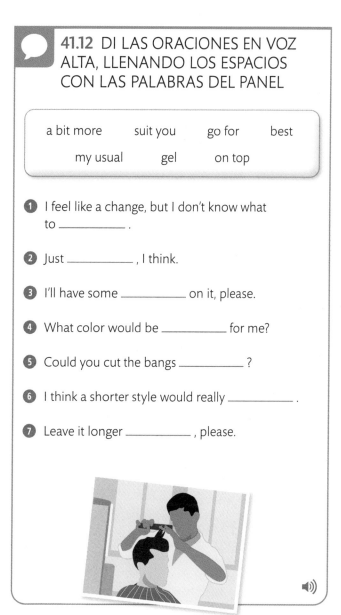

41.13 USA EL ESQUEMA PARA FORMAR NUEVE ORACIONES Y DILAS EN VOZ ALTA

What style would be best for me?

| What | style / color / highlights | would be best for me? / would suit me? / should I go for? |

42 Enviar y recibir

42.1 EN LA OFICINA DE CORREOS

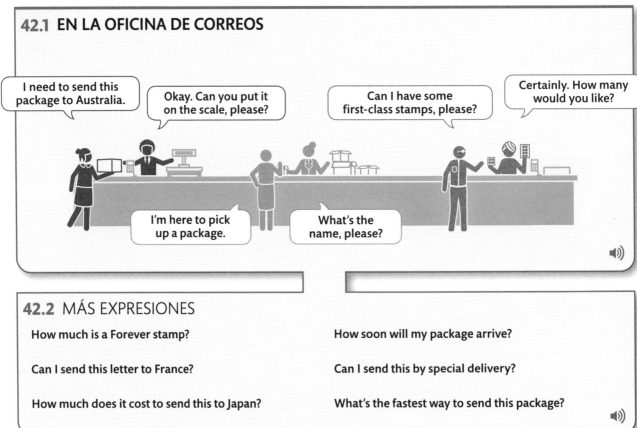

I need to send this package to Australia.

Okay. Can you put it on the scale, please?

Can I have some first-class stamps, please?

Certainly. How many would you like?

I'm here to pick up a package.

What's the name, please?

42.2 MÁS EXPRESIONES

How much is a Forever stamp?

Can I send this letter to France?

How much does it cost to send this to Japan?

How soon will my package arrive?

Can I send this by special delivery?

What's the fastest way to send this package?

42.3 SERVICIO DE MENSAJERÍA

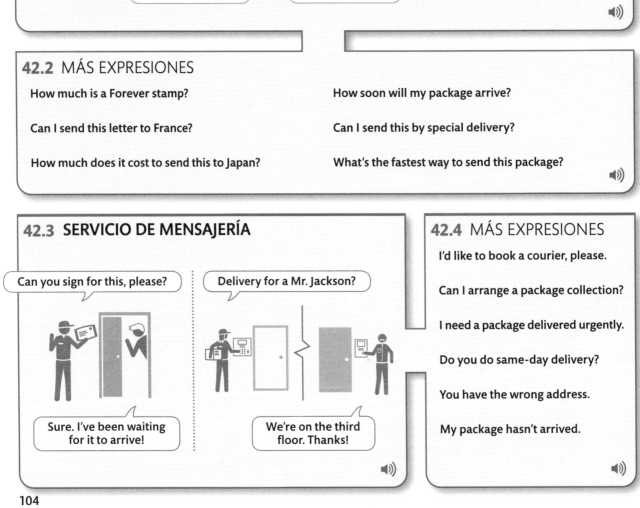

Can you sign for this, please?

Delivery for a Mr. Jackson?

Sure. I've been waiting for it to arrive!

We're on the third floor. Thanks!

42.4 MÁS EXPRESIONES

I'd like to book a courier, please.

Can I arrange a package collection?

I need a package delivered urgently.

Do you do same-day delivery?

You have the wrong address.

My package hasn't arrived.

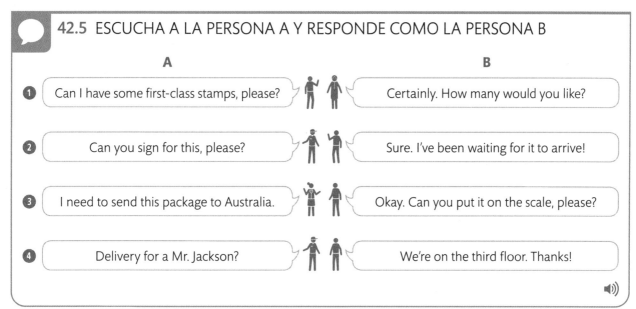

42.5 ESCUCHA A LA PERSONA A Y RESPONDE COMO LA PERSONA B

A

B

1. Can I have some first-class stamps, please? — Certainly. How many would you like?

2. Can you sign for this, please? — Sure. I've been waiting for it to arrive!

3. I need to send this package to Australia. — Okay. Can you put it on the scale, please?

4. Delivery for a Mr. Jackson? — We're on the third floor. Thanks!

42.6 ESCUCHA Y NUMERA LAS IMÁGENES EN EL ORDEN EN QUE SE DESCRIBEN

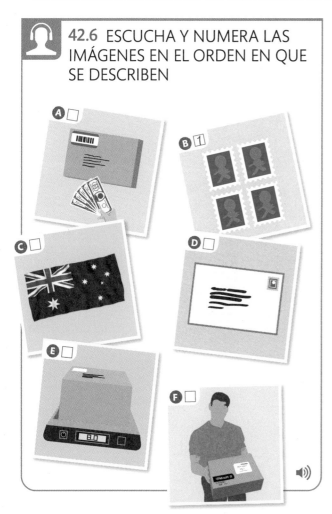

A ☐
B ☐ 1
C ☐
D ☐
E ☐
F ☐

42.7 DI LAS ORACIONES EN VOZ ALTA, LLENANDO LOS ESPACIOS CON LAS PALABRAS DEL PANEL

cost   send   like   put

waiting   pick up   sign   arrive

1. How many would you _____ ?

2. Can you _____ it on the scale, please?

3. How much does it _____ to send this to Japan?

4. I'm here to _____ a package.

5. Can you _____ for this, please?

6. How soon will my package _____ ?

7. Can I _____ this letter to France?

8. Sure. I've been _____ for it to arrive!

105

43 Dinero y finanzas

43.1 ABRIR UNA CUENTA BANCARIA

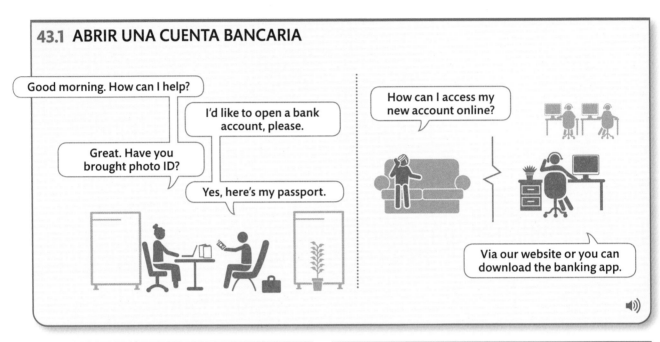

Good morning. How can I help?

I'd like to open a bank account, please.

Great. Have you brought photo ID?

Yes, here's my passport.

How can I access my new account online?

Via our website or you can download the banking app.

43.2 DEPOSITAR Y RETIRAR DINERO

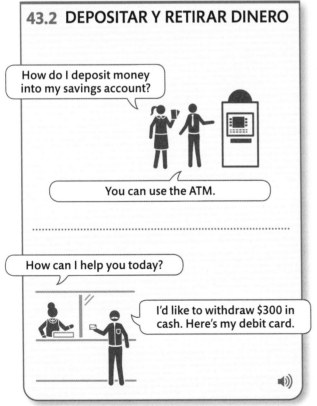

How do I deposit money into my savings account?

You can use the ATM.

How can I help you today?

I'd like to withdraw $300 in cash. Here's my debit card.

43.3 VOCABULARIO EN EL BANCO

cash

photo ID

ATM

debit card

credit card

currency

bank statement

mobile banking

online banking

to deposit money

to withdraw money

to transfer money

43.4 ESCUCHA A LA PERSONA A Y RESPONDE COMO LA PERSONA B

A	B
1 Good morning. How can I help?	I'd like to open a bank account, please.
2 Great. Have you brought photo ID?	Yes, here's my passport.
3 How do I deposit money into my savings account?	You can use the ATM.
4 How can I access my new account online?	Via our website or you can download the banking app.

43.5 RODEA CON UN CÍRCULO LO QUE OYES

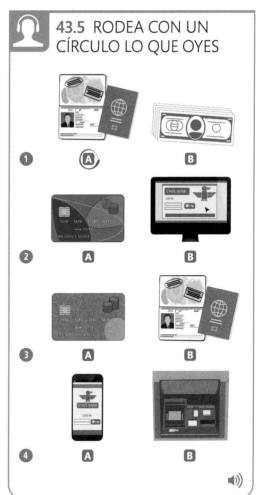

1 Ⓐ B

2 A B

3 A B

4 A B

43.6 USA EL ESQUEMA PARA FORMAR CINCO ORACIONES Y DILAS EN VOZ ALTA

I'd like to open a bank account, please.

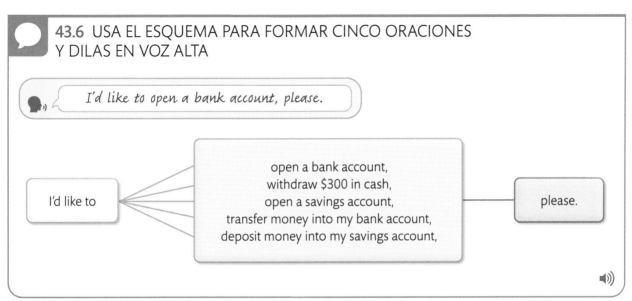

I'd like to

open a bank account,
withdraw $300 in cash,
open a savings account,
transfer money into my bank account,
deposit money into my savings account,

please.

43.7 COMPRAR DIVISAS

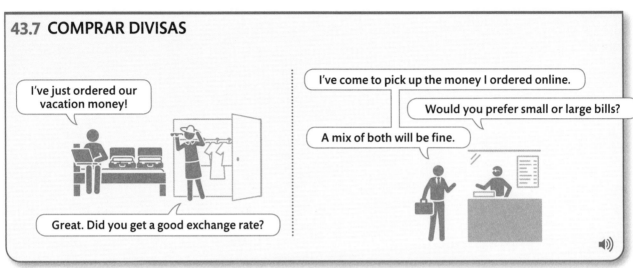

43.8 PROBLEMAS CON LA TARJETA DE CRÉDITO

43.9 FORMAS DE PAGO

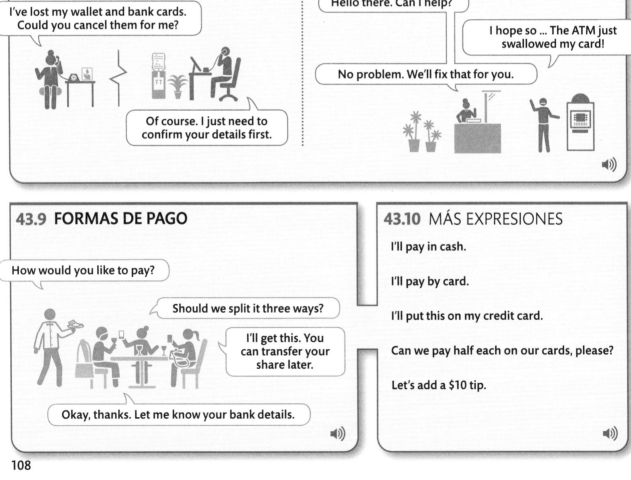

43.10 MÁS EXPRESIONES

I'll pay in cash.

I'll pay by card.

I'll put this on my credit card.

Can we pay half each on our cards, please?

Let's add a $10 tip.

43.11 ESCUCHA A LA PERSONA A Y RESPONDE COMO LA PERSONA B

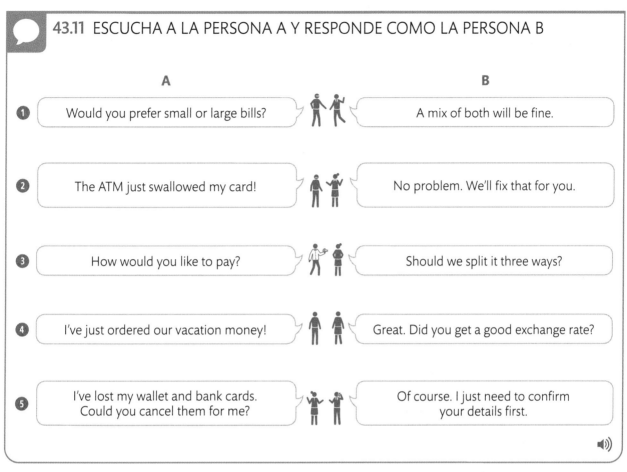

	A		B
1	Would you prefer small or large bills?		A mix of both will be fine.
2	The ATM just swallowed my card!		No problem. We'll fix that for you.
3	How would you like to pay?		Should we split it three ways?
4	I've just ordered our vacation money!		Great. Did you get a good exchange rate?
5	I've lost my wallet and bank cards. Could you cancel them for me?		Of course. I just need to confirm your details first.

43.12 CONECTA LAS ORACIONES Y DILAS EN VOZ ALTA

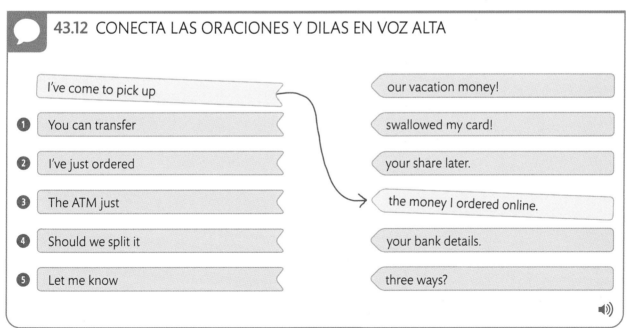

I've come to pick up —— the money I ordered online.

1. You can transfer — our vacation money!
2. I've just ordered — swallowed my card!
3. The ATM just — your share later.
4. Should we split it — your bank details.
5. Let me know — three ways?

44 En la biblioteca

44.1 HACERSE SOCIO

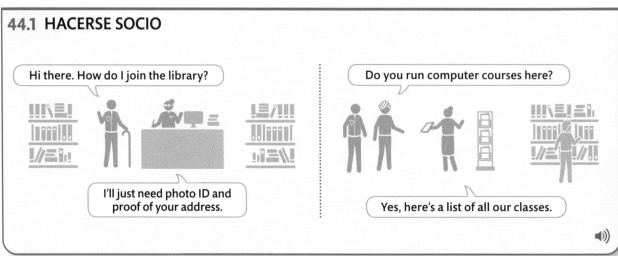

Hi there. How do I join the library?

I'll just need photo ID and proof of your address.

Do you run computer courses here?

Yes, here's a list of all our classes.

44.2 USAR LA BIBLIOTECA

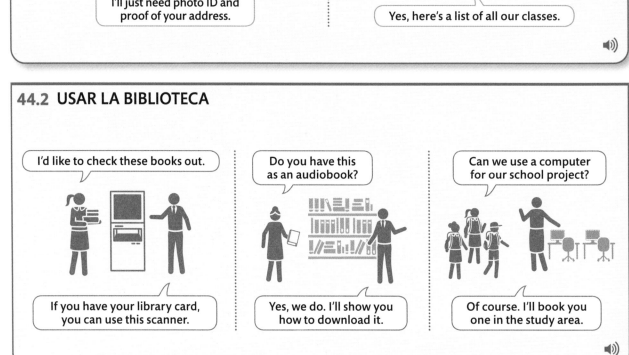

I'd like to check these books out.

If you have your library card, you can use this scanner.

Do you have this as an audiobook?

Yes, we do. I'll show you how to download it.

Can we use a computer for our school project?

Of course. I'll book you one in the study area.

44.3 MÁS EXPRESIONES

I need to renew these books, please.

Where do I return these books?

Can you help me find a book, please?

Where is the children's section?

Could you recommend a good thriller?

Can I see your newspaper archive?

44.4 ESCUCHA A LA PERSONA A Y RESPONDE COMO LA PERSONA B

A

B

1 Hi there. How do I join the library?

I'll just need photo ID and proof of your address.

2 Can we use a computer for our school project?

Of course. I'll book you one in the study area.

3 Do you have this as an audiobook?

Yes, we do. I'll show you how to download it.

4 Do you run computer courses here?

Yes, here's a list of all our classes.

5 I'd like to check these books out.

If you have your library card, you can use this scanner.

44.5 ESCUCHA Y NUMERA LAS IMÁGENES EN EL ORDEN EN QUE SE DESCRIBEN

A 1
B ☐
C ☐
D ☐
UNICORNS
E ☐
F ☐

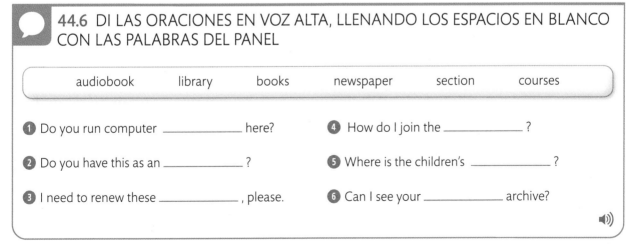

44.6 DI LAS ORACIONES EN VOZ ALTA, LLENANDO LOS ESPACIOS EN BLANCO CON LAS PALABRAS DEL PANEL

audiobook   library   books   newspaper   section   courses

1 Do you run computer _____ here?

2 Do you have this as an _____ ?

3 I need to renew these _____ , please.

4 How do I join the _____ ?

5 Where is the children's _____ ?

6 Can I see your _____ archive?

45 Trabajo y estudio

45.1 TRABAJOS / EMPLEOS

server

chef

teacher

cleaner

receptionist

lawyer

doctor

nurse

dentist

pharmacist

paramedic

childcare provider

courier

police officer

firefighter

security guard

pilot

flight attendant

mechanic

real estate agent

librarian

accountant

vet

sales assistant

electrician   carpenter   engineer

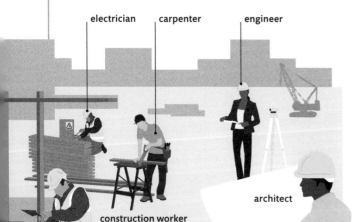
architect

construction worker

app developer

farmer

hairdresser

plumber

artist

gardener

45.2 ESCUELA Y UNIVERSIDAD

school / college

classroom

lesson

students / pupils

homework

university

timetable

to take an exam / a test

to pass an exam / a test

to fail an exam / a test

lecture

dissertation

graduation

degree

diploma

45.3 MUNDO LABORAL

employer

employee

freelancer

office worker

site worker

permanent job

temporary job

full-time job

part-time job

shift

overtime

flextime

to go on maternity leave

to resign

to retire

wages

salary

hourly rate

paycheck

benefits

raise

pay cut

bonus

vacation

sick leave

46 En la escuela

46.1 ELEGIR UNA ESCUELA

We offer a wide range of subjects.

Is music part of the curriculum?

The children have math every day.

How often do they have science lessons?

46.2 MÁS PREGUNTAS

How many children are in each class?

How much homework is there?

What clubs do you offer?

Do you have a school uniform?

Is there an after-school club?

46.3 COMENZAR LA ESCUELA

You must be our new student. Welcome!

Yes, this is Tom. He's a bit nervous for his first day!

There's no need to worry, Tom. Let's go and meet your new class.

46.4 REUNIONES DE PADRES

Zia is settling in very well.

Oh, good. How is she doing with English?

She's making really good progress.

46.5 VOCABULARIO ASIGNATURAS

English

math

science

computing

history

geography

languages

physical education (PE)

art

music

theater

religious studies

46.6 ESCUCHA A LA PERSONA A Y RESPONDE COMO LA PERSONA B

A	B
1 You must be our new student. Welcome!	Yes, this is Tom. He's a bit nervous for his first day!
2 The children have math every day.	How often do they have science lessons?
3 Zia is settling in very well.	Oh, good. How is she doing with English?
4 We offer a wide range of subjects.	Is music part of the curriculum?

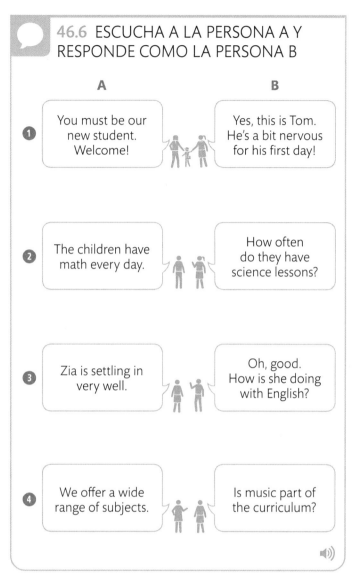

46.7 RODEA CON UN CÍRCULO LO QUE OYES

46.8 USA EL ESQUEMA PARA FORMAR CINCO ORACIONES Y DILAS EN VOZ ALTA

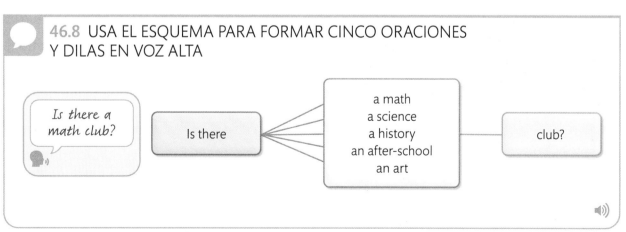

Is there a math club?

Is there → a math / a science / a history / an after-school / an art → club?

47 Formación continua y superior

47.1 ESCOGER UN CURSO

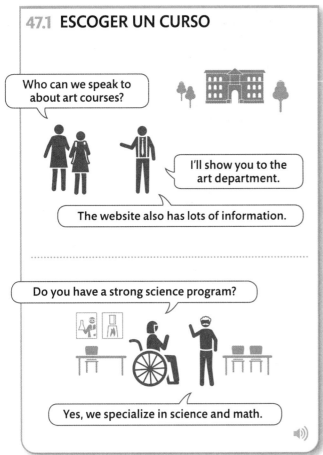

47.2 CURSOS VOCACIONALES

47.3 MÁS PREGUNTAS

What qualifications do I need?

What are your entry requirements?

What qualification will I get?

How long does the course last?

How do I apply?

Is there a chance to study abroad?

47.4 CURSOS DE TARDE

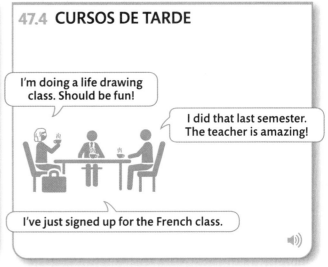

47.5 ESCUCHA A LA PERSONA A Y RESPONDE COMO LA PERSONA B

A

B

1. May I ask about your cooking course?
   Sure. It's a two-year, full-time program.

2. Do you have a strong science program?
   Yes, we specialize in science and math.

3. I've just signed up for the French class.
   I did that last semester.

4. Who can we speak to about art courses?
   I'll show you to the art department.

47.6 ESCUCHA Y NUMERA LAS ORACIONES EN EL ORDEN EN QUE LAS OYES

A. May I ask about your cooking course? ☐

B. Does the hairdressing course include work experience? ☐1☐

C. Who can we speak to about art courses? ☐

D. Yes. Students work once a week in a salon. ☐

E. I'll show you to the art department. ☐

F. I'm doing a life drawing class. Should be fun! ☐

47.7 DI LAS ORACIONES EN VOZ ALTA, LLENANDO LOS ESPACIOS CON LAS PALABRAS DEL PANEL

full-time   qualifications   website   salon

teacher   class   requirements   abroad

1. What are your entry _____ ?

2. Sure. It's a two-year, _____ program.

3. I've just signed up for the French _____ .

4. The _____ is amazing!

5. The _____ also has lots of information.

6. What _____ do I need?

7. Is there a chance to study _____ ?

8. Students work once a week in a _____ .

47.8 VOCABULARIO DEPARTAMENTOS Y ASIGNATURAS

humanities

social sciences

chemistry

physics

biology

medicine

law

engineering

art and design

business

economics

politics

47.9 EL PRIMER DÍA DE UNIVERSIDAD

Excuse me, I'm new here. Do you know where I can leave my bike?

Yes, the bike rack is around the corner. Enjoy your first day!

Hi, I'm Amy. I'm here for the business lecture.

Me, too. I'm Lucas.

Hello. I'm your lecturer, Professor Li. Take a seat.

47.10 ORIENTARSE EN EL CAMPUS

Can you tell me where the biology department is?

I'm going there, too. I'll show you.

Any idea where the art school is?

It's right next to the coffee shop. I can show you the way.

47.11 ESCUCHA A LA PERSONA A Y RESPONDE COMO LA PERSONA B

A

B

1. Do you know where I can leave my bike?

Yes, the bike rack is around the corner.

2. Hi, I'm Amy. I'm here for the business lecture.

Hello. I'm your lecturer, Professor Li.

3. Can you tell me where the biology department is?

I'm going there, too. I'll show you.

4. Any idea where the art school is?

It's right next to the coffee shop.

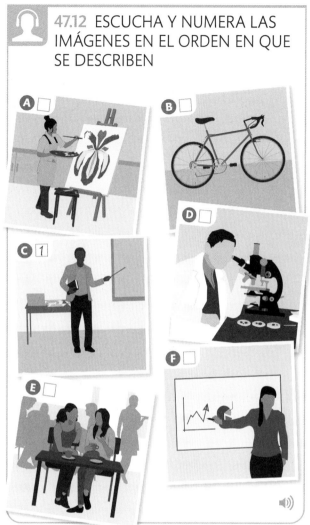

47.12 ESCUCHA Y NUMERA LAS IMÁGENES EN EL ORDEN EN QUE SE DESCRIBEN

A ☐

B ☐

C 1

D ☐

E ☐

F ☐

47.13 USA EL ESQUEMA PARA FORMAR 12 ORACIONES Y DILAS EN VOZ ALTA

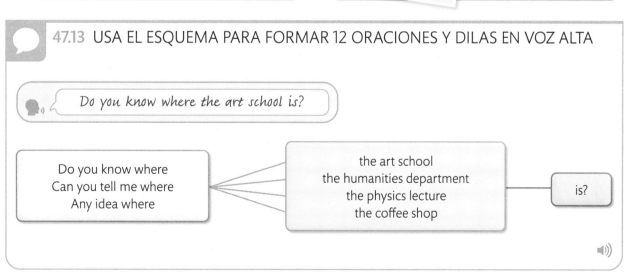

Do you know where the art school is?

| Do you know where Can you tell me where Any idea where | the art school the humanities department the physics lecture the coffee shop | is? |

47.14 VIDA UNIVERSITARIA

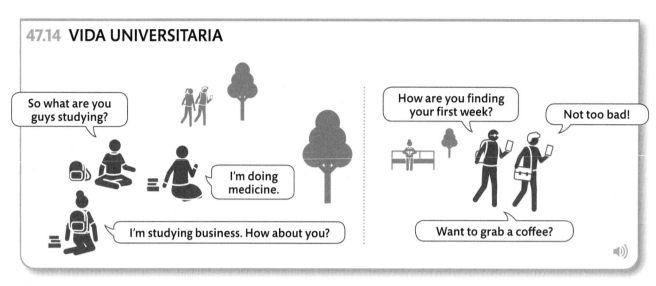

So what are you guys studying?

I'm doing medicine.

I'm studying business. How about you?

How are you finding your first week?

Not too bad!

Want to grab a coffee?

47.15 TUTORÍAS

How are you coping?

I'm really enjoying my course ...

... but I'm feeling a bit homesick ...

... and I'm finding it hard to make friends.

47.16 OTROS ASUNTOS

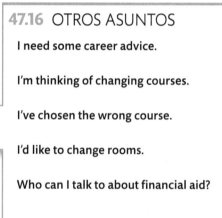

I need some career advice.

I'm thinking of changing courses.

I've chosen the wrong course.

I'd like to change rooms.

Who can I talk to about financial aid?

47.17 UNIRSE A UN CLUB

Are you coming to the Activities Fair?

Wanna try out for the basketball team?

Yes, I want to sign up for some new clubs.

Sounds good, thanks!

47.18 DECIR QUE SÍ O QUE NO

Sounds like fun!

I'm in!

I'd be up for that!

I'd rather not, actually.

It's not for me, sorry.

I think I'll pass.

47.19 RODEA CON UN CÍRCULO LO QUE OYES

47.20 RESPONDE EN VOZ ALTA AL AUDIO, LLENANDO LOS ESPACIOS EN BLANCO CON LAS PALABRAS DEL PANEL

47.21 CONECTA LAS ORACIONES Y DILAS EN VOZ ALTA

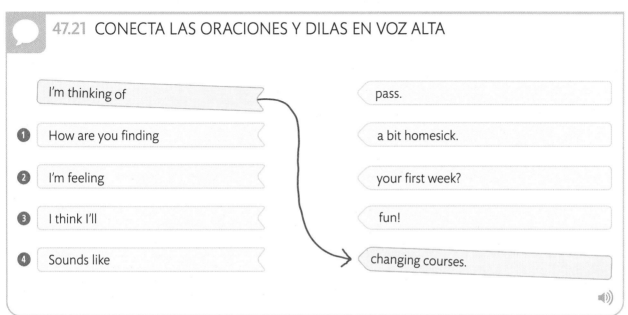

121

48 Buscar trabajo

48.1 BÚSQUEDA DE EMPLEO

This job looks interesting ...

... flexible hours ...

... no experience needed ...

... sounds ideal!

Have you used this job search website?

Yes, I found my current job on there.

Is the job in the window still open?

BAR STAFF WANTED

Yes. Can you email us your resume?

48.2 EN LA OFICINA DE EMPLEO

How can I help?

I'm looking for a part-time sales job.

Okay, let me get some details about you.

Have you worked in a restaurant before?

I worked as a server last summer.

48.3 PREGUNTAS QUE PODRÍAS OÍR

What skills do you have?

What hours can you work?

What experience do you have?

What salary are you looking for?

Why did you leave your last job?

48.4 ESCUCHA A LA PERSONA A Y RESPONDE COMO LA PERSONA B

A	B
1 How can I help?	I'm looking for a part-time sales job.
2 Is the job in the window still open?	Yes. Can you email us your resume?
3 Have you used this job search website?	Yes, I found my current job on there.
4 Have you worked in a restaurant before?	I worked as a server last summer.

48.5 ESCUCHA Y NUMERA LAS ORACIONES EN EL ORDEN EN QUE LAS OYES

A What hours can you work? ☐

B What skills do you have? ☐

C What salary are you looking for? ☐

D What experience do you have? ☐

E Have you worked in a restaurant before? ☐

F How can I help? [1]

G Is the job in the window still open? ☐

48.6 DI LAS ORACIONES EN VOZ ALTA, LLENANDO LOS ESPACIOS CON LAS PALABRAS DEL PANEL

skills	website	part-time
details	window	job
	hours	resume

1 Okay, let me get some _____ about you.

2 This _____ looks interesting ...

3 I'm looking for a _____ sales job.

4 What _____ can you work?

5 Have you used this job search _____ ?

6 Yes. Can you email us your _____ ?

7 What _____ do you have?

8 Is the job in the _____ still open?

49.1 PREPARAR UN CURRÍCULUM

I really want to apply for this job. I need to update my resume!

There are tons of examples online to help you.

It says the deadline for applications is tomorrow.

Really? I'd better email my resume tonight, then.

My resume is all checked and ready to go ...

Don't forget to send your cover letter, too!

49.2 FORMULARIOS DE SOLICITUD

Have you finished your application yet?

I just need to fill in my personal details and it'll be ready.

This application form is taking ages!

Why don't you save it and take a break?

49.3 VOCABULARIO SOLICITUDES DE EMPLEO

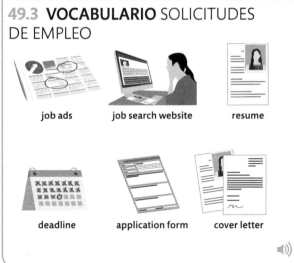

job ads

job search website

resume

deadline

application form

cover letter

49.4 ESCUCHA A LA PERSONA A Y RESPONDE COMO LA PERSONA B

	A	B
1	I need to update my resume!	There are tons of examples online to help you.
2	It says the deadline for applications is tomorrow.	Really? I'd better email my resume tonight, then.
3	Have you finished your application yet?	I just need to fill in my personal details and it'll be ready.
4	This application form is taking ages!	Why don't you save it and take a break?

49.5 RODEA CON UN CÍRCULO LO QUE OYES

49.6 CONECTA LAS ORACIONES Y DILAS EN VOZ ALTA

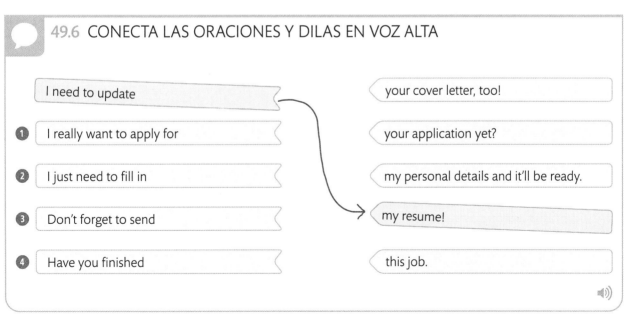

I need to update ——→ my resume!

1 I really want to apply for — this job.

2 I just need to fill in — my personal details and it'll be ready.

3 Don't forget to send — your cover letter, too!

4 Have you finished — your application yet?

50 Entrevistas de trabajo

50.1 PREGUNTAS DEL EMPLEADOR

Why are you right for this position?

I have the qualifications and experience you're looking for.

What can you bring to our company?

Enthusiasm, energy, and lots of ideas.

Why did you apply for this job?

I'm really eager to use my planning skills.

50.2 OTRAS PREGUNTAS QUE TE PUEDEN HACER

What experience do you have in ...?

What are your strengths?

What do you enjoy doing outside work?

What are your goals for the future?

Why do you want to leave your current job?

What salary are you expecting?

What's the notice period in your current job?

How soon could you start?

50.3 HABLAR DE UNO MISMO

Tell me about yourself.

I'm reliable and organized.

I work well in a team.

I'm good with customers.

I'm used to working under pressure.

50.4 MÁS EXPRESIONES

I can adapt to new situations.

I'm a quick learner.

I'm self-motivated.

I have an excellent track record.

I enjoy solving problems.

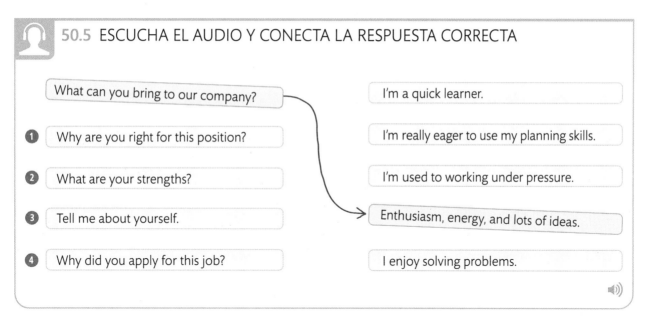

50.5 ESCUCHA EL AUDIO Y CONECTA LA RESPUESTA CORRECTA

What can you bring to our company? → Enthusiasm, energy, and lots of ideas.

I'm a quick learner.

1 Why are you right for this position?

I'm really eager to use my planning skills.

2 What are your strengths?

I'm used to working under pressure.

3 Tell me about yourself.

4 Why did you apply for this job?

I enjoy solving problems.

50.6 DI LAS ORACIONES EN VOZ ALTA, LLENANDO LOS ESPACIOS EN BLANCO CON LAS PALABRAS DEL PANEL

working   notice   company   start   customers   salary

1 What can you bring to our _____ ?

2 What _____ are you expecting?

3 What's the _____ period in your current job?

4 How soon could you _____ ?

5 I'm used to _____ under pressure.

6 I'm good with _____ .

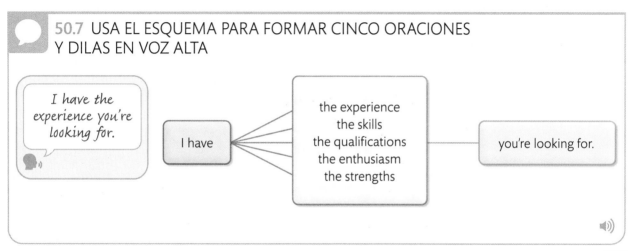

50.7 USA EL ESQUEMA PARA FORMAR CINCO ORACIONES Y DILAS EN VOZ ALTA

I have the experience you're looking for.

I have →

the experience
the skills
the qualifications
the enthusiasm
the strengths

you're looking for.

51 Empezar en un nuevo trabajo

51.1 PREPARATIVOS

Hello, I'm Christina. It's my first day.

Welcome! Here's your pass. I'll let the manager know you're here.

I've set up your email account. Can you type in a password?

Okay. How long does it have to be?

51.2 MÁS EXPRESIONES

Your supervisor will show you where everything is.

Let's find you a locker.

Anything you need, just ask.

You'll need to clock out at the end of your shift.

Your first break is at 12:30.

51.3 CONOCER A LOS COLEGAS

How's it going so far?

There's lots to remember, but I'm getting there!

Let me know if you need help.

51.4 MÁS EXPRESIONES

It's great to have you on the team.

How's your morning been?

Do you have everything you need?

Have you met everybody now?

Want to grab some lunch?

51.5 SALUD Y SEGURIDAD

You need to read these safety rules carefully.

And always wear your hard hat!

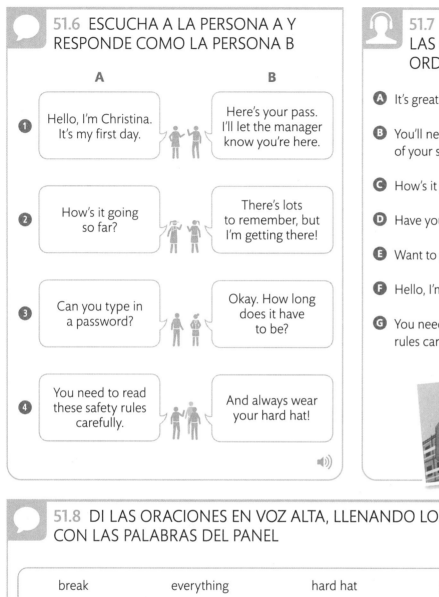

51.6 ESCUCHA A LA PERSONA A Y RESPONDE COMO LA PERSONA B

A

B

1 Hello, I'm Christina. It's my first day.

Here's your pass. I'll let the manager know you're here.

2 How's it going so far?

There's lots to remember, but I'm getting there!

3 Can you type in a password?

Okay. How long does it have to be?

4 You need to read these safety rules carefully.

And always wear your hard hat!

🔊

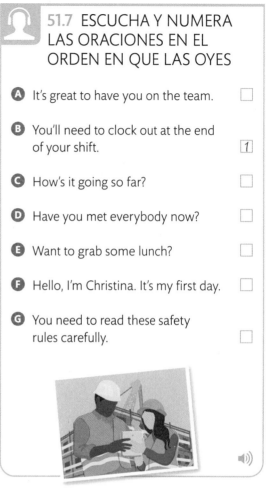

51.7 ESCUCHA Y NUMERA LAS ORACIONES EN EL ORDEN EN QUE LAS OYES

A It's great to have you on the team. ☐

B You'll need to clock out at the end of your shift. [1]

C How's it going so far? ☐

D Have you met everybody now? ☐

E Want to grab some lunch? ☐

F Hello, I'm Christina. It's my first day. ☐

G You need to read these safety rules carefully. ☐

🔊

51.8 DI LAS ORACIONES EN VOZ ALTA, LLENANDO LOS ESPACIOS EN BLANCO CON LAS PALABRAS DEL PANEL

break	everything	hard hat	password
email	lunch	morning	team

1 Your first _____ is at 12:30.

2 And always wear your _____ !

3 It's great to have you on the _____ .

4 I've set up your _____ account.

5 Want to grab some _____ ?

6 How's your _____ been?

7 Do you have _____ you need?

8 Can you type in a _____ ?

🔊

52.1 RUTINAS LABORALES

We have a team meeting at 4 p.m. on Tuesdays.

And a full staff meeting once a month.

Thanks. I'll put it in my calendar.

What time is your lunch break?

It's in half an hour. How about yours?

52.2 PROBLEMAS EN EL TRABAJO

Sorry, I have to change my shift on Monday.

Which one are you down for?

I'm scheduled for the morning shift. Could I change to the afternoon?

This station is down again. It keeps crashing!

Not again! Okay, let's call the supervisor.

52.3 VOCABULARIO EN EL TRABAJO

meeting

lunch break

coffee break

morning shift

afternoon shift

evening shift

manager

supervisor

colleague

team

to clock in / out

locker

52.4 ESCUCHA A LA PERSONA A Y RESPONDE COMO LA PERSONA B

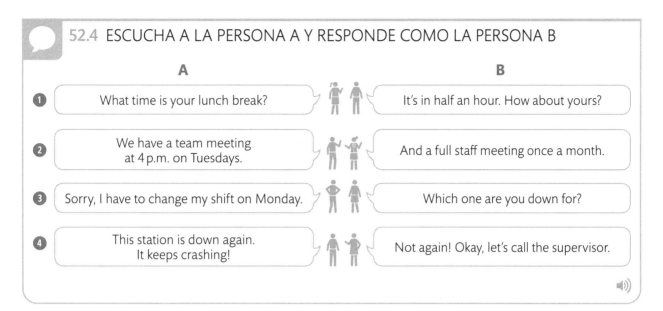

A

① What time is your lunch break?

② We have a team meeting at 4 p.m. on Tuesdays.

③ Sorry, I have to change my shift on Monday.

④ This station is down again. It keeps crashing!

B

① It's in half an hour. How about yours?

② And a full staff meeting once a month.

③ Which one are you down for?

④ Not again! Okay, let's call the supervisor.

52.5 RODEA CON UN CÍRCULO LO QUE OYES

52.6 RESPONDE EN VOZ ALTA AL AUDIO, LLENANDO LOS ESPACIOS EN BLANCO CON LAS PALABRAS DEL PANEL

scheduled for   let's call   How about   put it in

① What time is your lunch break?

It's in half an hour. _____ yours?

② This station is down again. It keeps crashing!

Not again! Okay, _____ the supervisor.

③ Which one are you down for?

I'm _____ the morning shift.

④ We have a team meeting at 4 p.m. on Tuesdays.

Thanks. I'll _____ my calendar.

53 Hacer una presentación

53.1 EMPEZAR A HABLAR

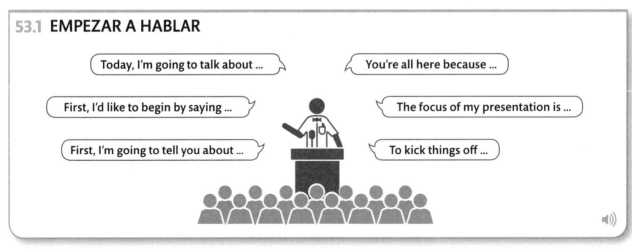

Today, I'm going to talk about ...

You're all here because ...

First, I'd like to begin by saying ...

The focus of my presentation is ...

First, I'm going to tell you about ...

To kick things off ...

53.2 CAMBIAR DE TEMA

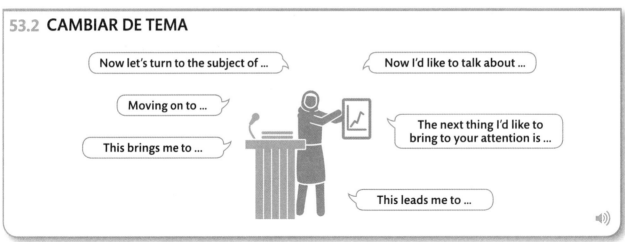

Now let's turn to the subject of ...

Now I'd like to talk about ...

Moving on to ...

The next thing I'd like to bring to your attention is ...

This brings me to ...

This leads me to ...

53.3 TERMINAR LA CHARLA

Last, I'd like to finish by saying ...

I think I've covered everything. Any questions?

Finally, I want to let you know that ...

Does anyone have anything to add?

So, to sum up, I'd say ...

53.4 ESCUCHA Y NUMERA LAS ORACIONES EN EL ORDEN EN QUE LAS OYES

A To kick things off ... ☐

B So, to sum up, I'd say ... 1

C Moving on to ... ☐

D First, I'm going to tell you about ... ☐

E Last, I'd like to finish by saying ... ☐

F This leads me to ... ☐

G First, I'd like to begin by saying ... ☐

H Does anyone have anything to add? ☐

53.5 CONECTA LAS ORACIONES Y DILAS EN VOZ ALTA

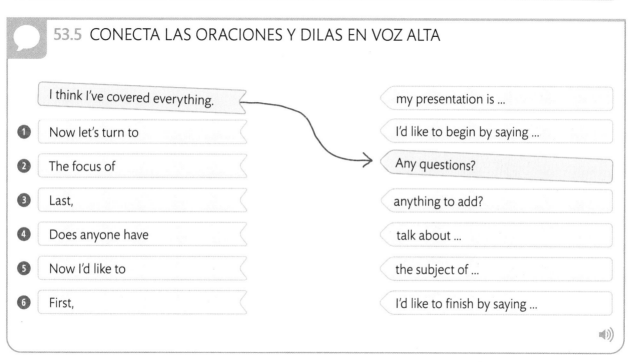

I think I've covered everything.

1 Now let's turn to

2 The focus of

3 Last,

4 Does anyone have

5 Now I'd like to

6 First,

my presentation is ...

I'd like to begin by saying ...

Any questions?

anything to add?

talk about ...

the subject of ...

I'd like to finish by saying ...

53.6 USA EL ESQUEMA PARA FORMAR 10 ORACIONES Y DILAS EN VOZ ALTA

Today, I'd like to talk about ...

Today,
First,
Now
Last,
Finally,

I'd like to
I'm going to

talk about ...

54 Reuniones de trabajo

54.1 ESTABLECER EL ORDEN DEL DÍA

I think we're all here, so let's get started.

What's on today's agenda?

We're starting with how to improve our customer service.

Listen up, everyone! There's a lot to get through.

First up is deciding next week's menus …

… then we'll move on to the schedules.

54.2 TURNARSE PARA HABLAR

So that's the situation. Let's hear your thoughts.

If I can just add … It will be a slow process.

May I go first? For me, these changes are important.

Let's hear from James on this point.

Just to clarify … Which changes exactly?

Can I jump in? I totally agree.

54.3 DAR UNA OPINIÓN

Let's go around the table and see where we all stand.

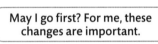

I'm 100% on board with this.

If you ask me, it's a nonstarter.

54.4 MÁS EXPRESIONES

Why don't we try …?

The way I see it is …

How about if we …?

I see where you're coming from, so …

I'm wondering if we could …?

54.5 ESCUCHA EL AUDIO Y CONECTA LAS ORACIONES

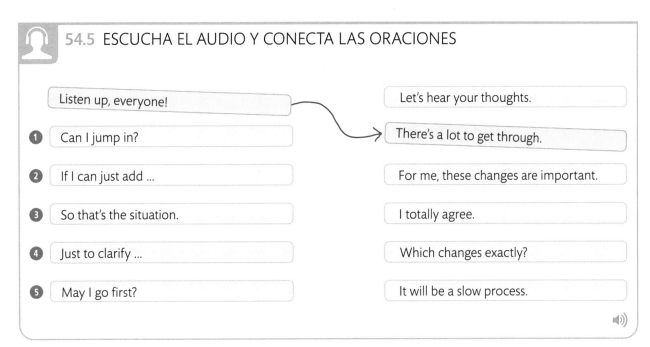

Listen up, everyone!	Let's hear your thoughts.
1 Can I jump in?	There's a lot to get through.
2 If I can just add ...	For me, these changes are important.
3 So that's the situation.	I totally agree.
4 Just to clarify ...	Which changes exactly?
5 May I go first?	It will be a slow process.

54.6 ESCUCHA A LA PERSONA A Y RESPONDE COMO LA PERSONA B

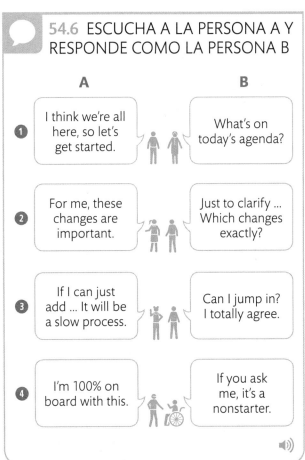

A — **B**

1 I think we're all here, so let's get started. — What's on today's agenda?

2 For me, these changes are important. — Just to clarify ... Which changes exactly?

3 If I can just add ... It will be a slow process. — Can I jump in? I totally agree.

4 I'm 100% on board with this. — If you ask me, it's a nonstarter.

54.7 DI LAS ORACIONES EN VOZ ALTA, LLENANDO LOS ESPACIOS CON LAS PALABRAS DEL PANEL

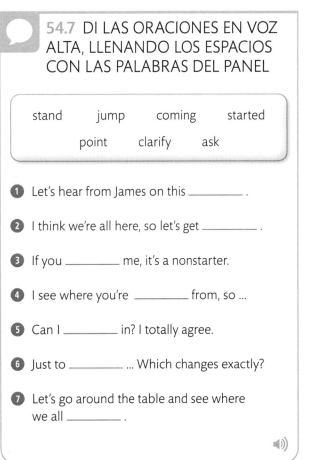

stand   jump   coming   started
point   clarify   ask

1 Let's hear from James on this _____ .

2 I think we're all here, so let's get _____ .

3 If you _____ me, it's a nonstarter.

4 I see where you're _____ from, so ...

5 Can I _____ in? I totally agree.

6 Just to _____ ... Which changes exactly?

7 Let's go around the table and see where we all _____ .

54.8 TERMINAR LA REUNIÓN

To sum up, we're going ahead with the new designs.

Any questions before we wrap up?

To recap, we've agreed to change the timetable.

I'll email the action points to you all later.

Great. Thanks everyone for your input!

54.9 HACER CONTACTOS

I understand you work for AbiCo.

That's right. Sorry, I didn't catch your name.

It was great meeting you.

You, too. Let's stay in touch. Here's my card.

Thanks. I'll let you know if something suitable comes up.

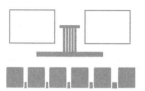

Your project sounds really interesting.

I'd love to keep the conversation going.

I've enjoyed our discussion.

Me, too. Let's follow up in the office.

54.10 ESCUCHA A LA PERSONA A Y RESPONDE COMO LA PERSONA B

A		B
1 To sum up, we're going ahead with the new designs.		Any questions before we wrap up?
2 To recap, we've agreed to change the timetable.		I'll email the action points to you all later.
3 I've enjoyed our discussion.		Me, too. Let's follow up in the office.
4 Your project sounds really interesting.		I'd love to keep the conversation going.

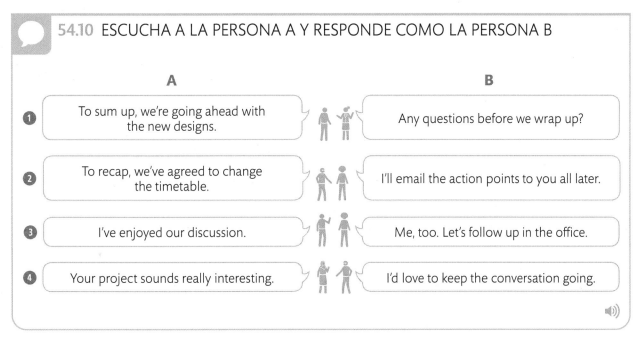

54.11 ESCUCHA Y NUMERA LAS ORACIONES EN EL ORDEN EN QUE LAS OYES

A Your project sounds really interesting. ☐

B Any questions before we wrap up? ☐

C Sorry, I didn't catch your name. ☐ 1

D Thanks everyone for your input! ☐

E To sum up, we're going ahead with the new designs. ☐

F Thanks. I'll let you know if something suitable comes up. ☐

G You, too. Let's stay in touch. Here's my card. ☐

H Me, too. Let's follow up in the office. ☐

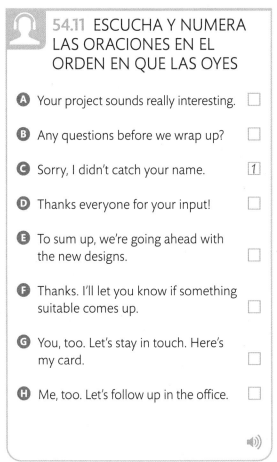

54.12 RESPONDE EN VOZ ALTA AL AUDIO, LLENANDO LOS ESPACIOS CON LAS PALABRAS DEL PANEL

your name   in touch   follow up

1 It was great meeting you.

You, too. Let's stay _____ .

2 I understand you work for AbiCo.

That's right. Sorry, I didn't catch _____ .

3 I've enjoyed our discussion.

Me, too. Let's _____ in the office.

137

55 Reuniones virtuales

55.1 EMPEZAR

55.2 MÁS EXPRESIONES

Would you like to speak first?

Could you repeat that, please?

Can you enlarge it on your screen?

Sorry for interrupting, please keep going.

55.3 PROBLEMAS DE CONEXIÓN

55.4 LA SIGUIENTE REUNIÓN

55.5 ESCUCHA A LA PERSONA A Y RESPONDE COMO LA PERSONA B

A | B

1 Let's get started, shall we? 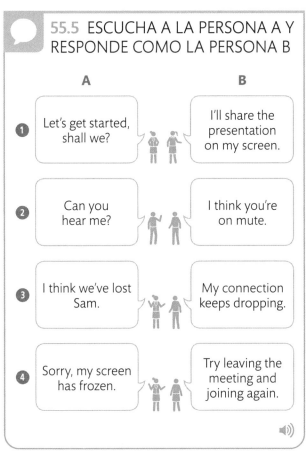 I'll share the presentation on my screen.

2 Can you hear me? I think you're on mute.

3 I think we've lost Sam. My connection keeps dropping.

4 Sorry, my screen has frozen. Try leaving the meeting and joining again.

🔊

55.6 ESCUCHA Y NUMERA LAS ORACIONES EN EL ORDEN EN QUE LAS OYES

- **A** Let's get started, shall we? ☐
- **B** I think you're on mute. ☐
- **C** Sorry, my screen has frozen. ☐
- **D** Try leaving the meeting and joining again. [1]
- **E** Can you hear me? ☐
- **F** I'll share the presentation on my screen. ☐
- **G** My connection keeps dropping. ☐

🔊

55.7 CONECTA LAS ORACIONES Y DILAS EN VOZ ALTA

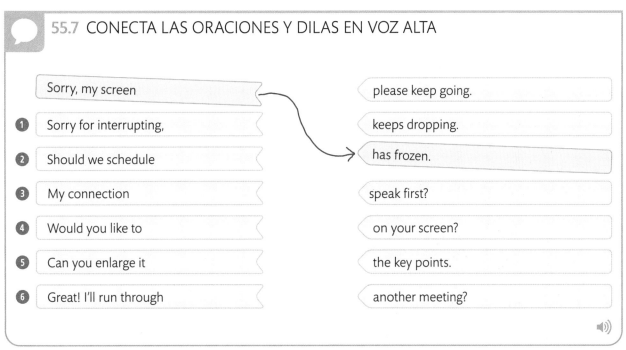

Sorry, my screen — please keep going.

1 Sorry for interrupting, — keeps dropping.

2 Should we schedule → has frozen.

3 My connection — speak first?

4 Would you like to — on your screen?

5 Can you enlarge it — the key points.

6 Great! I'll run through — another meeting?

🔊

56 El hogar

56.1 VIVIENDAS Y VECINDARIOS

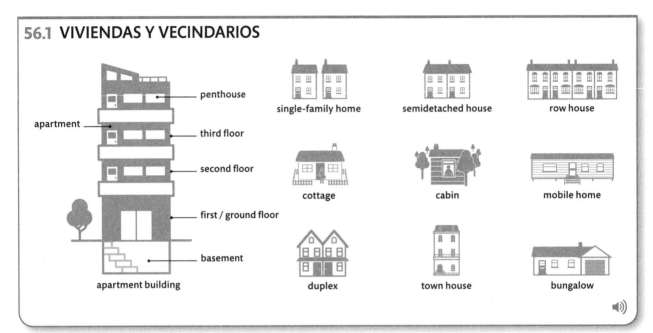

penthouse

apartment

third floor

second floor

first / ground floor

basement

apartment building

single-family home

semidetached house

row house

cottage

cabin

mobile home

duplex

town house

bungalow

56.2 HABITACIONES Y ZONAS DE LA CASA

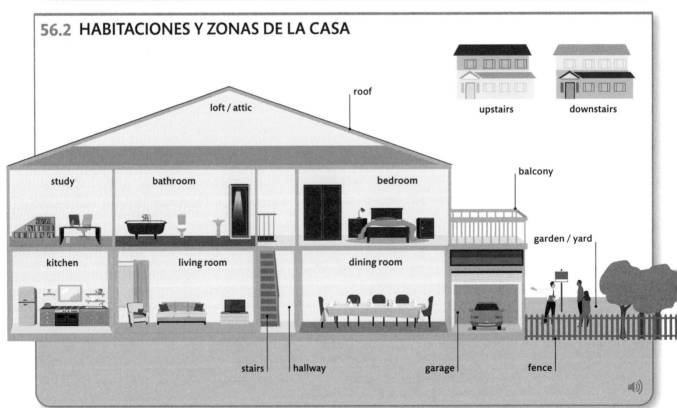

roof

loft / attic

upstairs

downstairs

balcony

study

bathroom

bedroom

garden / yard

kitchen

living room

dining room

stairs

hallway

garage

fence

56.3 MEJORAS EN CASA

to paint a door

to grout tiles

to strip the walls

to fill a crack

to rewire the house

to fix a fence

to hang shelves

to lay a carpet

to sew curtains

to build an extension

56.4 ELECTRODOMÉSTICOS Y MOBILIARIO

top-freezer fridge

oven

washing machine

dishwasher

kitchen sink

bathtub

shower

toilet

bathroom sink

mirror

bed

crib

closet

nightstand

chest of drawers

couch

armchair

coffee table

ottoman

toy box

shelf
bookcase

dining table

dining chair

television / TV

sideboard

57 Encontrar un nuevo hogar

57.1 BUSCAR VIVIENDA

What sort of property are you looking for?

A one-bedroom place in the city center.

57.3 VISITAR UNA VIVIENDA

Thanks for showing us around. I love the location!

What do you think of the inside?

It's a good size, but it needs a lot of work.

57.2 DECIR QUÉ QUIERES

I'm looking for an apartment on the ground floor.

We'd like a house with a yard.

I want a property close to the subway.

We'd prefer somewhere near a school.

We need at least two bedrooms.

57.4 DAR TU OPINIÓN

I think it's too small for us.

It's on a busy road.

I really like the layout.

We'd need to put in a new kitchen.

We like it, but the price is too high.

57.5 HACER UNA OFERTA

How do you feel after seeing it again?

We love it even more!

Would you like to put in an offer?

Yes, for $5,000 under the asking price.

FOR SALE

57.6 ESCUCHA A LA PERSONA A Y RESPONDE COMO LA PERSONA B

	A		B
1	What sort of property are you looking for?		A one-bedroom place in the city center.
2	What do you think of the inside?		It's a good size, but it needs a lot of work.
3	How do you feel after seeing it again?		We love it even more!
4	Would you like to put in an offer?		Yes, for $5,000 under the asking price.

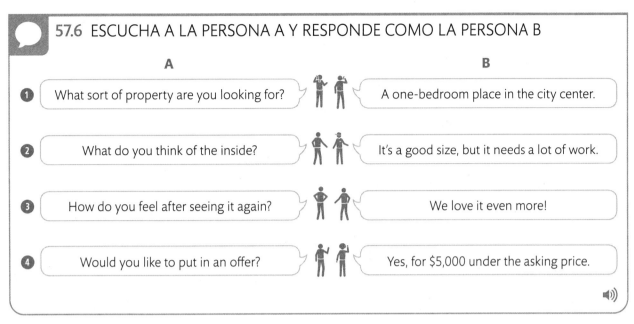

57.7 CONECTA LAS ORACIONES Y DILAS EN VOZ ALTA

It's on — a busy road.

1 We'd need to — put in a new kitchen.

2 I want a property — the layout.

3 I really like — it's too small for us.

4 I think — close to the subway.

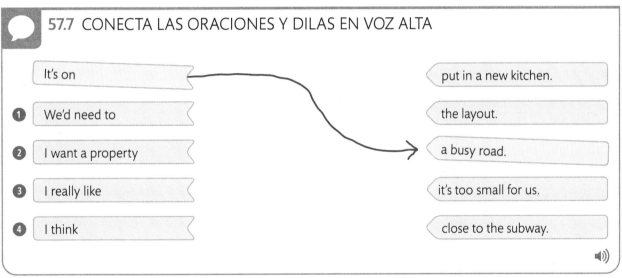

57.8 USA EL ESQUEMA PARA FORMAR NUEVE ORACIONES Y DILAS EN VOZ ALTA

We'd like a house with a yard.

We'd like

a house
an apartment
a property

with a yard.
close to the subway.
near a school.

57.9 ALQUILAR UNA VIVIENDA

How long is the lease?

One year, with an option to renew.

How soon could we move in?

As soon as you've signed the rental agreement!

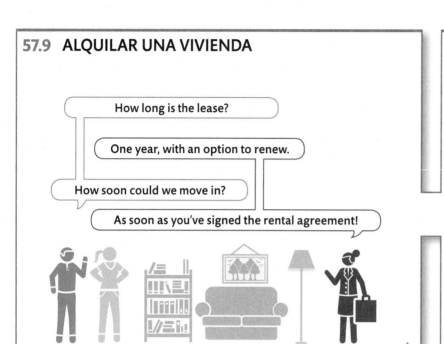

57.10 MÁS PREGUNTAS

How much is the rent?

Do I pay the rent monthly?

Does it have a washer and dryer?

Do you need a deposit?

Are utility bills included?

Are pets allowed?

Can I have a roommate?

What references do you need?

57.11 DURANTE EL ALQUILER

Can I put this picture up?

Yes, as long as it doesn't leave marks on the wall.

The washing machine is leaking.

I'll get maintenance to come and look at it.

57.12 VOCABULARIO ALQUILAR UNA VIVIENDA

landlord / landlady

tenant

roommate

rent

deposit

rental agreement

furnished

unfurnished

utility bills

57.13 ESCUCHA Y NUMERA LAS ORACIONES EN EL ORDEN EN QUE LAS OYES

A How soon could we move in? ☐

B One year, with an option to renew. 1

C Does it have a washer and dryer? ☐

D The washing machine is leaking. ☐

E Can I have a roommate? ☐

F How much is the rent? ☐

57.14 DI LAS ORACIONES EN VOZ ALTA, REEMPLAZANDO LAS IMÁGENES CON PALABRAS

1 How much is the ___ ?

2 Are ___ included?

3 Can I put this ___ up?

4 The ___ is leaking.

5 Are ___ allowed?

6 As soon as you've signed the ___ !

57.15 DI LAS ORACIONES EN VOZ ALTA, LLENANDO LOS ESPACIOS EN BLANCO CON LAS PALABRAS DEL PANEL

bills	roommate	pay	renew	deposit	references

1 Can I have a _____ ?

2 One year, with an option to _____ .

3 Are utility _____ included?

4 Do you need a _____ ?

5 Do I _____ the rent monthly?

6 What _____ do you need?

58 Mudarse

58.1 HACER CAJAS

I'm moving! Do you have any spare boxes?

There are lots in the back. Help yourself!

Is everything packed and ready?

Yes, we're done. Let's load the van!

58.2 EL DÍA DE LA MUDANZA

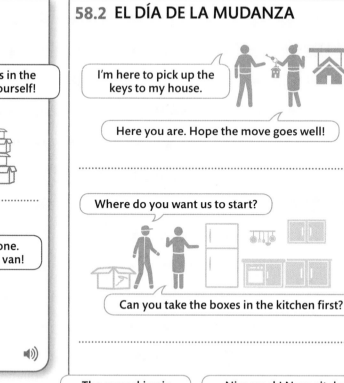

I'm here to pick up the keys to my house.

Here you are. Hope the move goes well!

Where do you want us to start?

Can you take the boxes in the kitchen first?

The unpacking is all done!

Nice work! Now, sit down and have some coffee.

58.3 VOCABULARIO TRASLADO

moving date

to move out

to move in

keys

to pack

to unpack

boxes

to load

moving van

58.4 MÁS EXPRESIONES

I've told everyone our moving date.

We have to move out by the weekend.

I've packed up the bedroom.

Let's load the moving van!

We can unpack in the morning.

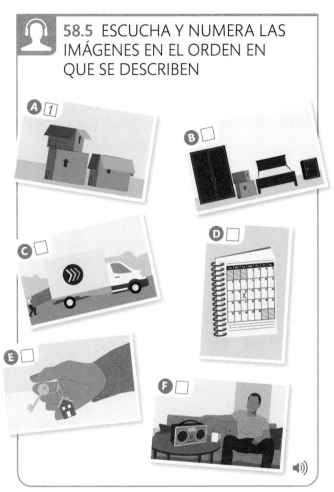

58.5 ESCUCHA Y NUMERA LAS IMÁGENES EN EL ORDEN EN QUE SE DESCRIBEN

58.6 DI LAS ORACIONES EN VOZ ALTA, LLENANDO LOS ESPACIOS CON LAS PALABRAS DEL PANEL

unpack	ready	the move	packed
weekend	load	boxes	moving

1 Is everything packed and _____ ?

2 Hope _____ goes well!

3 Do you have any spare _____ ?

4 I've told everyone our _____ date.

5 We have to move out by the _____ .

6 I've _____ up the bedroom.

7 Let's _____ the moving van!

8 We can _____ in the morning.

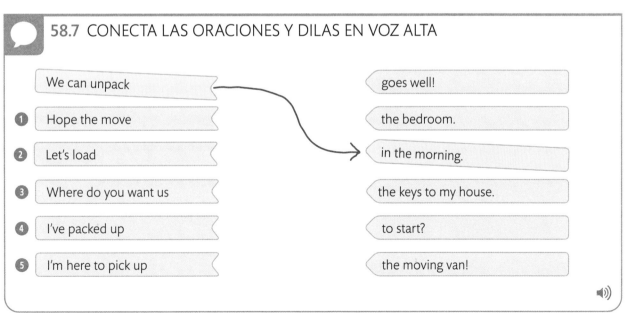

58.7 CONECTA LAS ORACIONES Y DILAS EN VOZ ALTA

We can unpack ⟶ in the morning.

goes well!

the bedroom.

the keys to my house.

to start?

the moving van!

1 Hope the move

2 Let's load

3 Where do you want us

4 I've packed up

5 I'm here to pick up

59 Conocer a los vecinos

59.1 PRESENTARSE

Hi! I've just moved in next door.

Yes, I saw you arrive. Welcome to the neighborhood!

Hello. I live downstairs. I've brought you a housewarming gift.

That's so kind of you!

59.2 MÁS EXPRESIONES

It's so nice to meet you.

We've moved here from Beijing.

I'm your new neighbor.

I wanted to introduce myself.

I just came over to say hello.

59.3 SOCIALIZAR

We're having a housewarming party on Saturday. Would you like to join us?

I'd love to, thank you!

59.4 MÁS EXPRESIONES

Would you like to stop by for drinks later?

Are you free for lunch on Sunday?

Can you come over for coffee tomorrow?

I'm having a cookout next week, if you'd like to come?

59.5 COMPARTIR INFORMACIÓN

Would you like to join our local group chat?

Yes, please! I'd love to get to know the neighbors.

Street Chat

Does anyone know a good plumber?

I do! I'll find their number and send it to you.

I know one, too!

59.6 ESCUCHA A LA PERSONA A Y RESPONDE COMO LA PERSONA B

A		B
1 Hi! I've just moved in next door.		Yes, I saw you arrive. Welcome to the neighborhood!
2 Hello. I live downstairs. I've brought you a housewarming gift.		That's so kind of you!
3 We're having a housewarming party on Saturday. Would you like to join us?		I'd love to, thank you!
4 Would you like to join our local group chat?		Yes, please! I'd love to get to know the neighbors.
5 Does anyone know a good plumber?		I do! I'll find their number and send it to you.

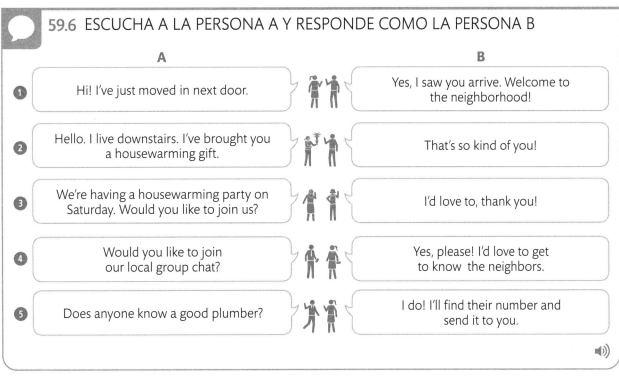

59.7 ESCUCHA Y NUMERA LAS ORACIONES EN EL ORDEN EN QUE LAS OYES

A It's so nice to meet you. ☐

B Can you come over for coffee tomorrow? ☐

C I'm your new neighbor. 1

D I wanted to introduce myself.

E I just came over to say hello. ☐

F Are you free for lunch on Sunday? ☐

G We've moved here from Beijing. ☐

H Would you like to stop by for drinks later? ☐

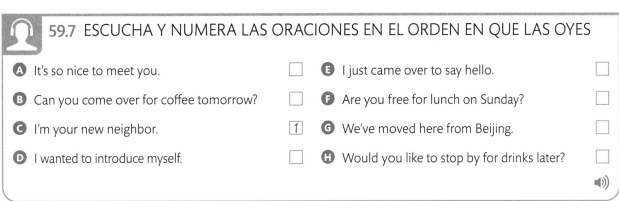

59.8 USA EL ESQUEMA PARA FORMAR NUEVE ORACIONES Y DILAS EN VOZ ALTA

Are you free for drinks later?

Are you free for

drinks	later?
lunch	tomorrow?
coffee	on Sunday?

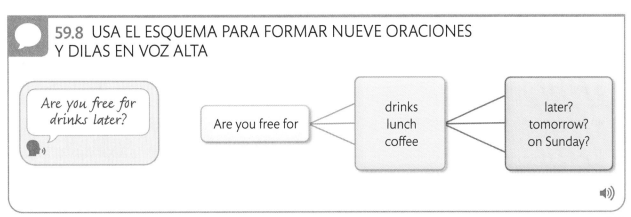

60 Tareas domésticas

60.1 COMPARTIR TAREAS

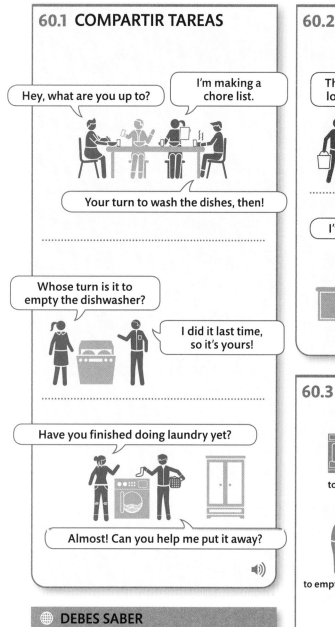

Hey, what are you up to?

I'm making a chore list.

Your turn to wash the dishes, then!

Whose turn is it to empty the dishwasher?

I did it last time, so it's yours!

Have you finished doing laundry yet?

Almost! Can you help me put it away?

60.2 LIMPIEZA DE PRIMAVERA

There we go. The house looks much tidier now!

Phew! That was a major spring-clean!

I've cleaned the counters and the oven.

Great job! The kitchen was in a bad state.

60.3 VOCABULARIO TAREAS DOMÉSTICAS

to do laundry

to wash dishes

to do the vacuuming

to empty the dishwasher

to clean the bathtub

to sweep the floor

to put the trash out

to tidy up

to make the bed

60.4 ESCUCHA A LA PERSONA A Y RESPONDE COMO LA PERSONA B

A	B

1
Hey, what are you up to?

I'm making a chore list.

2
Have you finished doing laundry yet?

Almost! Can you help me put it away?

3
I've cleaned the counters and the oven.

Great job! The kitchen was in a bad state.

4
There we go. The house looks much tidier now!

Phew! That was a major spring-clean!

🔊

60.5 RODEA CON UN CÍRCULO LO QUE OYES

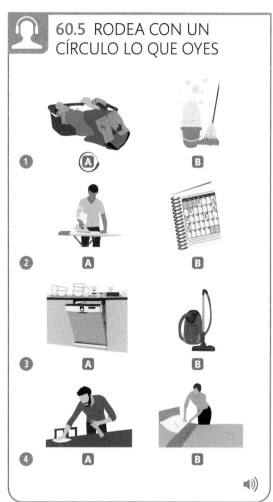

1 Ⓐ   B

2 A   B

3 A   B

4 A   B

🔊

60.6 CONECTA LAS ORACIONES Y DILAS EN VOZ ALTA

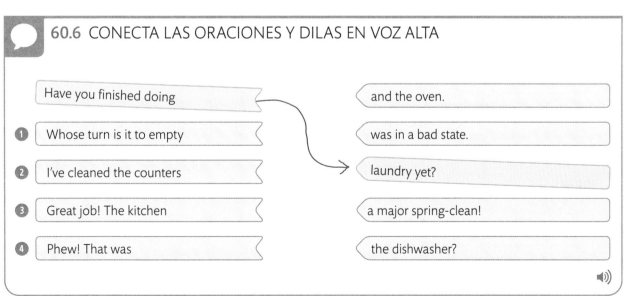

Have you finished doing → laundry yet?

and the oven.

1 Whose turn is it to empty

was in a bad state.

2 I've cleaned the counters

laundry yet?

3 Great job! The kitchen

a major spring-clean!

4 Phew! That was

the dishwasher?

🔊

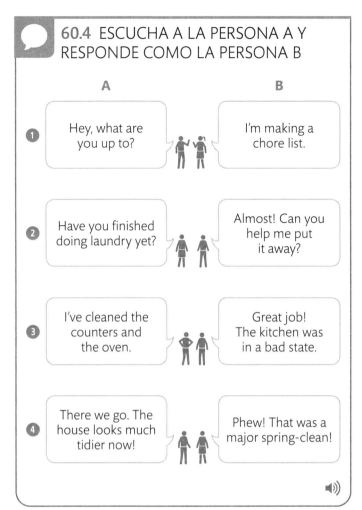

61 Mejoras en el hogar

61.1 HACER UNO MISMO LAS OBRAS

How are you coming along?

The tiles are all up. Just the grouting to go and I'm done!

I've finished stripping the walls.

Great! Let's hang this new wallpaper, then.

It's looking good!

Thank you. One more coat of paint should do it, I think.

61.2 CONTRATAR A UN PROFESIONAL

ABC Decorators, how can I help?

Hi, we need someone to hang some shelves.

Sure, we can do that for you.

Are you able to come over and give us a quote?

I could come over on Thursday.

61.3 MÁS EXPRESIONES

Could you put together this chest of drawers?

Can you give us a quote for fixing our fence?

We need someone to paint our kitchen walls.

I'd like a quote for laying a carpet.

Is that your best quote?

Will you supply the materials?

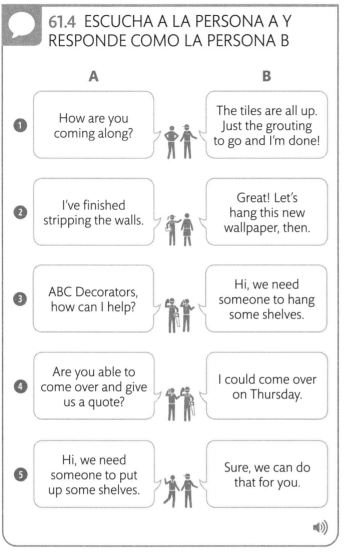

61.4 ESCUCHA A LA PERSONA A Y RESPONDE COMO LA PERSONA B

A   **B**

1. How are you coming along? — The tiles are all up. Just the grouting to go and I'm done!

2. I've finished stripping the walls. — Great! Let's hang this new wallpaper, then.

3. ABC Decorators, how can I help? — Hi, we need someone to hang some shelves.

4. Are you able to come over and give us a quote? — I could come over on Thursday.

5. Hi, we need someone to put up some shelves. — Sure, we can do that for you.

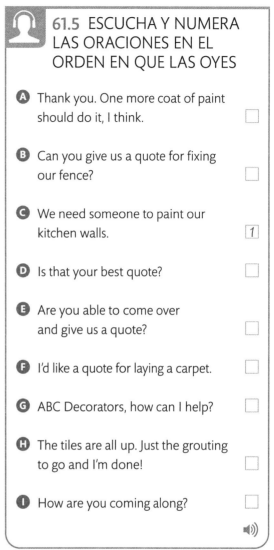

61.5 ESCUCHA Y NUMERA LAS ORACIONES EN EL ORDEN EN QUE LAS OYES

A Thank you. One more coat of paint should do it, I think. ☐

B Can you give us a quote for fixing our fence? ☐

C We need someone to paint our kitchen walls. ☐ 1

D Is that your best quote? ☐

E Are you able to come over and give us a quote? ☐

F I'd like a quote for laying a carpet. ☐

G ABC Decorators, how can I help? ☐

H The tiles are all up. Just the grouting to go and I'm done! ☐

I How are you coming along? ☐

61.6 USA EL ESQUEMA PARA FORMAR OCHO ORACIONES Y DILAS EN VOZ ALTA

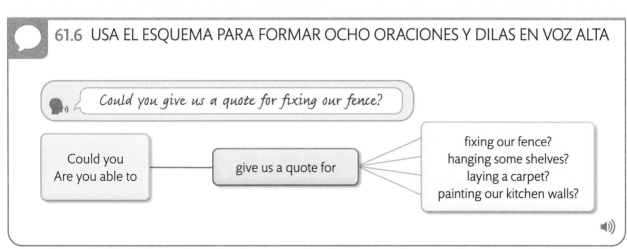

Could you give us a quote for fixing our fence?

| Could you / Are you able to | give us a quote for | fixing our fence? / hanging some shelves? / laying a carpet? / painting our kitchen walls? |

62 Mascotas

62.1 ADOPTAR UN ANIMAL ABANDONADO

Hi, I'd like to adopt a cat.

I'm looking to adopt one of your dogs.

Does she like other cats?

Is anyone home during the day?

Are you looking for a particular breed?

Is she good with children?

Yes, I work from home.

62.2 VISITA AL VETERINARIO

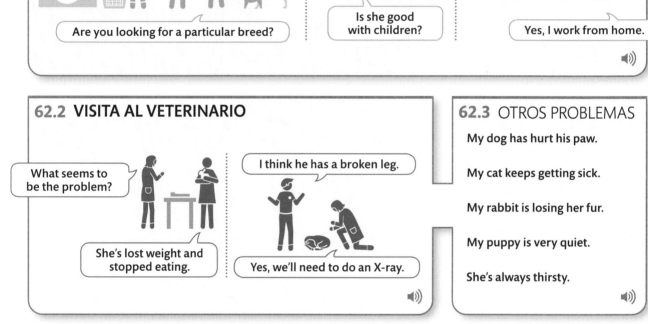

What seems to be the problem?

I think he has a broken leg.

She's lost weight and stopped eating.

Yes, we'll need to do an X-ray.

62.3 OTROS PROBLEMAS

My dog has hurt his paw.

My cat keeps getting sick.

My rabbit is losing her fur.

My puppy is very quiet.

She's always thirsty.

62.4 VOCABULARIO CUIDADOS

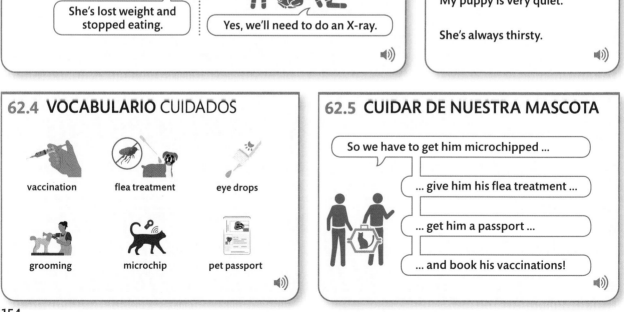

vaccination

flea treatment

eye drops

grooming

microchip

pet passport

62.5 CUIDAR DE NUESTRA MASCOTA

So we have to get him microchipped ...

... give him his flea treatment ...

... get him a passport ...

... and book his vaccinations!

62.6 ESCUCHA A LA PERSONA A Y RESPONDE COMO LA PERSONA B

A	B
1 I'm looking to adopt one of your dogs.	Are you looking for a particular breed?
2 Is anyone home during the day?	Yes, I work from home.
3 What seems to be the problem?	She's lost weight and stopped eating.
4 I think he has a broken leg.	Yes, we'll need to do an X-ray.

🔊

62.7 ESCUCHA Y NUMERA LAS IMÁGENES EN EL ORDEN EN QUE SE DESCRIBEN

Ⓐ 1   Ⓑ ☐

Ⓒ ☐   Ⓓ ☐

Ⓔ ☐   Ⓕ ☐

🔊

62.8 CONECTA LAS ORACIONES Y DILAS EN VOZ ALTA

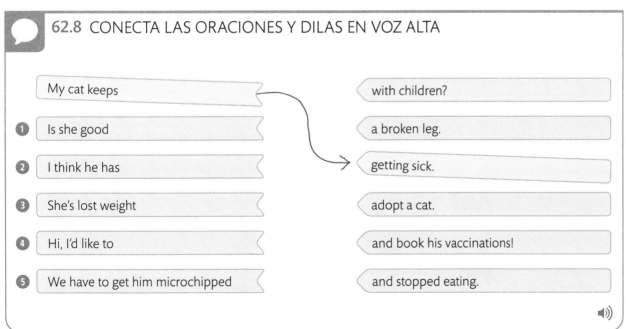

My cat keeps	with children?
1 Is she good	a broken leg.
2 I think he has	getting sick.
3 She's lost weight	adopt a cat.
4 Hi, I'd like to	and book his vaccinations!
5 We have to get him microchipped	and stopped eating.

🔊

63 Emergencias domésticas

63.1 PROBLEMAS ELÉCTRICOS

What's happening?

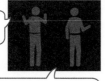

The power has gone out. I'll check the fuse box.

A breaker has tripped. Let's see if I can get it working …

Try turning the lights on now …

The power is back on!

63.2 AYUDA PROFESIONAL

My dishwasher's leaking …

I can be there in an hour. My callout fee is $80.

Okay, so what seems to be the problem?

The faucet has been dripping for days.

My shower keeps turning cold!

When was the furnace last serviced?

63.3 MÁS EXPRESIONES

I have a leaking roof.

My toilet is overflowing.

There's no hot water.

The heat won't come on.

The window is broken.

63.4 VOCABULARIO PROBLEMAS EN EL HOGAR

broken window

burst pipe

broken-down furnace

overflowing toilet

leaking roof

clogged sink

dripping faucet

power outage

63.5 ESCUCHA A LA PERSONA A Y RESPONDE COMO LA PERSONA B

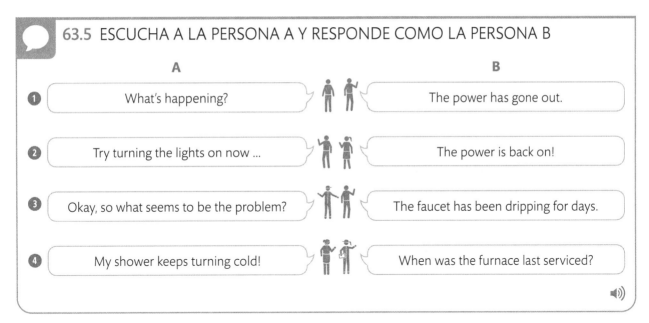

A	B
1 What's happening?	The power has gone out.
2 Try turning the lights on now ...	The power is back on!
3 Okay, so what seems to be the problem?	The faucet has been dripping for days.
4 My shower keeps turning cold!	When was the furnace last serviced?

63.6 ESCUCHA Y NUMERA LAS ORACIONES EN EL ORDEN EN QUE LAS OYES

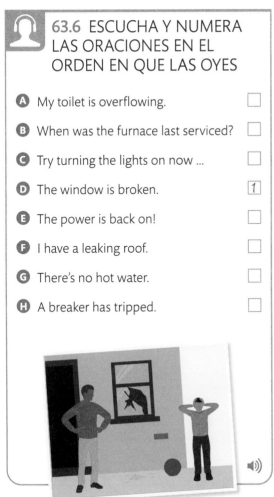

A My toilet is overflowing. ☐

B When was the furnace last serviced? ☐

C Try turning the lights on now ... ☐

D The window is broken. ☑ 1

E The power is back on! ☐

F I have a leaking roof. ☐

G There's no hot water. ☐

H A breaker has tripped. ☐

63.7 RESPONDE EN VOZ ALTA AL AUDIO, LLENANDO LOS ESPACIOS CON LAS PALABRAS DEL PANEL

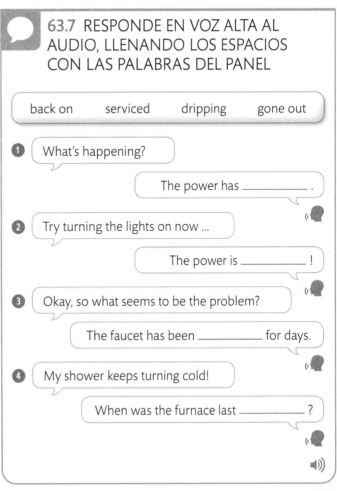

back on   serviced   dripping   gone out

1 What's happening?

The power has _____ .

2 Try turning the lights on now ...

The power is _____ !

3 Okay, so what seems to be the problem?

The faucet has been _____ for days.

4 My shower keeps turning cold!

When was the furnace last _____ ?

64 Ocio en el hogar

64.1 VER LA TELEVISIÓN

What should we watch tonight?

We could try this new detective series.

That was great—want to check out the next episode?

It's not streaming yet. How about some sports?

Do you have the remote? I can't hear anything.

Yes, here it is. I'll turn it up.

64.2 VIDEOJUEGOS

I'm so gonna win this!

Oh no! You got me again!

Your screen time's up now.

But I really want to finish this game! Just five more minutes ...

Should we play the next level?

I'm just grabbing a bite to eat—be right back!

64.3 MÁS EXPRESIONES

Can you turn on the subtitles?

Do you have another controller?

My tablet has frozen!

Is the console plugged in?

64.4 VOCABULARIO OCIO EN CASA

smart TV

remote

subtitles

headphones

console

smart speakers

controller

tablet

64.5 ESCUCHA A LA PERSONA A Y RESPONDE COMO LA PERSONA B

	A		B
1	What should we watch tonight?		We could try this new detective series.
2	Do you have the remote? I can't hear anything.		Yes, here it is. I'll turn it up.
3	I'm so gonna win this!		Oh no! You got me again!
4	Should we play the next level?		I'm just grabbing a bite to eat—be right back!

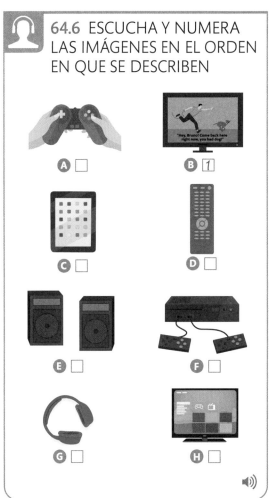

64.6 ESCUCHA Y NUMERA LAS IMÁGENES EN EL ORDEN EN QUE SE DESCRIBEN

A ☐   B 1
C ☐   D ☐
E ☐   F ☐
G ☐   H ☐

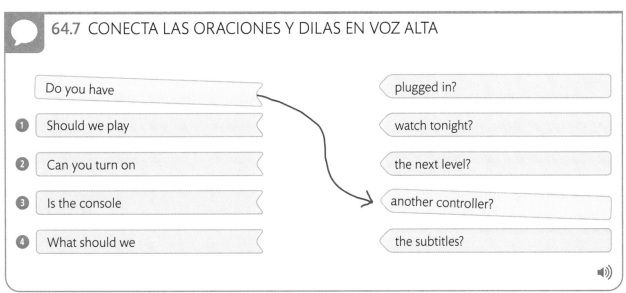

64.7 CONECTA LAS ORACIONES Y DILAS EN VOZ ALTA

Do you have → another controller?

1 Should we play — plugged in?

2 Can you turn on — watch tonight?

3 Is the console — the next level?

4 What should we — the subtitles?

65.1 TRANSPORTE

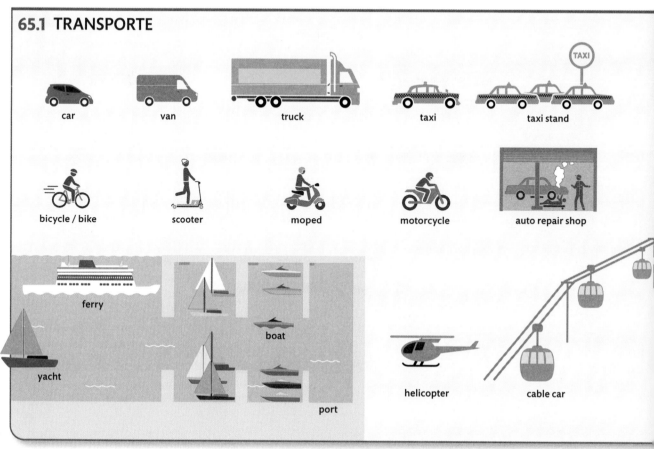

car

van

truck

taxi

taxi stand

bicycle / bike

scooter

moped

motorcycle

auto repair shop

ferry

boat

yacht

port

helicopter

cable car

65.2 VERBOS

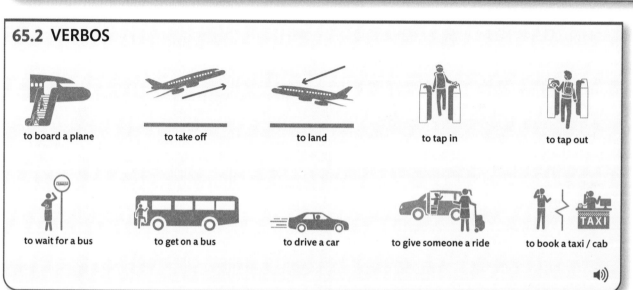

to board a plane

to take off

to land

to tap in

to tap out

to wait for a bus

to get on a bus

to drive a car

to give someone a ride

to book a taxi / cab

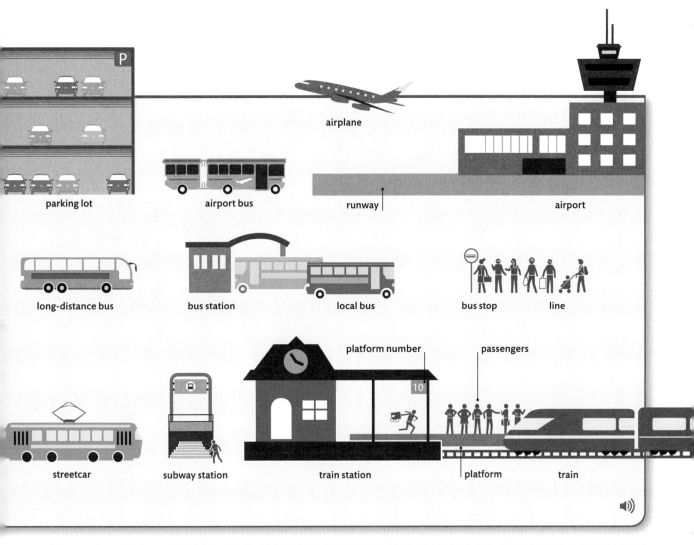

parking lot

airplane

airport bus

runway

airport

long-distance bus

bus station

local bus

bus stop

line

streetcar

subway station

platform number

train station

passengers

platform

train

65.3 DOCUMENTACIÓN Y HORARIOS

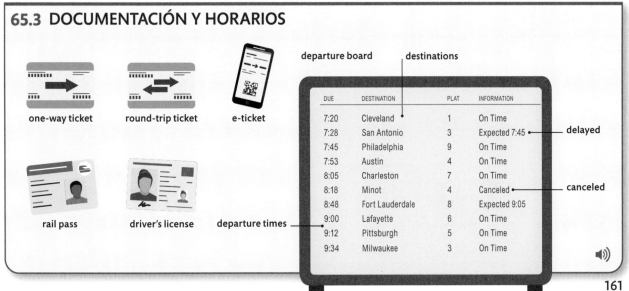

one-way ticket

round-trip ticket

e-ticket

rail pass

driver's license

departure board

destinations

departure times

DUE	DESTINATION	PLAT	INFORMATION	
7:20	Cleveland	1	On Time	
7:28	San Antonio	3	Expected 7:45	delayed
7:45	Philadelphia	9	On Time	
7:53	Austin	4	On Time	
8:05	Charleston	7	On Time	
8:18	Minot	4	Canceled	canceled
8:48	Fort Lauderdale	8	Expected 9:05	
9:00	Lafayette	6	On Time	
9:12	Pittsburgh	5	On Time	
9:34	Milwaukee	3	On Time	

66 Autobuses y ómnibus

66.1 TOMAR EL AUTOBÚS

Does this bus go to the town center?

Yes, via the railway station.

Can I have a one-way ticket to the museum, please?

That's $3, please.

Thanks. I'll pay by contactless.

Are we nearly at the library?

We're almost there—it's the next stop.

66.2 MORE QUESTIONS

Where is the nearest bus stop?

Are you stopping at the shopping center?

Is this the right stop for the airport bus?

What time is the next bus?

How much is the fare?

What time is the last bus from this stop?

66.3 VIAJE EN ÓMNIBUS

Could I see your ticket, please?

Here you go.

Great. We arrive in Atlanta at 4:45.

Hello. Are there bathrooms on the bus?

Yes, they're right at the back.

And is there Wi-Fi on board?

Yup, just log on to our network.

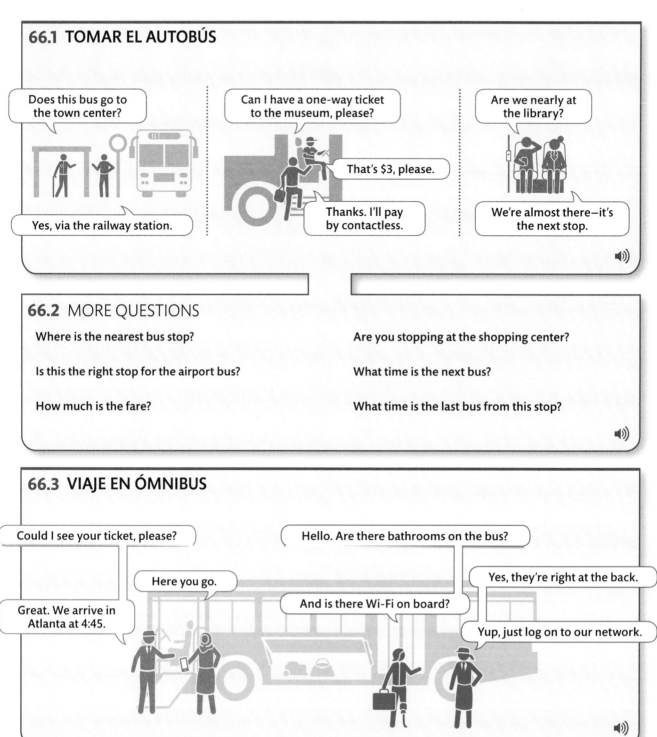

66.4 ESCUCHA A LA PERSONA A Y RESPONDE COMO LA PERSONA B

A		B
1 Could I see your ticket, please?		Here you go.
2 Does this bus go to the town center?		Yes, via the railway station.
3 That's $3, please.		Thanks. I'll pay by contactless.
4 Are we nearly at the library?		We're almost there—it's the next stop.

66.5 ESCUCHA EL AUDIO Y CONECTA LA RESPUESTA CORRECTA

That's $3, please.

Yup, just log on to our network.

1 Are we nearly at the library?

Yes, via the railway station.

2 Does this bus go to the town center?

We're almost there—it's the next stop.

3 Hello. Are there bathrooms on the bus?

Thanks. I'll pay by contactless.

4 Is there Wi-Fi on board?

Yes, they're right at the back.

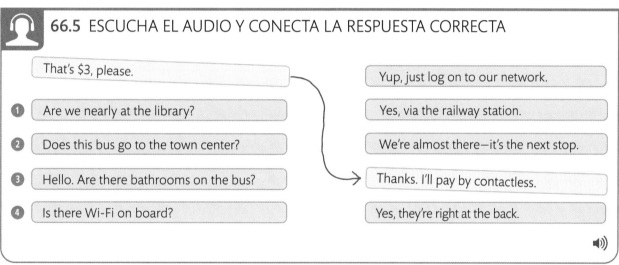

66.6 USA EL ESQUEMA PARA FORMAR NUEVE ORACIONES Y DILAS EN VOZ ALTA

Excuse me, does this bus go to the library?

Excuse me,	does this bus go to	the library?
	are we nearly at	the town center?
	is this the right stop for	the shopping center?

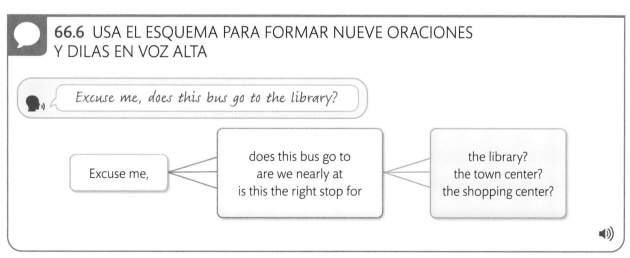

163

67 Viajar en tren y en metro

67.1 COMPRAR BOLETOS

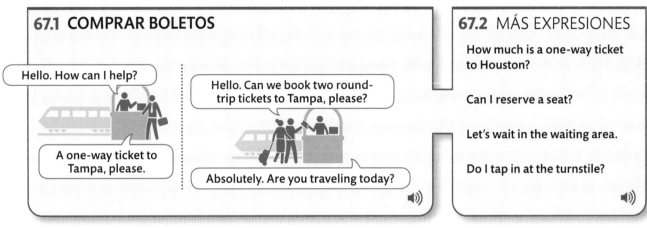

Hello. How can I help?

A one-way ticket to Tampa, please.

Hello. Can we book two round-trip tickets to Tampa, please?

Absolutely. Are you traveling today?

67.2 MÁS EXPRESIONES

How much is a one-way ticket to Houston?

Can I reserve a seat?

Let's wait in the waiting area.

Do I tap in at the turnstile?

67.3 PEDIR INFORMACIÓN

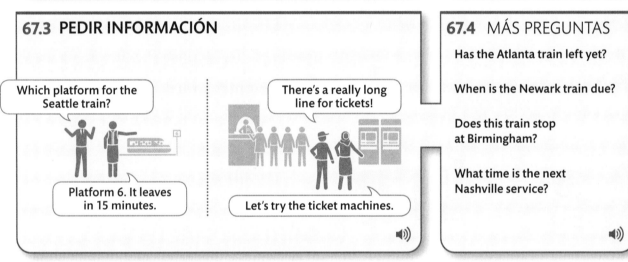

Which platform for the Seattle train?

Platform 6. It leaves in 15 minutes.

There's a really long line for tickets!

Let's try the ticket machines.

67.4 MÁS PREGUNTAS

Has the Atlanta train left yet?

When is the Newark train due?

Does this train stop at Birmingham?

What time is the next Nashville service?

67.5 VOCABULARIO VIAJAR EN TREN

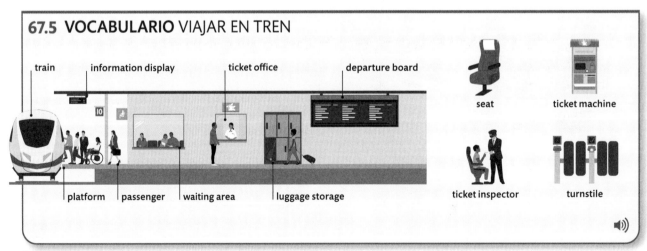

train

information display

ticket office

departure board

seat

ticket machine

platform

passenger

waiting area

luggage storage

ticket inspector

turnstile

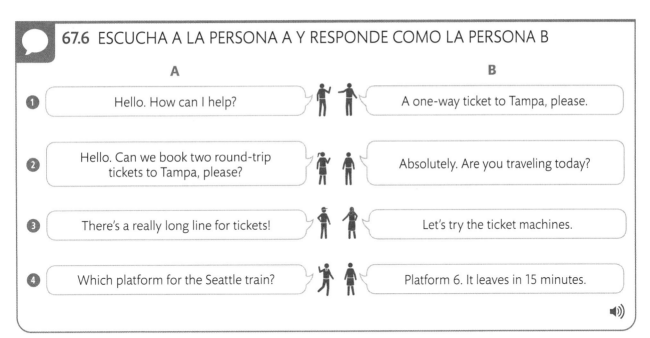

67.6 ESCUCHA A LA PERSONA A Y RESPONDE COMO LA PERSONA B

A

1. Hello. How can I help?
2. Hello. Can we book two round-trip tickets to Tampa, please?
3. There's a really long line for tickets!
4. Which platform for the Seattle train?

B

1. A one-way ticket to Tampa, please.
2. Absolutely. Are you traveling today?
3. Let's try the ticket machines.
4. Platform 6. It leaves in 15 minutes.

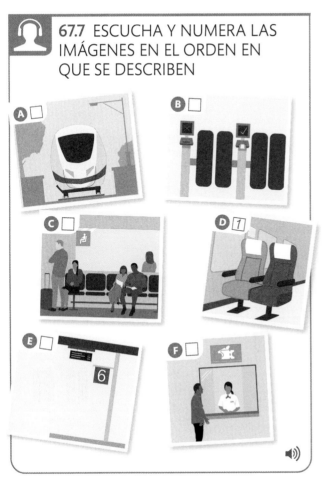

67.7 ESCUCHA Y NUMERA LAS IMÁGENES EN EL ORDEN EN QUE SE DESCRIBEN

A ☐
B ☐
C ☐
D ☐ 1
E ☐ 6
F ☐

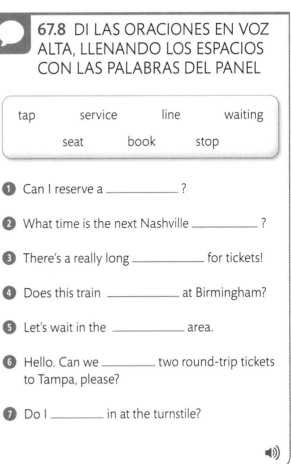

67.8 DI LAS ORACIONES EN VOZ ALTA, LLENANDO LOS ESPACIOS CON LAS PALABRAS DEL PANEL

tap	service	line	waiting
	seat	book	stop

1. Can I reserve a _____ ?

2. What time is the next Nashville _____ ?

3. There's a really long _____ for tickets!

4. Does this train _____ at Birmingham?

5. Let's wait in the _____ area.

6. Hello. Can we _____ two round-trip tickets to Tampa, please?

7. Do I _____ in at the turnstile?

67.9 PROBLEMAS Y AVISOS

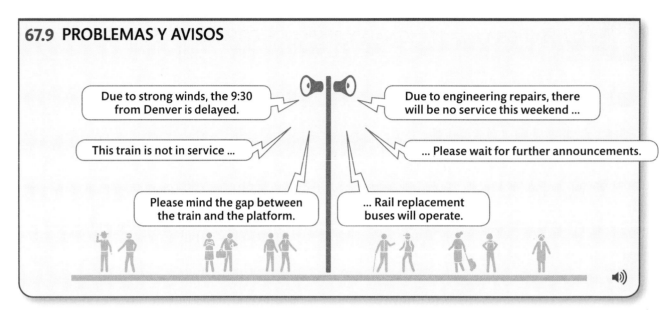

Due to strong winds, the 9:30 from Denver is delayed.

Due to engineering repairs, there will be no service this weekend ...

This train is not in service ...

... Please wait for further announcements.

Please mind the gap between the train and the platform.

... Rail replacement buses will operate.

67.10 EN EL TREN

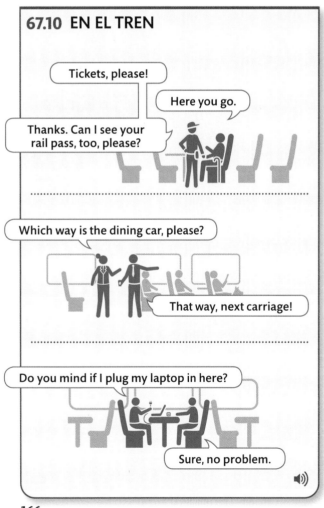

Tickets, please!

Here you go.

Thanks. Can I see your rail pass, too, please?

Which way is the dining car, please?

That way, next carriage!

Do you mind if I plug my laptop in here?

Sure, no problem.

67.11 EN EL METRO

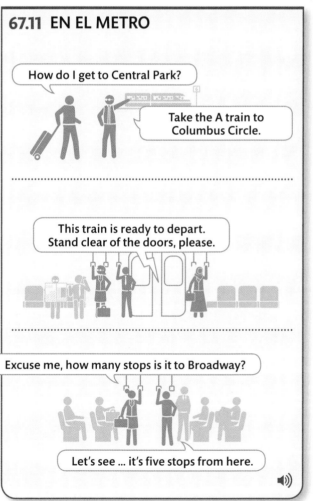

How do I get to Central Park?

Take the A train to Columbus Circle.

This train is ready to depart. Stand clear of the doors, please.

Excuse me, how many stops is it to Broadway?

Let's see ... it's five stops from here.

67.12 ESCUCHA A LA PERSONA A Y RESPONDE COMO LA PERSONA B

	A		B
1	Which way is the dining car, please?		That way, next carriage!
2	Do you mind if I plug my laptop in here?		Sure, no problem.
3	Excuse me, how many stops is it to Broadway?		Let's see ... it's five stops from here.
4	How do I get to Central Park?		Take the A train to Columbus Circle.

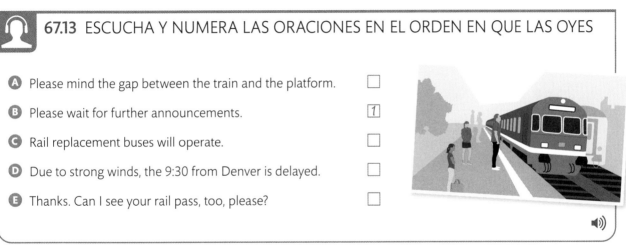

67.13 ESCUCHA Y NUMERA LAS ORACIONES EN EL ORDEN EN QUE LAS OYES

A Please mind the gap between the train and the platform. ☐

B Please wait for further announcements. ☐ 1

C Rail replacement buses will operate. ☐

D Due to strong winds, the 9:30 from Denver is delayed. ☐

E Thanks. Can I see your rail pass, too, please? ☐

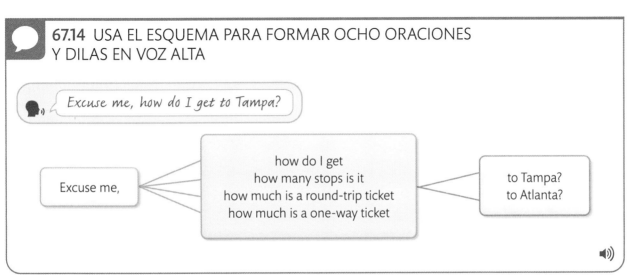

67.14 USA EL ESQUEMA PARA FORMAR OCHO ORACIONES Y DILAS EN VOZ ALTA

Excuse me, how do I get to Tampa?

Excuse me,	how do I get	to Tampa?
	how many stops is it	to Atlanta?
	how much is a round-trip ticket	
	how much is a one-way ticket	

167

68 En el aeropuerto

68.1 SALIDAS

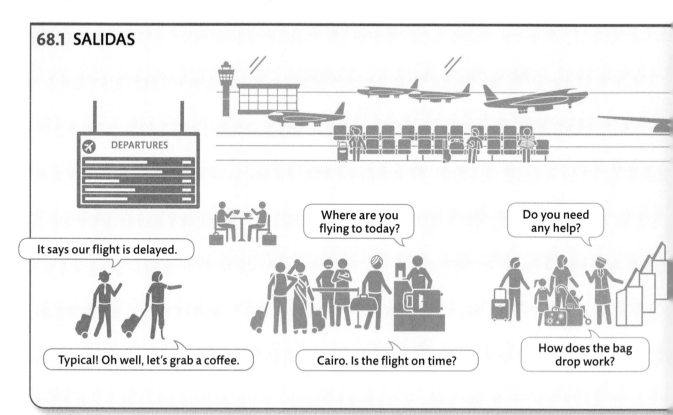

68.3 ESCUCHA A LA PERSONA A Y RESPONDE COMO LA PERSONA B

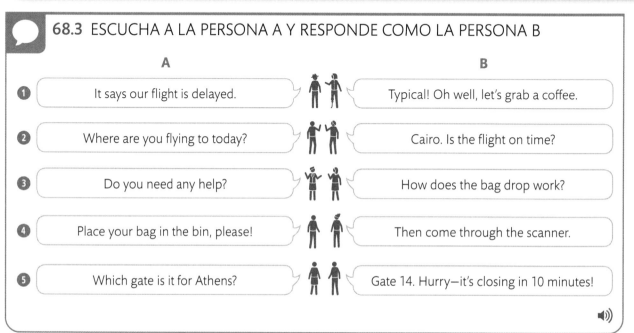

	A	B
1	It says our flight is delayed.	Typical! Oh well, let's grab a coffee.
2	Where are you flying to today?	Cairo. Is the flight on time?
3	Do you need any help?	How does the bag drop work?
4	Place your bag in the bin, please!	Then come through the scanner.
5	Which gate is it for Athens?	Gate 14. Hurry—it's closing in 10 minutes!

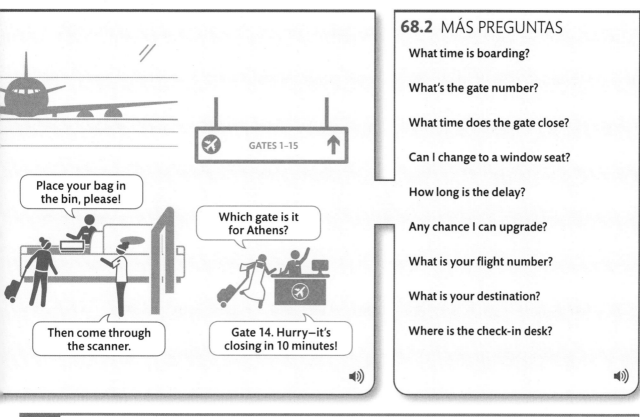

Place your bag in the bin, please!

Then come through the scanner.

GATES 1–15

Which gate is it for Athens?

Gate 14. Hurry—it's closing in 10 minutes!

68.2 MÁS PREGUNTAS

What time is boarding?

What's the gate number?

What time does the gate close?

Can I change to a window seat?

How long is the delay?

Any chance I can upgrade?

What is your flight number?

What is your destination?

Where is the check-in desk?

68.4 DI LAS ORACIONES EN VOZ ALTA, LLENANDO LOS ESPACIOS EN BLANCO CON LAS PALABRAS DEL PANEL

delay	bin	seat	time
upgrade	number	gate	check-in

1 What _____ is boarding?

2 Can I change to a window _____ ?

3 What's the gate _____ ?

4 How long is the _____ ?

5 Any chance I can _____ ?

6 What time does the _____ close?

7 Place your bag in the _____ , please!

8 Where is the _____ desk?

68.5 EMBARQUE Y DESPEGUE

Welcome! Can I see your boarding pass?

Hello! Here you go.

I'll put our stuff in the overhead bin.

Thanks. I'll keep my bag under the seat.

Ladies and gentlemen, welcome to Flight 86A for Beijing.

We are ready for departure.

68.6 DURANTE EL VUELO

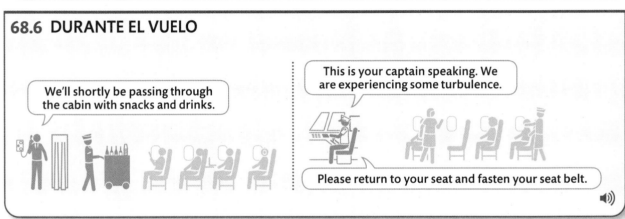

We'll shortly be passing through the cabin with snacks and drinks.

This is your captain speaking. We are experiencing some turbulence.

Please return to your seat and fasten your seat belt.

68.7 ATERRIZAJE

Your tray tables should be securely fastened.

Make sure your seat is in the upright position.

Please switch your digital devices to "airplane" mode.

We will arrive in Beijing at 9:20 local time.

68.8 VOCABULARIO EN LA CABINA

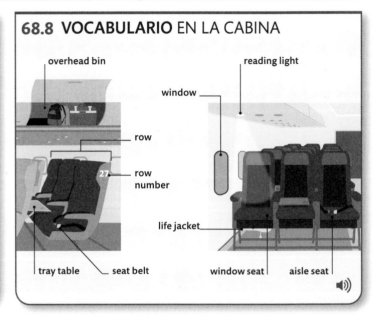

overhead bin

reading light

window

row

row number

life jacket

tray table

seat belt

window seat

aisle seat

68.9 ESCUCHA Y NUMERA LAS IMÁGENES EN EL ORDEN EN QUE SE DESCRIBEN

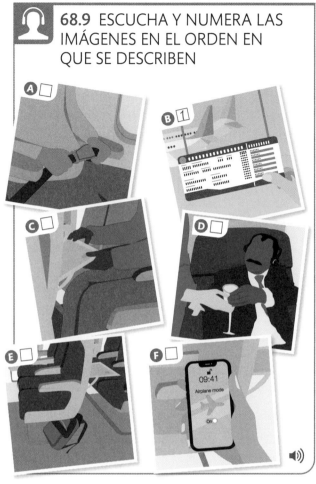

A ☐
B ☐ 1
C ☐
D ☐
E ☐
F ☐

09:41
Airplane mode
On

🔊

68.10 ESCUCHA Y NUMERA LAS ORACIONES EN EL ORDEN EN QUE LAS OYES

A I'll put our stuff in the overhead bin. ☐

B We are experiencing some turbulence. ☐

C Ladies and gentlemen, welcome to Flight 86A for Beijing. ☐

D Make sure your seat is in the upright position. ☐ 1

E We will arrive in Beijing at 9:20 local time. ☐

F We are ready for departure. ☐

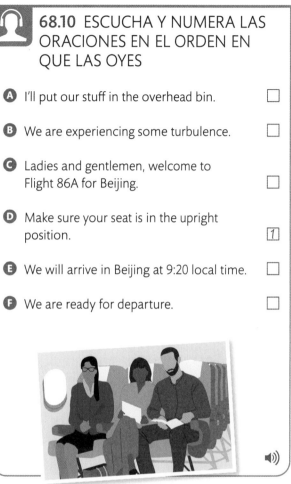

🔊

68.11 CONECTA LAS ORACIONES Y DILAS EN VOZ ALTA

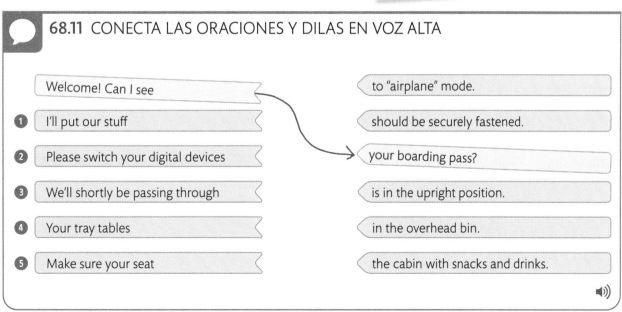

Welcome! Can I see — your boarding pass?

1 I'll put our stuff — in the overhead bin.

2 Please switch your digital devices — to "airplane" mode.

3 We'll shortly be passing through — the cabin with snacks and drinks.

4 Your tray tables — should be securely fastened.

5 Make sure your seat — is in the upright position.

🔊

68.12 LLEGADAS

What is the purpose of your trip?

I'm visiting friends.

Which baggage-claim carousel do we need to go to?

It's carousel 3.
I'll grab a cart.

I can't see our suitcases anywhere!

Let's go check at the baggage desk.

68.13 ALQUILAR UN AUTO

Hi! I'm here to pick up a rental car. Here's my booking confirmation.

Great! Can I see your driver's license, please?

Is the car ready for us?

6

Yes, it's in section 6. Enjoy your trip!

68.14 ESCUCHA Y RODEA CON UN CÍRCULO EL OBJETO QUE OYES

1. A   B
2. A   B
3. A   B
4. A   B

Can I see your customs declaration form?

CUSTOMS

Here it is!

Hi, can I help?

Yes, I need to exchange some Euros. What's your rate?

Where do we meet our taxi?

The driver should be waiting for us.

68.15 ESCUCHA A LA PERSONA A Y RESPONDE COMO LA B

A

B

1. What is the purpose of your trip? → I'm visiting friends.

2. Where do we meet our taxi? → The driver should be waiting for us.

3. I can't see our suitcases anywhere! → Let's go check at the baggage desk.

4. Hi, can I help? → Yes, I need to exchange some Euros. What's your rate?

68.16 DI LAS ORACIONES EN VOZ ALTA, REEMPLAZANDO LAS IMÁGENES CON PALABRAS

1. Where do we meet our ____?

2. I can't see our ____ anywhere!

3. It's carousel 3. I'll grab a ____.

4. Yes, I need to exchange some ____.

5. I'm here to pick up a rental ____.

69.1 COMPRAR UNA BICICLETA

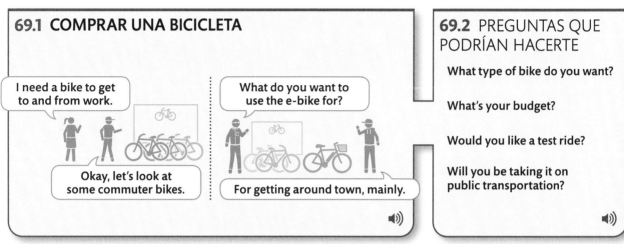

I need a bike to get to and from work.

Okay, let's look at some commuter bikes.

What do you want to use the e-bike for?

For getting around town, mainly.

69.2 PREGUNTAS QUE PODRÍAN HACERTE

What type of bike do you want?

What's your budget?

Would you like a test ride?

Will you be taking it on public transportation?

69.3 ALQUILAR UNA BICICLETA

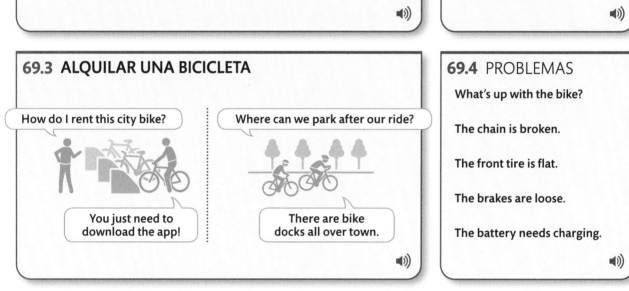

How do I rent this city bike?

You just need to download the app!

Where can we park after our ride?

There are bike docks all over town.

69.4 PROBLEMAS

What's up with the bike?

The chain is broken.

The front tire is flat.

The brakes are loose.

The battery needs charging.

69.5 VOCABULARIO PARTES DE UNA BICICLETA

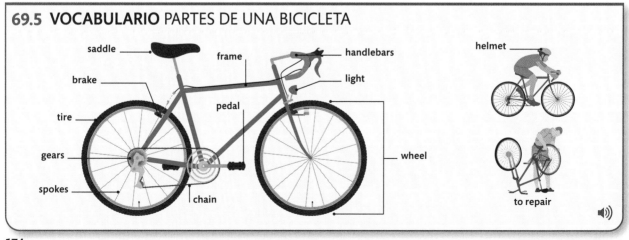

saddle

frame

handlebars

helmet

brake

light

pedal

tire

gears

wheel

spokes

chain

to repair

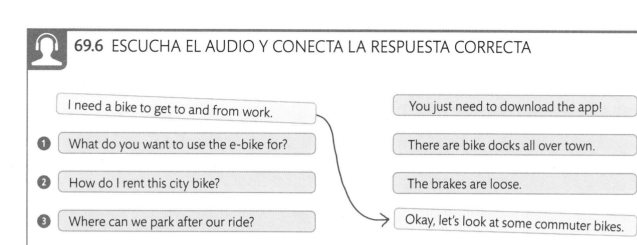

69.6 ESCUCHA EL AUDIO Y CONECTA LA RESPUESTA CORRECTA

I need a bike to get to and from work.

You just need to download the app!

1. What do you want to use the e-bike for?

There are bike docks all over town.

2. How do I rent this city bike?

The brakes are loose.

3. Where can we park after our ride?

Okay, let's look at some commuter bikes.

4. What's up with the bike?

For getting around town, mainly.

69.7 ESCUCHA Y NUMERA LAS IMÁGENES EN EL ORDEN EN QUE SE DESCRIBEN

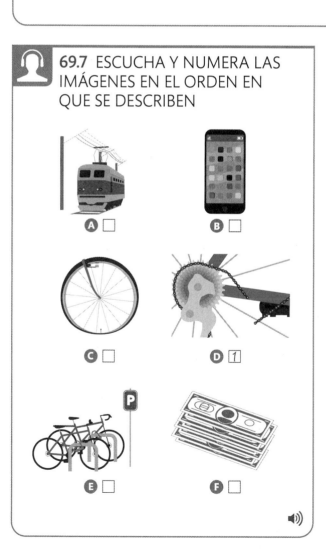

A ☐

B ☐

C ☐

D 1

E ☐

F ☐

69.8 DI LAS ORACIONES EN VOZ ALTA, LLENANDO LOS ESPACIOS CON LAS PALABRAS DEL PANEL

| brakes | tire | battery | work |
| bike | app | test ride | docks |

1. What type of _____ do you want?

2. The _____ needs charging.

3. The front _____ is flat.

4. Would you like a _____ ?

5. I need a bike to get to and from _____ .

6. There are bike _____ all over town.

7. You just need to download the _____ !

8. The _____ are loose.

70 Taxis

70.1 TOMAR UN TAXI

Where's the nearest taxi stand?

The cabs wait over there, across the street.

Can you take me to this address?

No problem. Let me put your suitcase in the trunk.

Can you drop me here, please?

Sure. That will be $19.10.

70.2 PEDIR UN TAXI CON ANTICIPACIÓN

Hello. Can I book a taxi from the airport?

For how many people and when do you need it?

Tomorrow at 11 a.m. There are four of us.

Where are you traveling to?

To Monroe Township.

How many pieces of luggage do you have?

One small suitcase and one large one.

Okay. That's all booked for you.

70.3 MÁS EXPRESIONES

How long will it take to get there?

Can we make an extra stop?

Keep the change.

Can I pay with contactless?

How soon will the cab be here?

I'll book a ride-share via the app.

I left my laptop in one of your taxis.

I'm traveling with my service dog.

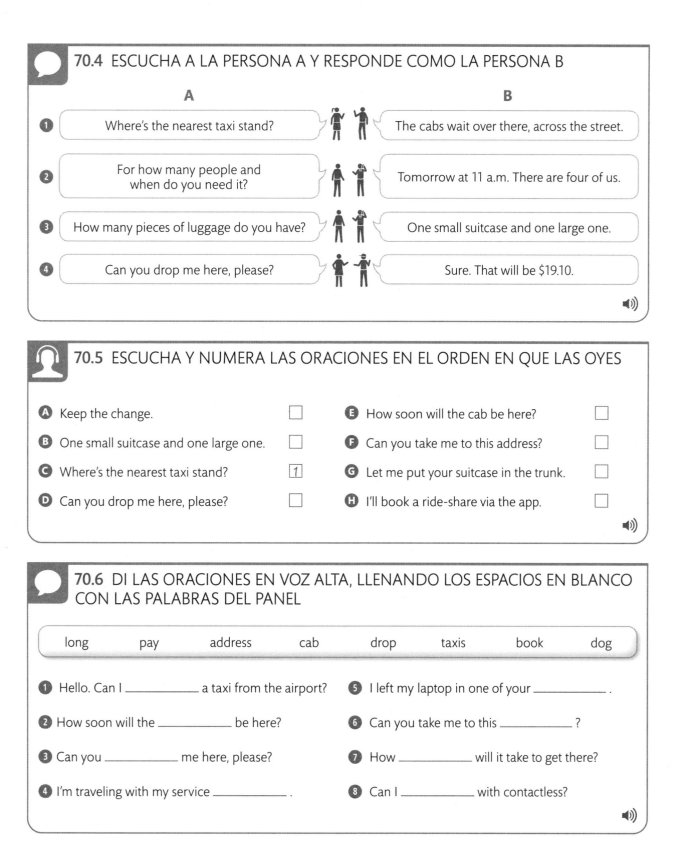

70.4 ESCUCHA A LA PERSONA A Y RESPONDE COMO LA PERSONA B

A		B
❶ Where's the nearest taxi stand?		The cabs wait over there, across the street.
❷ For how many people and when do you need it?		Tomorrow at 11 a.m. There are four of us.
❸ How many pieces of luggage do you have?		One small suitcase and one large one.
❹ Can you drop me here, please?		Sure. That will be $19.10.

70.5 ESCUCHA Y NUMERA LAS ORACIONES EN EL ORDEN EN QUE LAS OYES

Ⓐ Keep the change. ☐

Ⓑ One small suitcase and one large one. ☐

Ⓒ Where's the nearest taxi stand? ☐ 1

Ⓓ Can you drop me here, please? ☐

Ⓔ How soon will the cab be here? ☐

Ⓕ Can you take me to this address? ☐

Ⓖ Let me put your suitcase in the trunk. ☐

Ⓗ I'll book a ride-share via the app. ☐

70.6 DI LAS ORACIONES EN VOZ ALTA, LLENANDO LOS ESPACIOS EN BLANCO CON LAS PALABRAS DEL PANEL

long	pay	address	cab	drop	taxis	book	dog

❶ Hello. Can I _____ a taxi from the airport?

❷ How soon will the _____ be here?

❸ Can you _____ me here, please?

❹ I'm traveling with my service _____ .

❺ I left my laptop in one of your _____ .

❻ Can you take me to this _____ ?

❼ How _____ will it take to get there?

❽ Can I _____ with contactless?

71 En el taller mecánico

71.1 PEDIR CITA

ABC Autos, how can I help?

Could I book an appointment for my car, please?

When will my car be ready?

It should be ready to pick up at 5:30.

71.2 AVERÍAS Y REPARACIONES

What does this warning light mean? It keeps flashing ...

Looks like your oil level is too low. Let me check it.

So what seems to be the problem?

I think the engine's overheating.

Okay, I'll take a look.

71.3 OTROS PROBLEMAS

The headlight isn't working.

The oil needs to be changed.

The steering wheel is jammed.

The windshield is cracked.

The tire keeps going flat.

71.4 VOCABULARIO PARTES DE UN COCHE

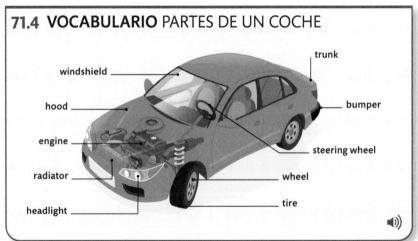

- trunk
- windshield
- hood
- bumper
- engine
- steering wheel
- radiator
- wheel
- headlight
- tire

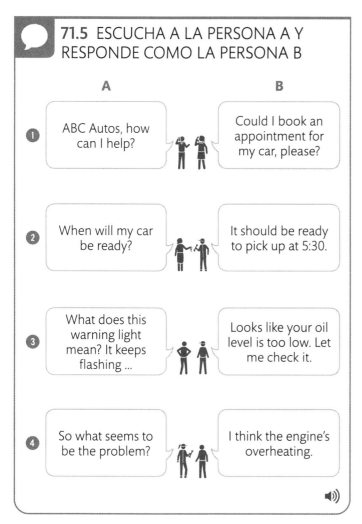

71.5 ESCUCHA A LA PERSONA A Y RESPONDE COMO LA PERSONA B

A	B
1 ABC Autos, how can I help?	Could I book an appointment for my car, please?
2 When will my car be ready?	It should be ready to pick up at 5:30.
3 What does this warning light mean? It keeps flashing ...	Looks like your oil level is too low. Let me check it.
4 So what seems to be the problem?	I think the engine's overheating.

71.6 RODEA CON UN CÍRCULO LO QUE OYES

1. Ⓐ   B
2. A   B
3. A   B
4. A   B

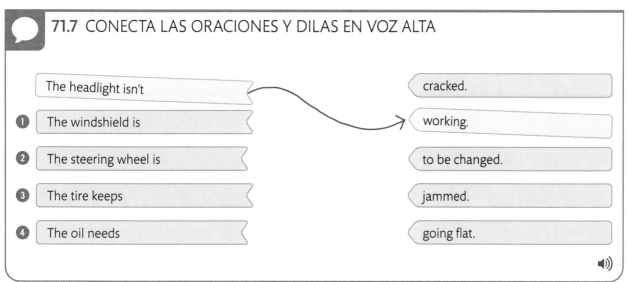

71.7 CONECTA LAS ORACIONES Y DILAS EN VOZ ALTA

The headlight isn't	cracked.
1 The windshield is	working.
2 The steering wheel is	to be changed.
3 The tire keeps	jammed.
4 The oil needs	going flat.

179

72 De vacaciones

72.1 ALOJAMIENTO

hotel · motel · bed and breakfast · hostel

chalet · cabin · campground · camper

accessible · pet-friendly · Wi-Fi · swimming pool

balcony · crib · room service · buffet

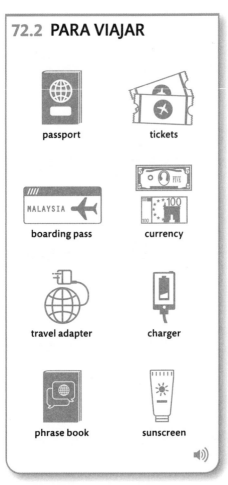

72.2 PARA VIAJAR

passport · tickets

boarding pass · currency

travel adapter · charger

phrase book · sunscreen

72.3 VERBOS

 to book a flight

 to make a reservation

 to go on vacation

 to rent a cottage

 to stay in a hotel

 to book a campsite

 to pack (a suitcase)

 to exchange money

 to go abroad

 to rent a car

 to check in

 to check out

72.4 ACTIVIDADES

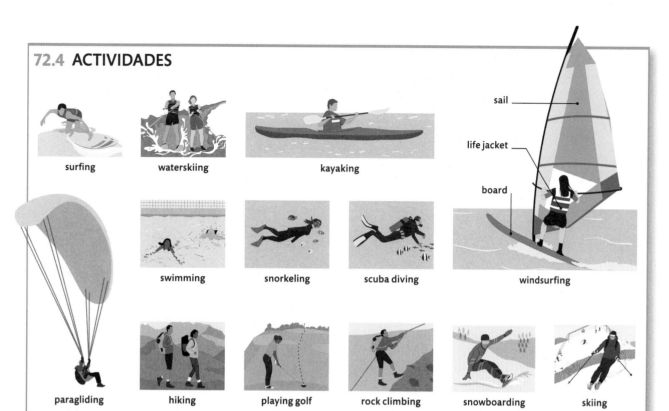

surfing

waterskiing

kayaking

sail

life jacket

board

paragliding

swimming

snorkeling

scuba diving

windsurfing

hiking

playing golf

rock climbing

snowboarding

skiing

72.5 VISITAS Y ATRACCIONES

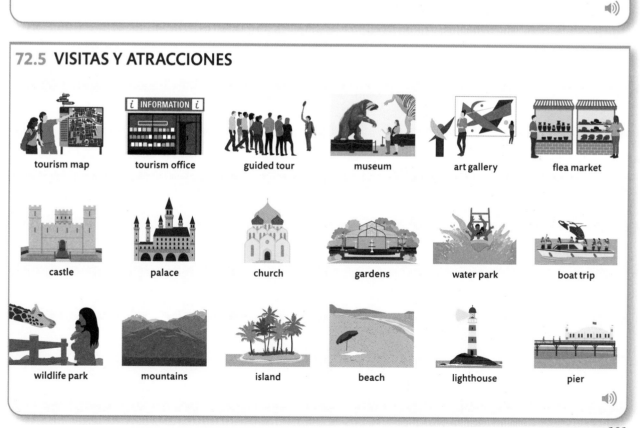

tourism map

i INFORMATION *i*

tourism office

guided tour

museum

art gallery

flea market

castle

palace

church

gardens

water park

boat trip

wildlife park

mountains

island

beach

lighthouse

pier

73 Reservar unas vacaciones

73.1 HABLAR CON LA AGENCIA DE VIAJES

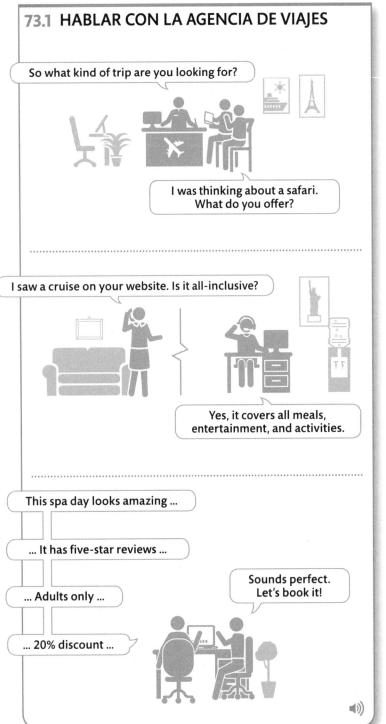

So what kind of trip are you looking for?

I was thinking about a safari. What do you offer?

I saw a cruise on your website. Is it all-inclusive?

Yes, it covers all meals, entertainment, and activities.

This spa day looks amazing ...

... It has five-star reviews ...

... Adults only ...

... 20% discount ...

Sounds perfect. Let's book it!

73.2 MÁS PREGUNTAS

What amenities are there?

What's your cancelation policy?

Do I need a visa?

Is it suitable for young children?

Can I bring my guide dog?

73.3 VOCABULARIO
TIPOS DE VACACIONES

beach vacation

city break

spa day

winter sports

camper

camping trip

hiking tour

cruise

safari

all-inclusive

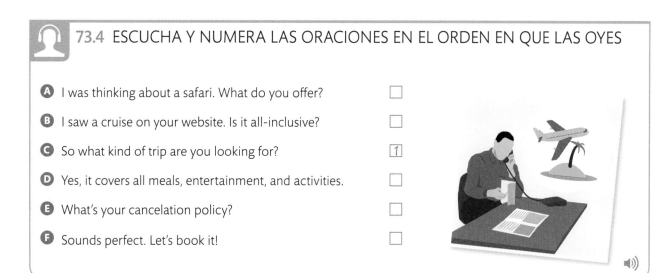

73.4 ESCUCHA Y NUMERA LAS ORACIONES EN EL ORDEN EN QUE LAS OYES

A I was thinking about a safari. What do you offer? ☐

B I saw a cruise on your website. Is it all-inclusive? ☐

C So what kind of trip are you looking for? 1

D Yes, it covers all meals, entertainment, and activities. ☐

E What's your cancelation policy? ☐

F Sounds perfect. Let's book it! ☐

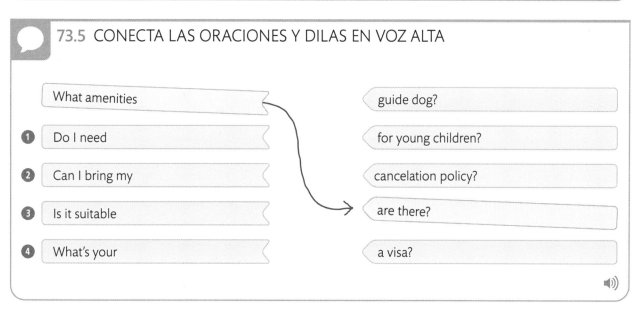

73.5 CONECTA LAS ORACIONES Y DILAS EN VOZ ALTA

What amenities	guide dog?
1 Do I need	for young children?
2 Can I bring my	cancelation policy?
3 Is it suitable	are there?
4 What's your	a visa?

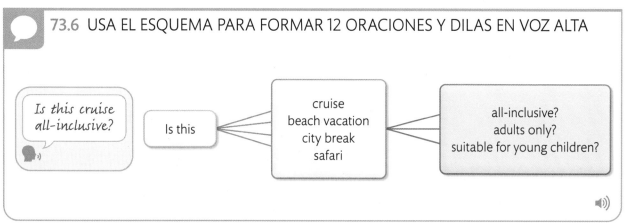

73.6 USA EL ESQUEMA PARA FORMAR 12 ORACIONES Y DILAS EN VOZ ALTA

Is this cruise all-inclusive?

Is this → cruise / beach vacation / city break / safari → all-inclusive? / adults only? / suitable for young children?

183

74 Alojarse en un hotel

74.1 LLEGADA Y REGISTRO

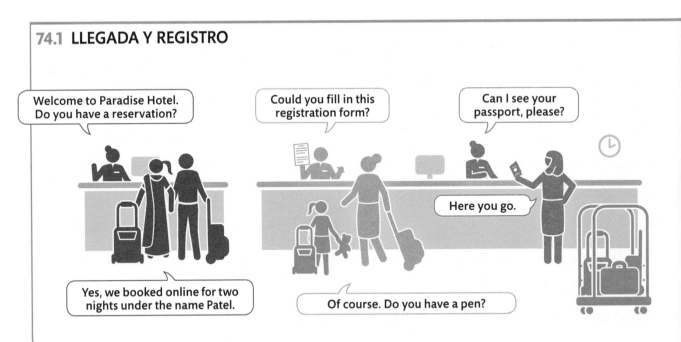

Welcome to Paradise Hotel. Do you have a reservation?

Could you fill in this registration form?

Can I see your passport, please?

Here you go.

Yes, we booked online for two nights under the name Patel.

Of course. Do you have a pen?

74.3 ESCUCHA A LA PERSONA A Y RESPONDE COMO LA PERSONA B

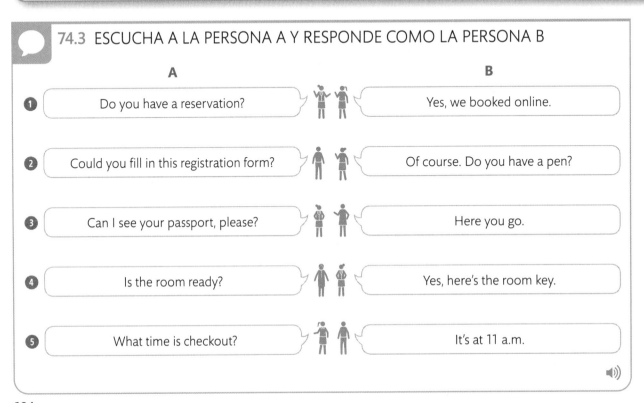

A	B
① Do you have a reservation?	Yes, we booked online.
② Could you fill in this registration form?	Of course. Do you have a pen?
③ Can I see your passport, please?	Here you go.
④ Is the room ready?	Yes, here's the room key.
⑤ What time is checkout?	It's at 11 a.m.

Is the room ready?

Yes, here's the room key.

What time is checkout?

It's at 11 a.m.

74.2 MÁS EXPRESIONES

I paid in advance on the booking site.

Do you have a king bed available?

We'd like a room with queen beds, please.

The restaurant serves dinner until 10 p.m.

The swimming pool opens again at 6 a.m.

Your room is on the second floor.

Breakfast is from 7:30 a.m. to 10 a.m.

74.4 ESCUCHA Y RODEA CON UN CÍRCULO EL OBJETO QUE OYES

74.5 PEDIR COSAS

Could I have some fresh towels, please?

Yes, I'll have some sent up right away.

74.6 MÁS EXPRESIONES

I'd like ...

... a hair dryer brought to my room.

... a club sandwich sent up, please.

... two extra pillows.

... a 7 a.m. wake-up call.

74.7 DESCRIBIR PROBLEMAS

The TV won't turn on.

Okay, let me take a look.

74.8 OTROS PROBLEMAS

The Wi-Fi password is wrong.

The lamp is broken.

The room is too hot.

My window doesn't close properly.

The shower is leaking.

My room key isn't working.

74.9 VOCABULARIO EN EL HOTEL

passport

registration form

king bed

queen beds

club sandwich

shower

room key

luggage

pillows

lamp

towels

hair dryer

74.10 ESCUCHA Y NUMERA LAS IMÁGENES EN EL ORDEN EN QUE SE DESCRIBEN

A □ B 1 C □ D □ E □ F □

🔊

74.11 CONECTA LAS ORACIONES Y DILAS EN VOZ ALTA

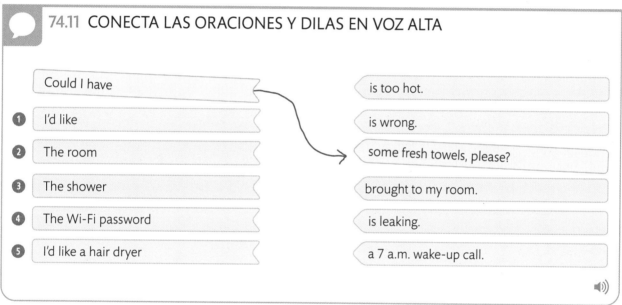

Could I have		is too hot.
1 I'd like		is wrong.
2 The room		some fresh towels, please?
3 The shower		brought to my room.
4 The Wi-Fi password		is leaking.
5 I'd like a hair dryer		a 7 a.m. wake-up call.

🔊

74.12 USA EL ESQUEMA PARA FORMAR OCHO ORACIONES Y DILAS EN VOZ ALTA

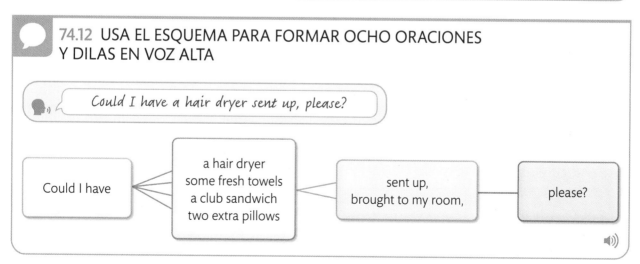

Could I have a hair dryer sent up, please?

| Could I have | a hair dryer
some fresh towels
a club sandwich
two extra pillows | sent up,
brought to my room, | please? |

🔊

74.13 EN EL DESAYUNO

Am I too late for breakfast?

No, you're just in time.

Can I get your room number?

Can we sit anywhere we like?

Yes, and help yourselves to the buffet.

Could I have some more coffee?

Sure, I'll bring it to your table.

74.14 SALIDA DEL HOTEL

Did you enjoy your stay?

It was great, thanks.

The room was a bit noisy.

Here's your bill if you'd like to check it.

That all looks fine.

Are you paying by card?

74.15 MÁS EXPRESIONES

Dinner was delicious.

Our breakfast was a bit cold.

The bed was a little hard.

Is it possible to stay an extra night?

Can I leave my luggage here?

Could you call me a cab, please?

🌐 DEBES SABER

En inglés hablado, solemos utilizar **a bit** o **a little** —en lugar de los más formales **quite** o **rather**— cuando queremos describir algo negativo. Por ejemplo, no diríamos que nuestro desayuno estaba "**a bit** delicious" (un poco delicioso), sino que estaba "**a bit** bland" (un poco soso) o "**a little** cold" (un poco frío).

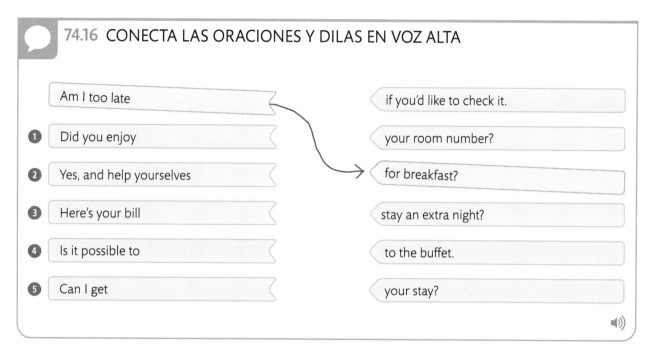

74.16 CONECTA LAS ORACIONES Y DILAS EN VOZ ALTA

Am I too late → for breakfast?

1. Did you enjoy — your stay?
2. Yes, and help yourselves — to the buffet.
3. Here's your bill — if you'd like to check it.
4. Is it possible to — stay an extra night?
5. Can I get — your room number?

74.17 DI LAS ORACIONES EN VOZ ALTA, REEMPLAZANDO LAS IMÁGENES CON PALABRAS

1. Could I have some more ☕ ?
2. Are you paying by 💳 ?
3. Could you call me a 🚕 , please?
4. The 🛏 was a little hard.
5. Can I leave my 🧳 here?

74.18 DI LAS ORACIONES EN VOZ ALTA, LLENANDO LOS ESPACIOS CON LAS PALABRAS DEL PANEL

room   checkout   floor
delicious   restaurant   queen beds
passport   king

1. Can I see your _____ , please?
2. What time is _____ ?
3. We'd like a room with _____ , please.
4. The _____ was a bit noisy.
5. Dinner was _____ .
6. Do you have a _____ bed available?
7. The _____ serves dinner until 10 p.m.
8. Your room is on the second _____ .

75 Visitar una ciudad

75.1 ATRACCIONES

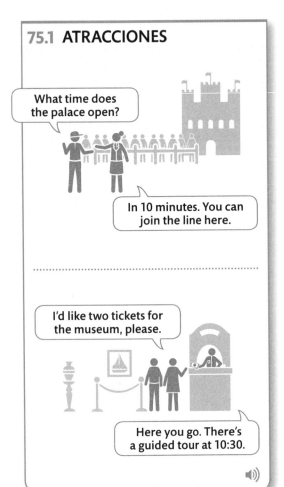

What time does the palace open?

In 10 minutes. You can join the line here.

I'd like two tickets for the museum, please.

Here you go. There's a guided tour at 10:30.

75.2 MÁS EXPRESIONES

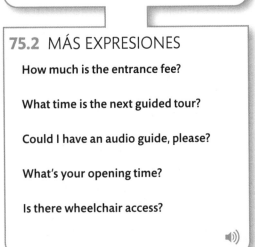

How much is the entrance fee?

What time is the next guided tour?

Could I have an audio guide, please?

What's your opening time?

Is there wheelchair access?

75.3 EN UN AUTOBÚS TURÍSTICO

On your right, you'll see the oldest building in the city.

Look—we're here on the map, and there's our hotel!

Wow! Check that out!

Quick! Take a picture!

Want to get off at the next stop?

75.4 VOCABULARIO LO BÁSICO

tour bus

line

guided tour

audio guide

ticket

tourism office

map

guidebook

souvenir

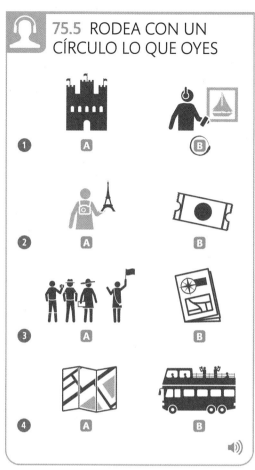

75.5 RODEA CON UN CÍRCULO LO QUE OYES

1. A / **B**
2. A / B
3. A / B
4. A / B

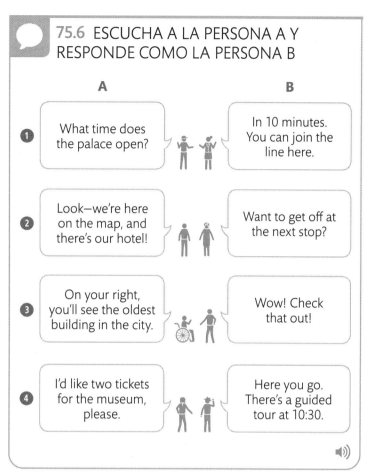

75.6 ESCUCHA A LA PERSONA A Y RESPONDE COMO LA PERSONA B

A — **B**

1. What time does the palace open? — In 10 minutes. You can join the line here.
2. Look—we're here on the map, and there's our hotel! — Want to get off at the next stop?
3. On your right, you'll see the oldest building in the city. — Wow! Check that out!
4. I'd like two tickets for the museum, please. — Here you go. There's a guided tour at 10:30.

75.7 CONECTA LAS ORACIONES Y DILAS EN VOZ ALTA

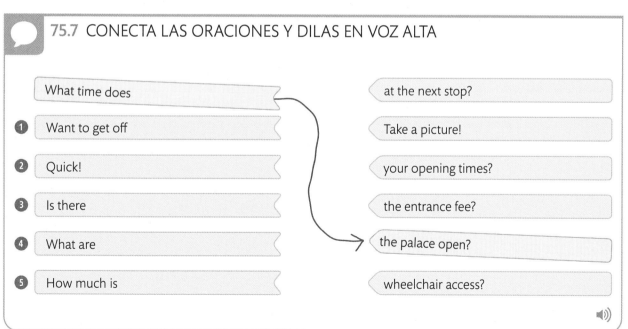

- What time does — the palace open?
1. Want to get off — at the next stop?
2. Quick! — Take a picture!
3. Is there — the entrance fee?
4. What are — your opening times?
5. How much is — wheelchair access?

De campamento

76.1 LLEGADA

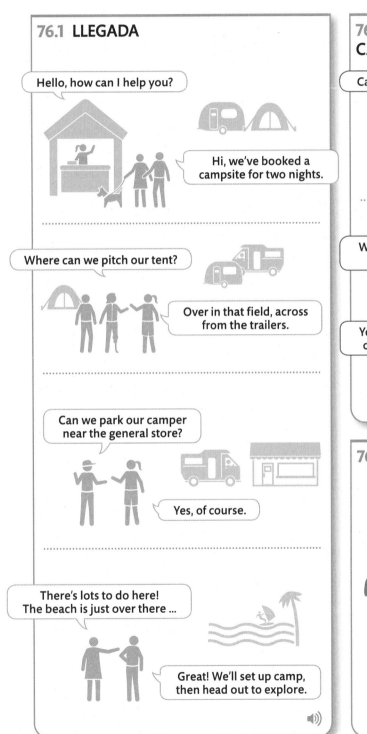

Hello, how can I help you?

Hi, we've booked a campsite for two nights.

Where can we pitch our tent?

Over in that field, across from the trailers.

Can we park our camper near the general store?

Yes, of course.

There's lots to do here! The beach is just over there ...

Great! We'll set up camp, then head out to explore.

76.2 EN LA TIENDA DEL CAMPAMENTO

Can we light a campfire?

Yes, you can. Do you need firewood?

We forgot to bring camping gas! Do you have any?

Sure, on that shelf over there. Anything else?

Yes. I'll take a box of matches, too.

76.3 VOCABULARIO CAMPAMENTO

tent

campfire

shower block

trailer

camper

general store

matches

camping stove

camping gas

76.4 ESCUCHA A LA PERSONA A Y RESPONDE COMO LA PERSONA B

A

B

1. Hello, how can I help you?

   Hi, we've booked a campsite for two nights.

2. Where can we pitch our tent?

   Over in that field, across from the trailers.

3. There's lots to do here! The beach is just over there ...

   Great! We'll set up camp, then head out to explore.

4. Can we light a campfire?

   Yes, you can. Do you need firewood?

5. Sure, on that shelf over there. Anything else?

   Yes. I'll take a box of matches, too.

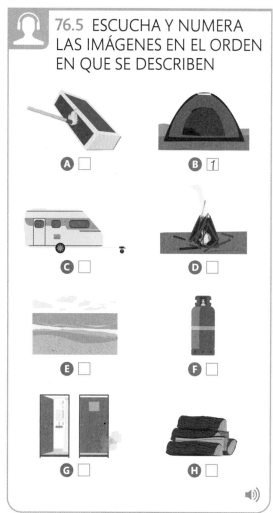

76.5 ESCUCHA Y NUMERA LAS IMÁGENES EN EL ORDEN EN QUE SE DESCRIBEN

A ☐

B 1

C ☐

D ☐

E ☐

F ☐

G ☐

H ☐

76.6 USA EL ESQUEMA PARA FORMAR NUEVE ORACIONES Y DILAS EN VOZ ALTA

Can we pitch our tent over in that field?

Can we

pitch our tent
set up camp
park our camper

over in that field?
near the shower block?
across from the trailers?

77 En la playa

77.1 LLEGAR A LA PLAYA

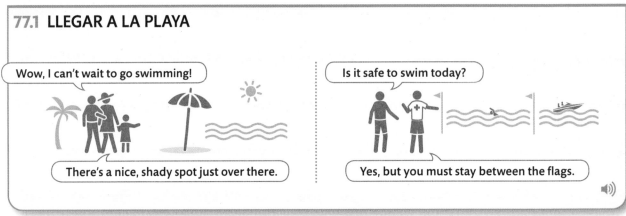

Wow, I can't wait to go swimming!

There's a nice, shady spot just over there.

Is it safe to swim today?

Yes, but you must stay between the flags.

77.2 ACTIVIDADES EN LA PLAYA

Do you do surfing lessons?

Can we hire a paddleboat here?

Do you sell children's wet suits?

How much is a bodyboard for the day?

Where can we buy a pail and shovel?

77.3 VOCABULARIO EN LA PLAYA

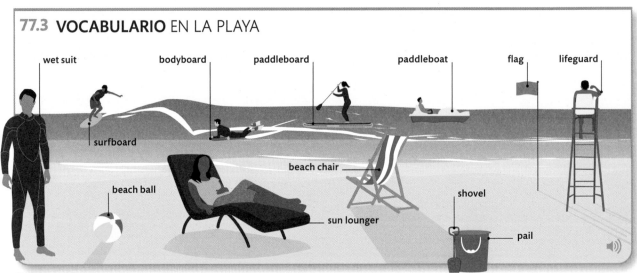

wet suit

bodyboard

paddleboard

paddleboat

flag

lifeguard

surfboard

beach chair

beach ball

sun lounger

shovel

pail

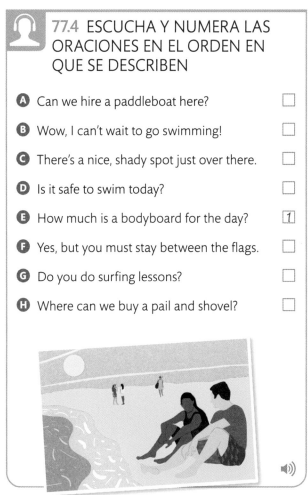

77.4 ESCUCHA Y NUMERA LAS ORACIONES EN EL ORDEN EN QUE SE DESCRIBEN

A Can we hire a paddleboat here? ☐

B Wow, I can't wait to go swimming! ☐

C There's a nice, shady spot just over there. ☐

D Is it safe to swim today? ☐

E How much is a bodyboard for the day? ☐1

F Yes, but you must stay between the flags. ☐

G Do you do surfing lessons? ☐

H Where can we buy a pail and shovel? ☐

77.5 DI LAS ORACIONES EN VOZ ALTA, REEMPLAZANDO LAS IMÁGENES CON PALABRAS

1 Can we hire a _____ here?

2 How much is a _____ for the day?

3 Where can we buy a _____ ?

4 Can we hire a _____ for the day?

5 Do you do _____ lessons?

77.6 CONECTA LAS ORACIONES Y DILAS EN VOZ ALTA

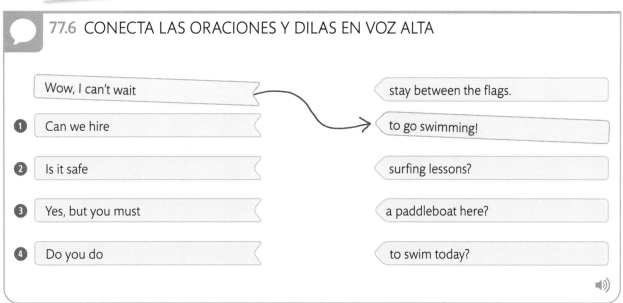

Wow, I can't wait → to go swimming!

stay between the flags.

1 Can we hire — a paddleboat here?

2 Is it safe — to swim today?

3 Yes, but you must — stay between the flags.

4 Do you do — surfing lessons?

78 Encontrar el camino

78.1 PEDIR INDICACIONES

Excuse me, do you know the way to the bus station?

Yes, go straight ahead and it's on your left.

Can you tell me how to get to the museum?

Let me think ... Take the first right after the library.

78.2 SEGUIR LAS INDICACIONES

Hi there, is the bank this way?

No, you need to go past the church ...

... and take the first left ...

... then cross the road ...

... and turn right at the traffic lights.

It's just next to the hospital.

Thanks for your help!

78.3 VOCABULARIO INDICACIONES DE LUGAR

turn left | turn right | go straight ahead | first right | second left | go around the corner

cross the road | go past | next to | behind | in front of | across from

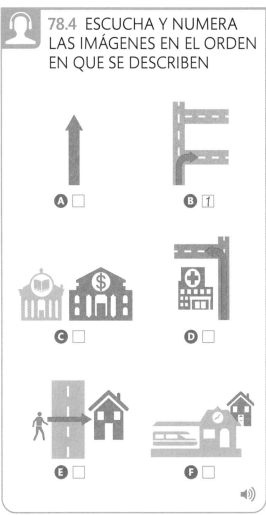

78.4 ESCUCHA Y NUMERA LAS IMÁGENES EN EL ORDEN EN QUE SE DESCRIBEN

A ☐

B 1

C ☐

D ☐

E ☐

F ☐

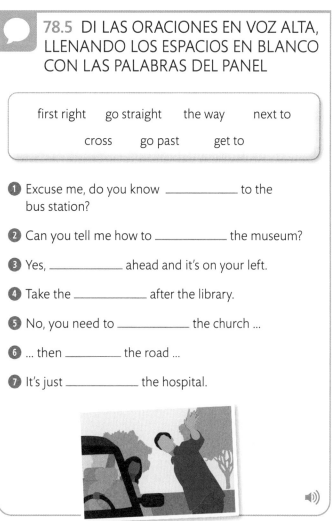

78.5 DI LAS ORACIONES EN VOZ ALTA, LLENANDO LOS ESPACIOS EN BLANCO CON LAS PALABRAS DEL PANEL

first right   go straight   the way   next to

cross   go past   get to

1 Excuse me, do you know _____ to the bus station?

2 Can you tell me how to _____ the museum?

3 Yes, _____ ahead and it's on your left.

4 Take the _____ after the library.

5 No, you need to _____ the church ...

6 ... then _____ the road ...

7 It's just _____ the hospital.

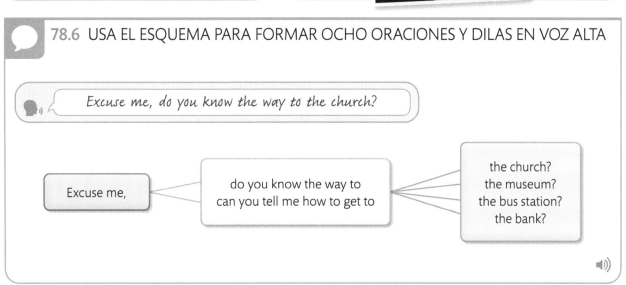

78.6 USA EL ESQUEMA PARA FORMAR OCHO ORACIONES Y DILAS EN VOZ ALTA

Excuse me, do you know the way to the church?

| Excuse me, | do you know the way to
can you tell me how to get to | the church?
the museum?
the bus station?
the bank? |

79 Problemas con las vacaciones

79.1 PERTENENCIAS PERDIDAS

My bag's been stolen with my passport inside!

Okay, let me take down some details.

Excuse me, my suitcase hasn't shown up.

The airline desk can help you.

Hello, you left your phone behind!

Oh gosh, thank you so much!

79.2 RETRASOS Y ANULACIONES

I'm sorry, your flight is delayed.

We'll let you know more as soon as we can.

I can't see our platform number anywhere ...

Look at the board. Our train has been canceled!

79.3 MÁS EXPRESIONES

Your luggage has an extra charge.

Your gate has just closed.

The baggage handlers are on strike.

The train is canceled due to lack of available train crew.

79.4 LESIONES Y ENFERMEDADES

Wanna come hiking tomorrow?

I can't—I've thrown my back out!

You look awful!

Yeah, I won't make it to the beach. I have a stomach bug!

Hello, I've had an accident on vacation and I can't fly home!

Your insurance should cover you if you get a doctor's note.

79.5 ESCUCHA A LA PERSONA A Y RESPONDE COMO LA PERSONA B

A		B
1 My bag's been stolen with my passport inside!	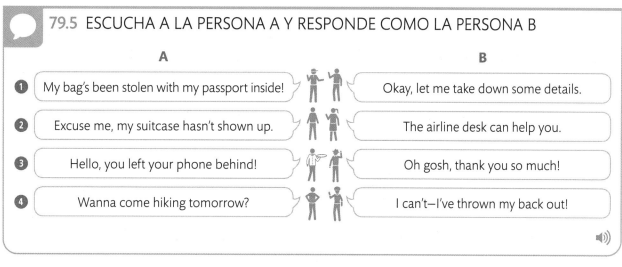	Okay, let me take down some details.
2 Excuse me, my suitcase hasn't shown up.		The airline desk can help you.
3 Hello, you left your phone behind!		Oh gosh, thank you so much!
4 Wanna come hiking tomorrow?		I can't—I've thrown my back out!

🔊

79.6 ESCUCHA Y NUMERA LAS ORACIONES EN EL ORDEN EN QUE LAS OYES

A We'll let you know more as soon as we can. ☐

B Your luggage has an extra charge. ☐

C Your gate has just closed. ☐ 1

D I'm sorry, your flight is delayed. ☐

E My bag's been stolen with my passport inside! ☐

F Your insurance should cover you if you get a doctor's note. ☐

G Okay, let me take down some details. ☐

H Hello, I've had an accident on vacation and I can't fly home! ☐

I The baggage handlers are on strike. ☐

🔊

79.7 CONECTA LAS ORACIONES Y DILAS EN VOZ ALTA

The baggage handlers	I have a stomach bug!
1 The train is canceled	if you get a doctor's note.
2 Yeah, I won't make it to the beach.	are on strike.
3 Look at the board.	due to lack of available train crew.
4 Your insurance should cover you	Our train has been canceled!

🔊

80 Salud y medicina

80.1 EL CUERPO HUMANO

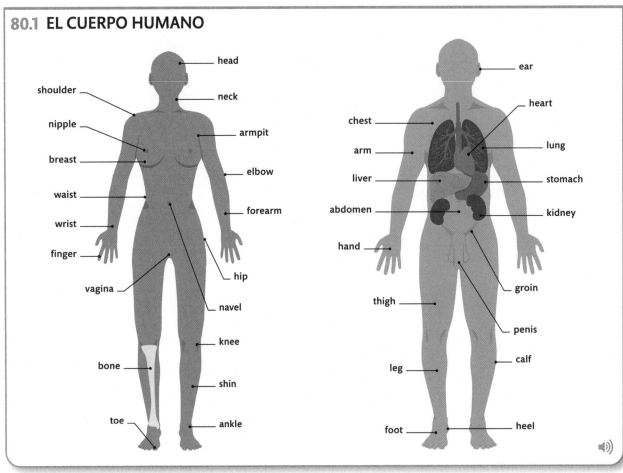

head
shoulder
nipple
breast
waist
wrist
finger
neck
armpit
elbow
forearm
hip
vagina
navel
knee
bone
shin
toe
ankle

ear
chest
arm
liver
abdomen
hand
thigh
leg
foot
heart
lung
stomach
kidney
groin
penis
calf
heel

80.2 PROFESIONALES DE LA SALUD

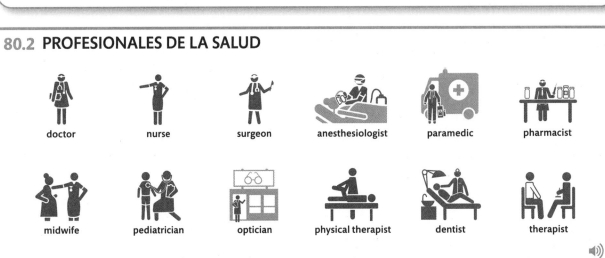

doctor
nurse
surgeon
anesthesiologist
paramedic
pharmacist

midwife
pediatrician
optician
physical therapist
dentist
therapist

80.3 LESIONES Y ENFERMEDADES

cough

cold

runny nose

virus

fever

sore throat

infection

allergy

headache

earache

nausea

diarrhea

food poisoning

upset stomach

rash

scrape

bruise

swelling

cut

burn

bite

cramp

sprain

broken bone

80.4 EMERGENCIAS, DIAGNÓSTICO Y TRATAMIENTO

ambulance

hospital

ER
(emergency room)

emergency

accident

hospital porter

temperature

blood pressure

blood work

heart rate

X-ray

scan

checkup

dressing

stitches

injection / shot

medication

antibiotics

81 En la farmacia

81.1 DESCRIBIR LOS SÍNTOMAS

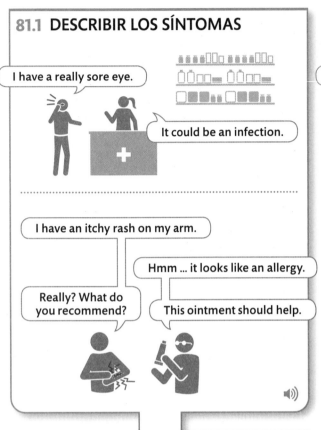

I have a really sore eye.

It could be an infection.

I have an itchy rash on my arm.

Hmm ... it looks like an allergy.

Really? What do you recommend?

This ointment should help.

81.2 MÁS EXPRESIONES

My knee really hurts.

I have a really bad headache.

My back is killing me.

🌐 DEBES SABER

En inglés hablado, utilizamos con frecuencia **really** para enfatizar algo: "I have a **really** sore eye", "My eye **really** hurts". **Really** tiene una función similar a **very**, pero es un poco más informal. También se utiliza para expresar interés o sorpresa: **Really? What do you recommend?**

81.3 POSIBLES PREGUNTAS

Do you have any other symptoms?

Yes, I also have a runny nose.

Do you have any allergies?

Yes, I'm allergic to aspirin.

Are you taking any other medication?

Yes, I'm taking antibiotics.

How long have you had symptoms?

For about a week.

81.4 ESCUCHA Y NUMERA LAS IMÁGENES EN EL ORDEN EN QUE SE DESCRIBEN

81.5 ESCUCHA A LA PERSONA A Y RESPONDE COMO LA PERSONA B

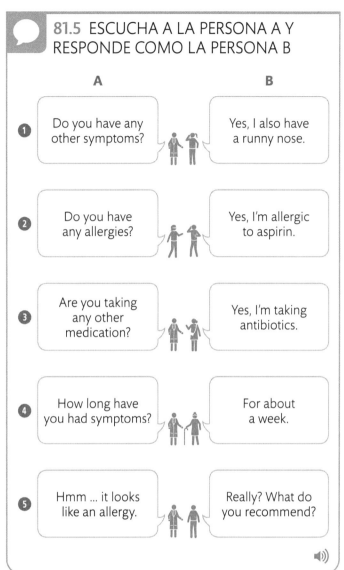

A **B**

1. Do you have any other symptoms? — Yes, I also have a runny nose.

2. Do you have any allergies? — Yes, I'm allergic to aspirin.

3. Are you taking any other medication? — Yes, I'm taking antibiotics.

4. How long have you had symptoms? — For about a week.

5. Hmm ... it looks like an allergy. — Really? What do you recommend?

81.6 USA EL ESQUEMA PARA FORMAR CINCO ORACIONES Y DILAS EN VOZ ALTA

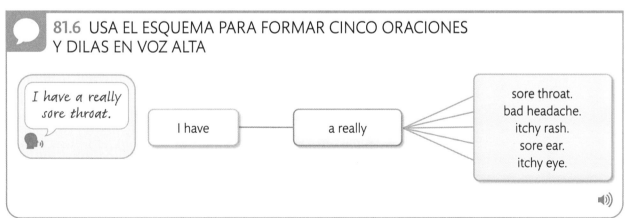

I have a really sore throat.

I have — a really —
sore throat.
bad headache.
itchy rash.
sore ear.
itchy eye.

81.7 TRATAMIENTO Y DOSIS

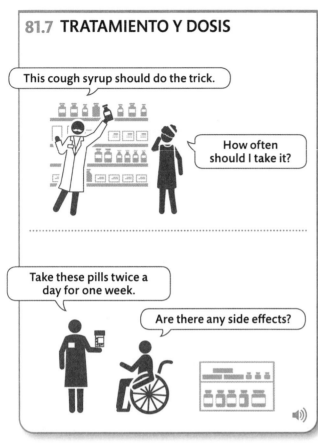

This cough syrup should do the trick.

How often should I take it?

Take these pills twice a day for one week.

Are there any side effects?

81.8 RECETAS MÉDICAS

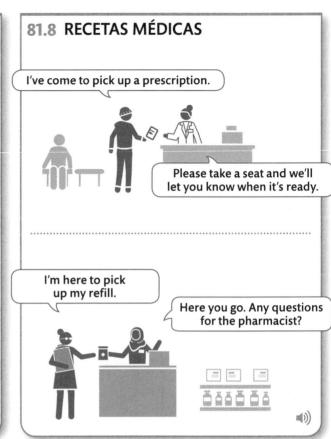

I've come to pick up a prescription.

Please take a seat and we'll let you know when it's ready.

I'm here to pick up my refill.

Here you go. Any questions for the pharmacist?

81.9 VOCABULARIO EN LA FARMACIA

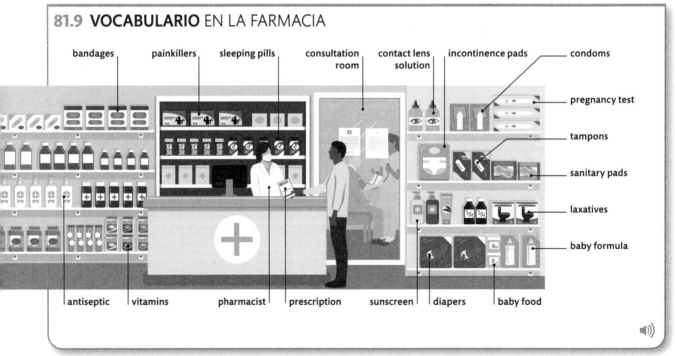

bandages · painkillers · sleeping pills · consultation room · contact lens solution · incontinence pads · condoms · pregnancy test · tampons · sanitary pads · laxatives · baby formula · antiseptic · vitamins · pharmacist · prescription · sunscreen · diapers · baby food

81.10 ESCUCHA EL AUDIO Y CONECTA LA RESPUESTA CORRECTA

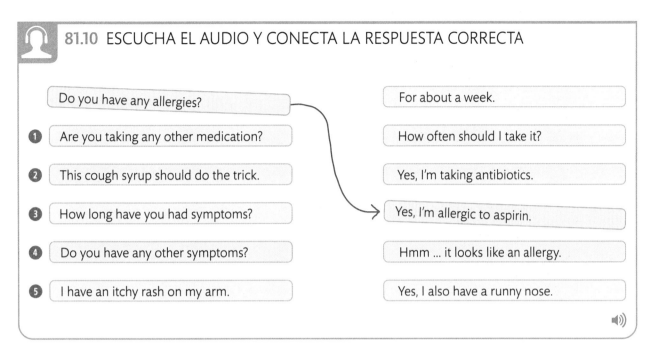

Do you have any allergies? ——→ Yes, I'm allergic to aspirin.

1 Are you taking any other medication?

2 This cough syrup should do the trick.

3 How long have you had symptoms?

4 Do you have any other symptoms?

5 I have an itchy rash on my arm.

For about a week.

How often should I take it?

Yes, I'm taking antibiotics.

Hmm ... it looks like an allergy.

Yes, I also have a runny nose.

81.11 ESCUCHA Y NUMERA LAS ORACIONES EN EL ORDEN EN QUE LAS OYES

A Are there any side effects? ☐

B This cough syrup should do the trick. ☐

C I've come to pick up a prescription. ☐ 1

D Any questions for the pharmacist? ☐

E Take these pills twice a day for one week. ☐

F I'm here to pick up my refill. ☐

G Please take a seat and we'll let you know when it's ready. ☐

H How often should I take it? ☐

I How long have you had symptoms? ☐

81.12 DI LAS ORACIONES EN VOZ ALTA, REEMPLAZANDO LAS IMÁGENES CON PALABRAS

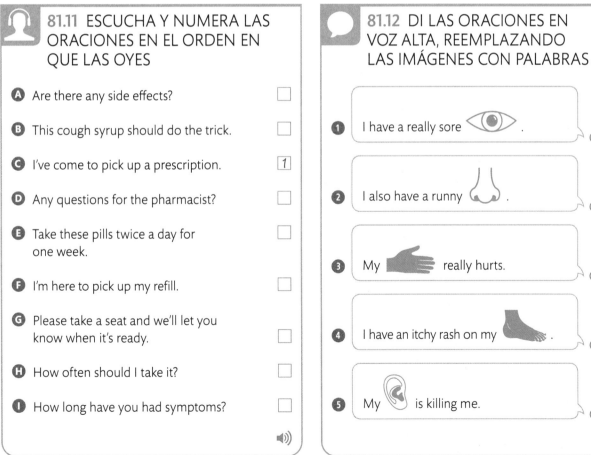

1 I have a really sore 👁 .

2 I also have a runny 👃 .

3 My ✋ really hurts.

4 I have an itchy rash on my 🦶 .

5 My 👂 is killing me.

82 Concertar una cita

82.1 EN LA CONSULTA DEL MÉDICO

Hi there, I'd like to book an appointment with Doctor Cole.

Can I ask what it's concerning?

I think I might have an eye infection.

We could squeeze you in later at 4:30?

That's great, thanks.

82.2 MÁS EXPRESIONES

When's the next available slot?

Do you have anything sooner?

I need to see the primary care nurse.

Can I reschedule my appointment?

Can I book an appointment for my daughter?

82.3 EN EL DENTISTA

I'd like to book a checkup, please.

Have you been with us before?

No, I haven't.

I'm sorry, we're not taking new patients.

I have an appointment next week, but I need to cancel it.

No problem. Can I take your name?

SMILE Dental

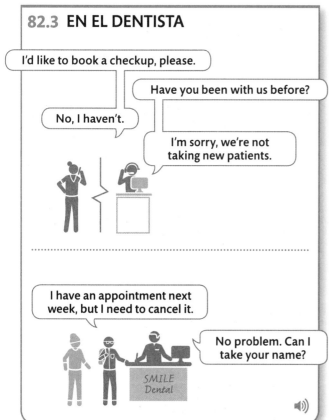

82.4 CITAS DE URGENCIAS

I need an emergency appointment. I have a really bad toothache.

We have a slot in half an hour if that's any good?

If you need an urgent appointment, we'll place you on the triage list ...

... and the doctor will call you back as soon as possible.

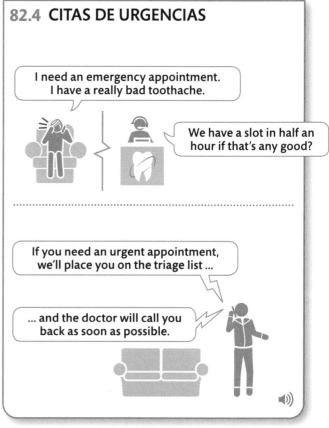

82.5 ESCUCHA A LA PERSONA A Y RESPONDE COMO LA PERSONA B

A   B

1. **A:** I'd like to book a checkup, please. **B:** Have you been with us before?

2. **A:** Can I ask what it's concerning? **B:** I think I might have an eye infection.

3. **A:** We could squeeze you in later at 4:30? **B:** That's great, thanks.

4. **A:** I have an appointment next week, but I need to cancel it. **B:** No problem. Can I take your name?

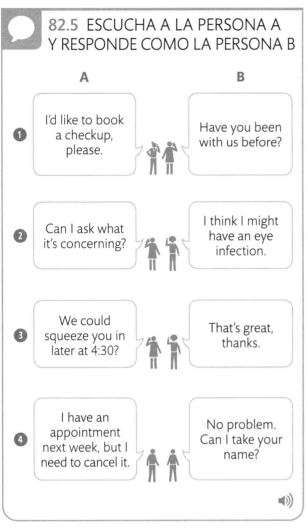

82.6 DI LAS ORACIONES EN VOZ ALTA, LLENANDO LOS ESPACIOS CON LAS PALABRAS DEL PANEL

eye   anything   reschedule   available

nurse   triage   appointment   Doctor

1. I need to see the primary care _____ .
2. Hi there, I'd like to book an appointment with _____ Cole.
3. Can I _____ my appointment?
4. Can I book an _____ for my daughter?
5. Do you have _____ sooner?
6. When's the next _____ slot?
7. If you need an urgent appointment, we'll place you on the _____ list ...
8. I think I might have an _____ infection.

82.7 USA EL ESQUEMA PARA FORMAR 12 ORACIONES Y DILAS EN VOZ ALTA

I'd like to book an appointment with the doctor.

| I'd like to | book an appointment
reschedule an appointment
book a checkup
cancel an appointment | with the doctor.
with the dentist.
for my daughter. |

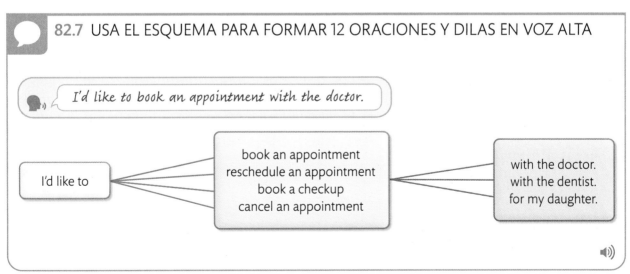

83 La visita médica

83.1 DESCRIBIR LOS SÍNTOMAS

What seems to be the problem?

I've had a bad cough for a week and it's getting worse.

I keep getting splitting headaches.

Okay, let me listen to your chest.

83.2 MÁS EXPRESIONES

I've been vomiting all night.

My shoulder has been hurting.

My son has a fever.

I've been under the weather.

I've found a lump in my breast.

83.3 CUIDADOS GENERALES

It seems to be healing up nicely ...

... I'll just change your bandage.

Which arm would you like the injection in?

Right, please! I'm left-handed.

83.4 MÁS EXPRESIONES

I'll refer you for some tests.

Can I book a flu shot?

Let's take your temperature.

I'd like a prescription refilled.

I'm due for a checkup.

83.5 DIAGNÓSTICOS Y CONSEJOS

What do you advise?

You need to rest and drink plenty of fluids.

It looks like a mild infection.

Will I need antibiotics?

Come back in two weeks and we'll see how it's looking.

83.6 ESCUCHA A LA PERSONA A Y RESPONDE COMO LA PERSONA B

A

B

1 Which arm would you like the injection in?

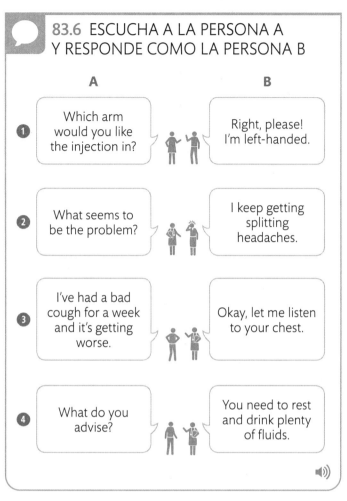

Right, please! I'm left-handed.

2 What seems to be the problem?

I keep getting splitting headaches.

3 I've had a bad cough for a week and it's getting worse.

Okay, let me listen to your chest.

4 What do you advise?

You need to rest and drink plenty of fluids.

🔊

83.7 ESCUCHA Y NUMERA LAS ORACIONES EN EL ORDEN EN QUE LAS OYES

A I've found a lump in my breast. ☐

B I'm due for a checkup. ☐1

C ... I'll just change your bandage. ☐

D I've been under the weather. ☐

E Come back in two weeks and we'll see how it's looking. ☐

F I've been vomiting all night. ☐

G It seems to be healing up nicely ... ☐

H I'd like a prescription refilled. ☐

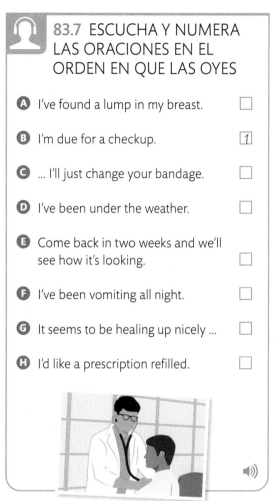

🔊

83.8 CONECTA LAS ORACIONES Y DILAS EN VOZ ALTA

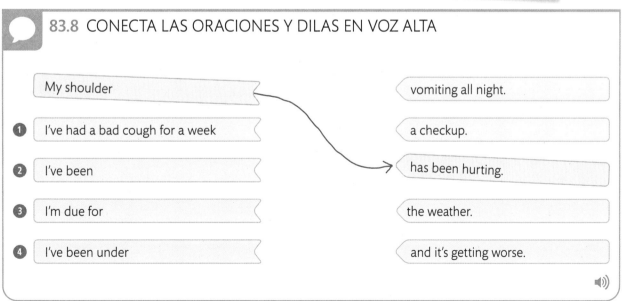

My shoulder — has been hurting.

1 I've had a bad cough for a week ⟩ ⟨ vomiting all night.

2 I've been ⟩ ⟨ a checkup.

3 I'm due for ⟩ ⟨ the weather.

4 I've been under ⟩ ⟨ and it's getting worse.

🔊

84 Lesiones y emergencias

84.1 EN UNA EMERGENCIA

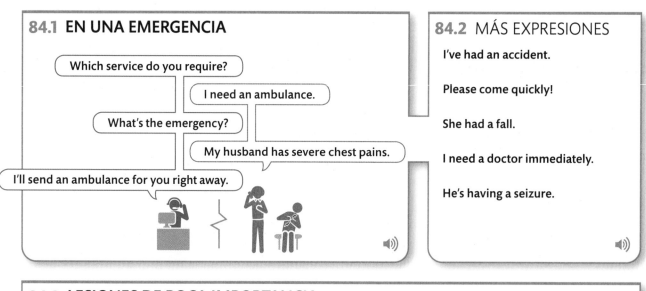

Which service do you require?

I need an ambulance.

What's the emergency?

My husband has severe chest pains.

I'll send an ambulance for you right away.

84.2 MÁS EXPRESIONES

I've had an accident.

Please come quickly!

She had a fall.

I need a doctor immediately.

He's having a seizure.

84.3 LESIONES DE POCA IMPORTANCIA

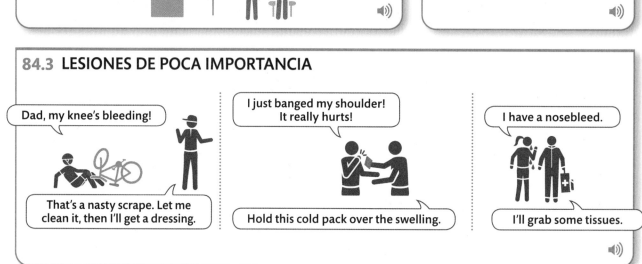

Dad, my knee's bleeding!

That's a nasty scrape. Let me clean it, then I'll get a dressing.

I just banged my shoulder! It really hurts!

Hold this cold pack over the swelling.

I have a nosebleed.

I'll grab some tissues.

84.4 LESIONES MÁS GRAVES

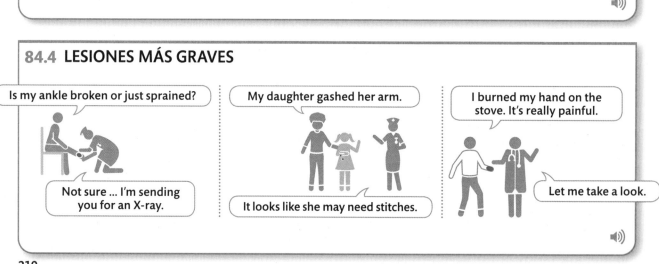

Is my ankle broken or just sprained?

Not sure ... I'm sending you for an X-ray.

My daughter gashed her arm.

It looks like she may need stitches.

I burned my hand on the stove. It's really painful.

Let me take a look.

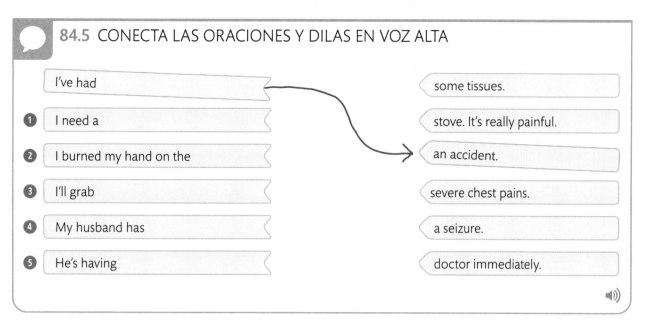

84.5 CONECTA LAS ORACIONES Y DILAS EN VOZ ALTA

I've had — an accident.

1 I need a — doctor immediately.

2 I burned my hand on the — stove. It's really painful.

3 I'll grab — some tissues.

4 My husband has — severe chest pains.

5 He's having — a seizure.

84.6 RODEA CON UN CÍRCULO LO QUE OYES

1 A / Ⓑ

2 A / B

3 A / B

4 A / B

84.7 RESPONDE EN VOZ ALTA AL AUDIO LLENANDO LOS ESPACIOS EN BLANCO CON LAS PALABRAS DEL PANEL

scrape   swelling   stitches   pains

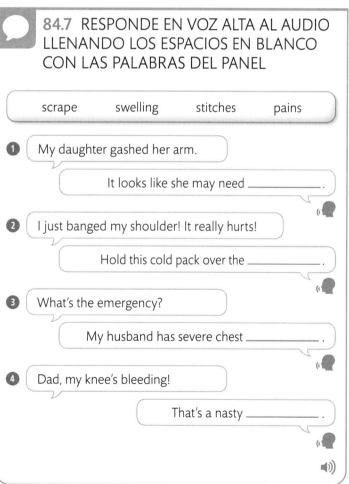

1 My daughter gashed her arm.

It looks like she may need _____.

2 I just banged my shoulder! It really hurts!

Hold this cold pack over the _____.

3 What's the emergency?

My husband has severe chest _____.

4 Dad, my knee's bleeding!

That's a nasty _____.

85 El hospital

85.1 EN EL HOSPITAL

We need to keep you overnight for observation.

I have a checkup with the nurse at 4:30.

Ward 1
EXIT

Waiting area

I need to see someone as soon as possible.

Do I need to have surgery?

Are you allergic to anything?

Okay, please fill out this paperwork and take a seat.

I'll take your details so we can get you seen.

Yes, I'm allergic to penicillin.

85.3 ESCUCHA Y NUMERA LAS IMÁGENES EN EL ORDEN EN QUE SE DESCRIBEN

A ☐

B ☐

C ☐

D ☐

E ☐ 1

85.4 DI LAS ORACIONES EN VOZ ALTA, LLENANDO LOS ESPACIOS CON LAS PALABRAS DEL PANEL

checkup	possible	examine
doctor	surgery	medical

1 I need to see someone as soon as _____ .

2 We have a _____ emergency.

3 How soon will I be seen by a _____ ?

4 I have a _____ with the nurse at 4:30.

5 Do I need to have _____ ?

6 I'm going to need to _____ you.

How long have you been feeling like this?

The pain started about two hours ago.

Okay, I'm going to do some blood work.

Good news! I got the all clear!

X-ray ➡

That's such a relief!

85.2 MÁS EXPRESIONES

We have a medical emergency.

Do you have health insurance?

Are you taking any regular medications?

Do you have someone you'd like to call?

I'm going to need to examine you.

I'm here for my scan.

How soon will I be seen by a doctor?

We'll move you to another ward for observation.

85.5 ESCUCHA A LA PERSONA A Y RESPONDE COMO LA PERSONA B

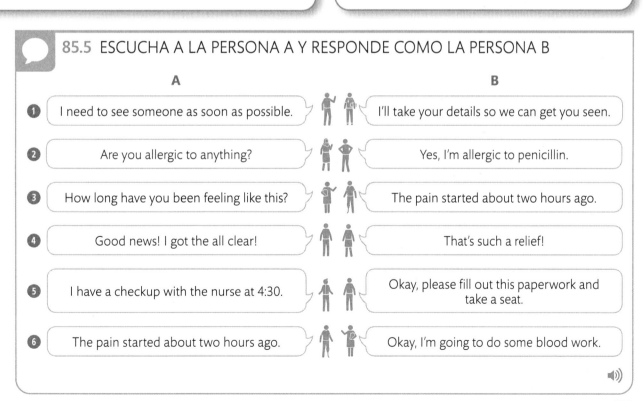

	A		B
1	I need to see someone as soon as possible.		I'll take your details so we can get you seen.
2	Are you allergic to anything?		Yes, I'm allergic to penicillin.
3	How long have you been feeling like this?		The pain started about two hours ago.
4	Good news! I got the all clear!		That's such a relief!
5	I have a checkup with the nurse at 4:30.		Okay, please fill out this paperwork and take a seat.
6	The pain started about two hours ago.		Okay, I'm going to do some blood work.

85.6 SOMETERSE A UNA OPERACIÓN

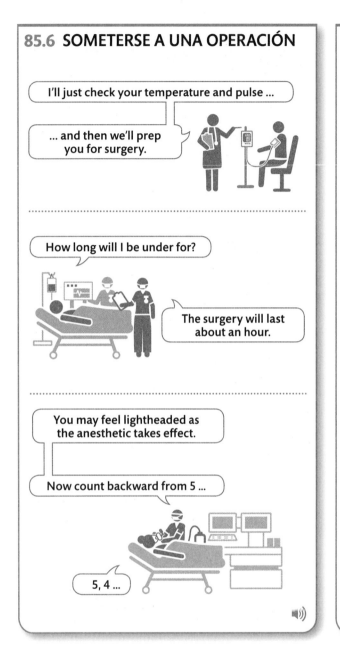

I'll just check your temperature and pulse ...

... and then we'll prep you for surgery.

How long will I be under for?

The surgery will last about an hour.

You may feel lightheaded as the anesthetic takes effect.

Now count backward from 5 ...

5, 4 ...

85.7 RECUPERARSE DE LA OPERACIÓN

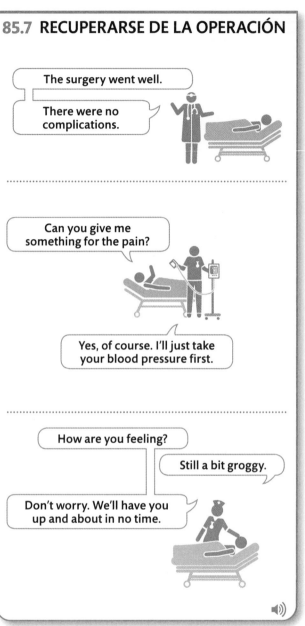

The surgery went well.

There were no complications.

Can you give me something for the pain?

Yes, of course. I'll just take your blood pressure first.

How are you feeling?

Still a bit groggy.

Don't worry. We'll have you up and about in no time.

85.8 VOCABULARIO TRATAMIENTO EN UN HOSPITAL

surgery

operating theater

anesthetic

ward

intensive care unit

visiting hours

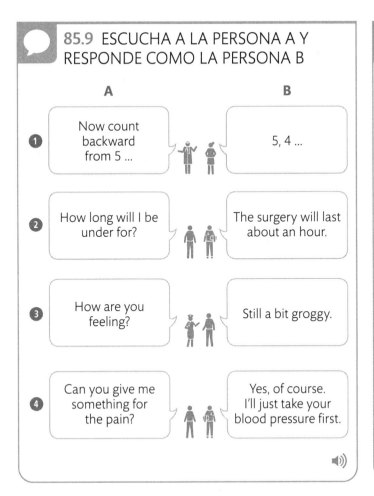

85.9 ESCUCHA A LA PERSONA A Y RESPONDE COMO LA PERSONA B

	A		B
❶	Now count backward from 5 ...		5, 4 ...
❷	How long will I be under for?		The surgery will last about an hour.
❸	How are you feeling?		Still a bit groggy.
❹	Can you give me something for the pain?		Yes, of course. I'll just take your blood pressure first.

◀))

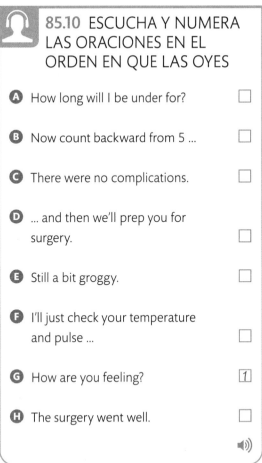

85.10 ESCUCHA Y NUMERA LAS ORACIONES EN EL ORDEN EN QUE LAS OYES

Ⓐ How long will I be under for? ☐

Ⓑ Now count backward from 5 ... ☐

Ⓒ There were no complications. ☐

Ⓓ ... and then we'll prep you for surgery. ☐

Ⓔ Still a bit groggy. ☐

Ⓕ I'll just check your temperature and pulse ... ☐

Ⓖ How are you feeling? ☐ 1

Ⓗ The surgery went well. ☐

◀))

85.11 DI LAS ORACIONES EN VOZ ALTA, LLENANDO LOS ESPACIOS EN BLANCO CON LAS PALABRAS DEL PANEL

complications	pressure	groggy	about
under	backward	anesthetic	temperature

❶ I'll just take your blood _____ first.

❷ Still a bit _____ .

❸ Don't worry. We'll have you up and _____ in no time.

❹ I'll just check your _____ and pulse ...

❺ You may feel lightheaded as the _____ takes effect.

❻ How long will I be _____ for?

❼ Now count _____ from 5 ...

❽ There were no _____ .

◀))

86 Cuidado dental

86.1 HABLAR CON EL DENTISTA

I have a bad toothache.

Do I need braces?

I think my crown has come loose.

My filling has come out.

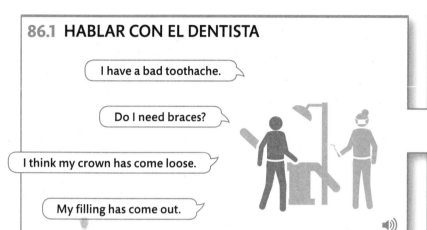

86.2 MÁS EXPRESIONES

Can I have my teeth whitened?

I brush my teeth twice a day.

I need to see the hygienist.

My son's first teeth are coming through.

86.3 DIAGNÓSTICOS Y CONSEJOS

Remember to floss regularly.

It looks like you need a small filling.

Would you like to rinse your mouth out?

Make sure you don't brush too hard.

86.4 MÁS EXPRESIONES

Open a bit wider for me, please.

You have a buildup of plaque.

You'll need this tooth pulled.

Let me know if you feel any pain.

You have a small cavity.

86.5 VOCABULARIO EN EL DENTISTA

dentist

whitening

toothache

to floss

to brush

to rinse

cavity

filling

plaque

crown

toothbrush

braces

86.6 ESCUCHA Y NUMERA LAS IMÁGENES EN EL ORDEN EN QUE SE DESCRIBEN

A 1   **B** ☐   **C** ☐   **D** ☐   **E** ☐   **F** ☐

86.7 ESCUCHA Y NUMERA LAS ORACIONES EN EL ORDEN EN QUE LAS OYES

A I have a bad toothache. ☐

B You have a small cavity. ☐

C Remember to floss regularly. 1

D You have a buildup of plaque. ☐

E Open a bit wider for me, please. ☐

F I need to see the hygienist. ☐

G Let me know if you feel any pain. ☐

H Make sure you don't brush too hard. ☐

I You'll need this tooth pulled. ☐

J It looks like you need a small filling. ☐

86.8 CONECTA LAS ORACIONES Y DILAS EN VOZ ALTA

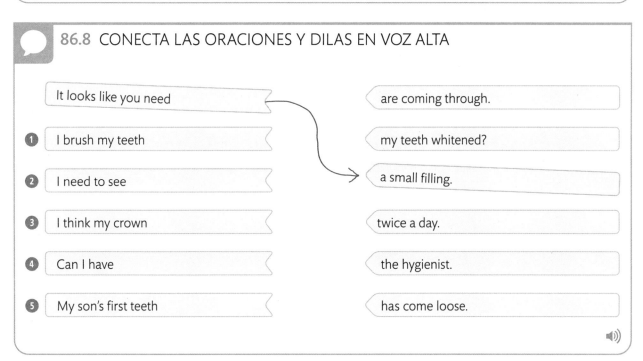

It looks like you need — a small filling.

1 I brush my teeth — twice a day.

2 I need to see — the hygienist.

3 I think my crown — has come loose.

4 Can I have — my teeth whitened?

5 My son's first teeth — are coming through.

87 Tratamiento psicológico

87.1 SOLICITAR TERAPIA

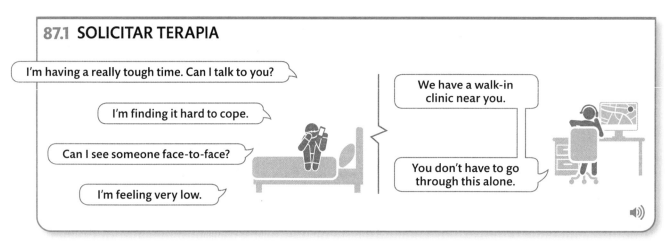

I'm having a really tough time. Can I talk to you?

I'm finding it hard to cope.

Can I see someone face-to-face?

I'm feeling very low.

We have a walk-in clinic near you.

You don't have to go through this alone.

87.2 PREGUNTAS DE TERAPIA

How did that make you feel?

How is this affecting you?

So what you're saying is ...

Can we explore this more?

87.3 TERAPIA DE GRUPO

Let's go around the group and say how we're feeling.

I've been a bit up and down.

I'm doing better this week.

These sessions are really helping me.

I'm anxious all the time.

87.4 MÁS EXPRESIONES

How are you feeling today?

That's a real trigger for me.

Your feelings are valid.

Talking about it really helps.

87.5 VOCABULARIO EMOCIONES

happy

calm

anxious

depressed

stressed

angry

87.6 ESCUCHA A LA PERSONA A Y RESPONDE COMO LA PERSONA B

A	B
1 Can I see someone face-to-face?	We have a walk-in clinic near you.
2 How is this affecting you?	I'm finding it hard to cope.
3 Let's go around the group and say how we're feeling.	I've been a bit up and down.
4 How are you feeling today?	I'm feeling very low.

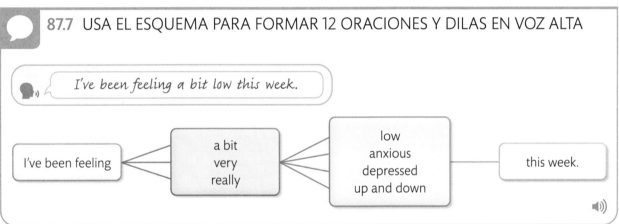

87.7 USA EL ESQUEMA PARA FORMAR 12 ORACIONES Y DILAS EN VOZ ALTA

I've been feeling a bit low this week.

I've been feeling → a bit / very / really → low / anxious / depressed / up and down → this week.

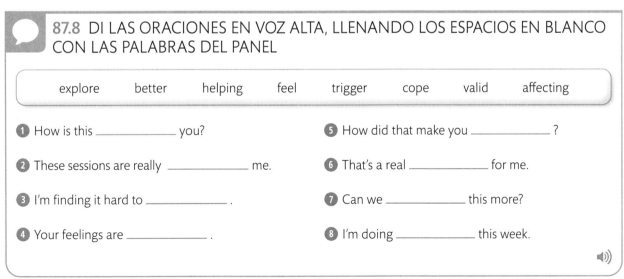

87.8 DI LAS ORACIONES EN VOZ ALTA, LLENANDO LOS ESPACIOS EN BLANCO CON LAS PALABRAS DEL PANEL

explore   better   helping   feel   trigger   cope   valid   affecting

1 How is this _____ you?

2 These sessions are really _____ me.

3 I'm finding it hard to _____ .

4 Your feelings are _____ .

5 How did that make you _____ ?

6 That's a real _____ for me.

7 Can we _____ this more?

8 I'm doing _____ this week.

88 Medios y comunicación

88.1 LLAMADAS DE TELÉFONO, MENSAJES DE TEXTO Y CORREOS ELECTRÓNICOS

to call · to leave a voicemail · to take a message · to put on hold · to transfer a call · to put on speaker

text / message · video call · email · email address · to click · to tap

88.2 DISPOSITIVOS

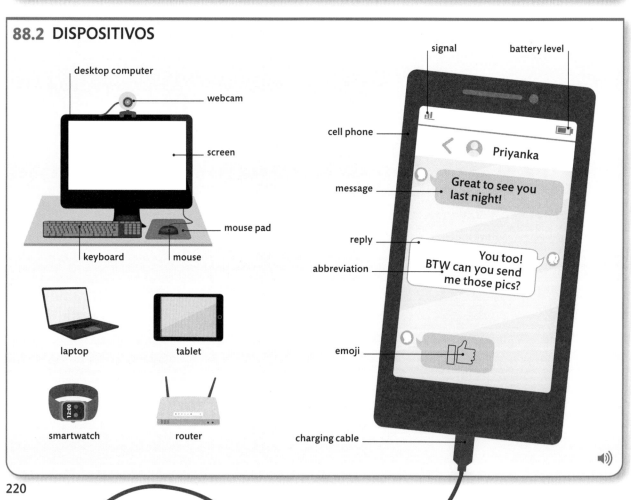

desktop computer · webcam · screen · mouse pad · keyboard · mouse

laptop · tablet

smartwatch · router

signal · battery level

cell phone

message

Priyanka

Great to see you last night!

reply

abbreviation

You too!
BTW can you send me those pics?

emoji

charging cable

88.3 INTERNET

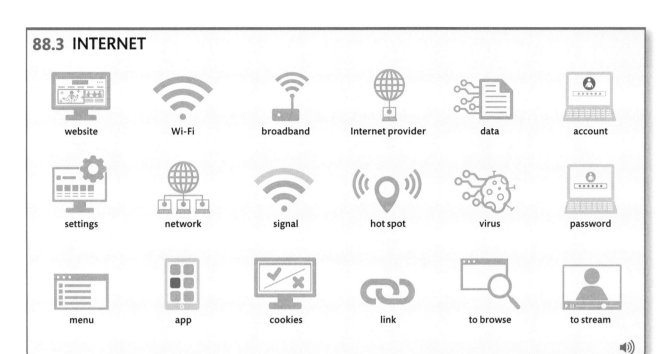

website · Wi-Fi · broadband · Internet provider · data · account

settings · network · signal · hot spot · virus · password

menu · app · cookies · link · to browse · to stream

88.4 REDES SOCIALES

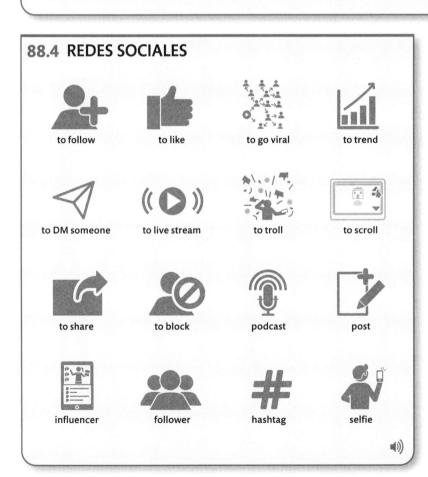

to follow · to like · to go viral · to trend

to DM someone · to live stream · to troll · to scroll

to share · to block · podcast · post

influencer · follower · hashtag · selfie

88.5 LECTURA

book · e-reader

magazine · subscription

article · headline

GIRL RAISES MONEY FOR CHARITY

newspaper

89 Llamadas formales

89.1 HACER UNA LLAMADA

Hi, could I speak to …?

Hello, I wonder if you can help me …

I'm calling about …

I'm calling you regarding …

89.2 LLAMAR A ATENCIÓN AL CLIENTE

Hello, customer service, how can I help?

I'll just put you on hold while I transfer you.

Thank you for waiting.

Thanks for calling.

89.3 DEJAR MENSAJES Y CONTESTAR LLAMADAS

Janos isn't available right now. Can I take a message?

Yes. Please ask him to call Ash at ABC Tech as soon as possible.

89.4 MÁS EXPRESIONES

Can I leave a message?

He knows where to reach me.

She'll call you back shortly.

We'll need to check our system and get back to you.

89.5 TERMINAR UNA LLAMADA

Is there anything else I can help you with?

I appreciate the call, thank you.

No, that's all. Thanks for your help. Goodbye.

My pleasure.

89.6 MÁS EXPRESIONES

Thanks for your call.

Thank you so much for calling.

Let's speak again soon.

You've been a great help.

Have a nice evening.

89.7 ESCUCHA A LA PERSONA A Y RESPONDE COMO LA PERSONA B

A
B

1 Janos isn't available right now. Can I take a message?

Yes. Please ask him to call Ash at ABC Tech as soon as possible.

2 I appreciate the call, thank you.

My pleasure.

3 Thank you so much for calling.

Let's speak again soon.

4 Is there anything else I can help you with?

No, that's all. Thanks for your help. Goodbye.

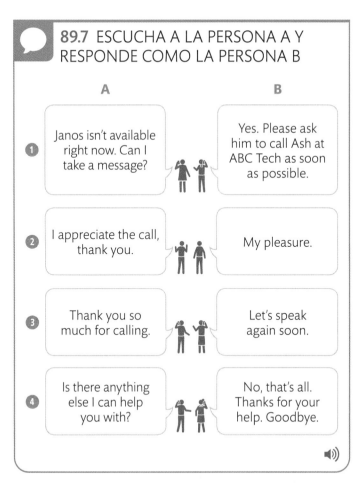

89.8 ESCUCHA Y NUMERA LAS ORACIONES EN EL ORDEN EN QUE LAS OYES

A I appreciate the call, thank you. ☐

B Hi, could I speak to …? ☐1

C I'm calling you regarding … ☐

D Have a nice evening. ☐

E Let's speak again soon. ☐

F She'll call you back shortly. ☐

G You've been a great help. ☐

H Thanks for your call. ☐

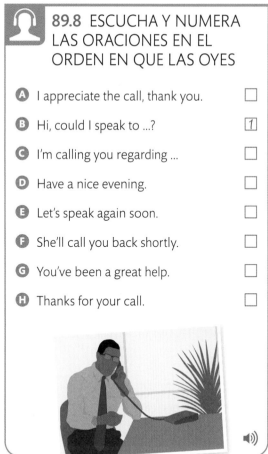

89.9 CONECTA LAS ORACIONES Y DILAS EN VOZ ALTA

Hello, customer service, — how can I help?

1 We'll need to check our system — and get back to you.

2 Is there anything else — I can help you with?

3 He knows where — to reach me.

4 Hello, I wonder — if you can help me …

5 Thank you so much — for calling.

223

90 Llamadas informales

90.1 HACER Y RECIBIR LLAMADAS

Hi, Mom. How's it going?

Good, thank you. I'm just checking in about tonight.

Hey bud, whereabouts are you?

Hey, I'm right here!

90.2 MÁS EXPRESIONES

You okay?

Lovely to hear from you!

Sorry, I can't talk now.

I'll message you back.

I'll put you on speaker.

90.3 PROBLEMAS CON EL TELÉFONO

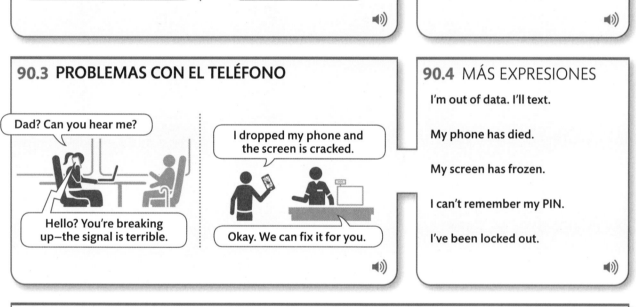

Dad? Can you hear me?

Hello? You're breaking up—the signal is terrible.

I dropped my phone and the screen is cracked.

Okay. We can fix it for you.

90.4 MÁS EXPRESIONES

I'm out of data. I'll text.

My phone has died.

My screen has frozen.

I can't remember my PIN.

I've been locked out.

90.5 TERMINAR UNA LLAMADA

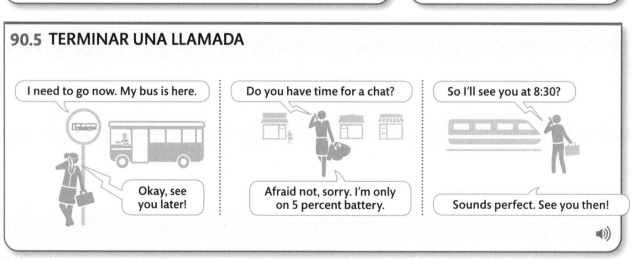

I need to go now. My bus is here.

Okay, see you later!

Do you have time for a chat?

Afraid not, sorry. I'm only on 5 percent battery.

So I'll see you at 8:30?

Sounds perfect. See you then!

90.6 ESCUCHA A LA PERSONA A Y RESPONDE COMO LA PERSONA B

A	B

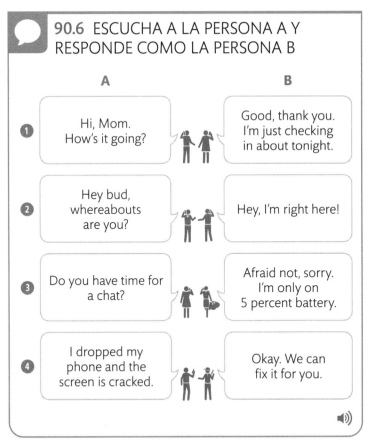

1
A: Hi, Mom. How's it going?
B: Good, thank you. I'm just checking in about tonight.

2
A: Hey bud, whereabouts are you?
B: Hey, I'm right here!

3
A: Do you have time for a chat?
B: Afraid not, sorry. I'm only on 5 percent battery.

4
A: I dropped my phone and the screen is cracked.
B: Okay. We can fix it for you.

90.7 DI LAS ORACIONES EN VOZ ALTA, LLENANDO LOS ESPACIOS CON LAS PALABRAS DEL PANEL

PIN   talk   message   locked
screen   died   speaker

1 Sorry, I can't _____ now.

2 I can't remember my _____ .

3 I'll _____ you back.

4 I'll put you on _____ .

5 My phone has _____ .

6 I've been _____ out.

7 My _____ has frozen.

90.8 RESPONDE EN VOZ ALTA AL AUDIO, LLENANDO LOS ESPACIOS EN BLANCO CON LAS PALABRAS DEL PANEL

See   breaking   fix   checking

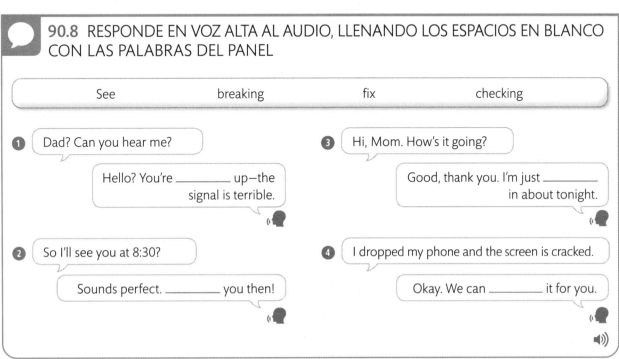

1
Dad? Can you hear me?
Hello? You're _____ up—the signal is terrible.

2
So I'll see you at 8:30?
Sounds perfect. _____ you then!

3
Hi, Mom. How's it going?
Good, thank you. I'm just _____ in about tonight.

4
I dropped my phone and the screen is cracked.
Okay. We can _____ it for you.

91 Usar internet

91.1 ACCEDER A UNA RED DE WIFI

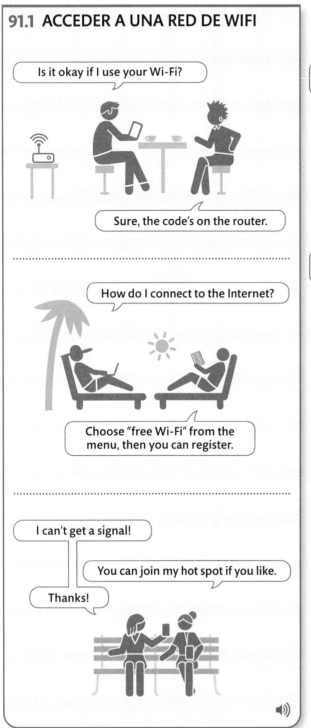

Is it okay if I use your Wi-Fi?

Sure, the code's on the router.

How do I connect to the Internet?

Choose "free Wi-Fi" from the menu, then you can register.

I can't get a signal!

You can join my hot spot if you like.

Thanks!

91.2 MEDIDAS DE SEGURIDAD

Molly just got her first cell phone. How do I set up parental controls?

Go to "settings," then tap "security."

Should I click this link? It looks a bit weird.

Yeah, that URL seems dicey. Let's try another site.

91.3 MÁS EXPRESIONES

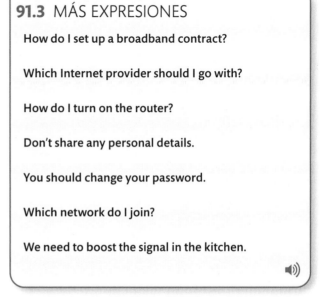

How do I set up a broadband contract?

Which Internet provider should I go with?

How do I turn on the router?

Don't share any personal details.

You should change your password.

Which network do I join?

We need to boost the signal in the kitchen.

91.4 ESCUCHA A LA PERSONA A Y RESPONDE COMO LA PERSONA B

A **B**

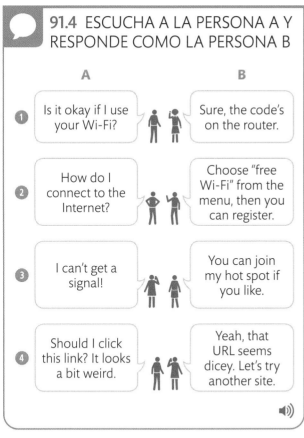

1. Is it okay if I use your Wi-Fi? — Sure, the code's on the router.

2. How do I connect to the Internet? — Choose "free Wi-Fi" from the menu, then you can register.

3. I can't get a signal! — You can join my hot spot if you like.

4. Should I click this link? It looks a bit weird. — Yeah, that URL seems dicey. Let's try another site.

91.5 ESCUCHA Y NUMERA LAS ORACIONES EN EL ORDEN EN QUE LAS OYES

A How do I set up a broadband contract? ☐

B Which Internet provider should I go with? ☐

C How do I turn on the router? ☐

D Which network do I join? [1]

E Don't share any personal details. ☐

F You should change your password. ☐

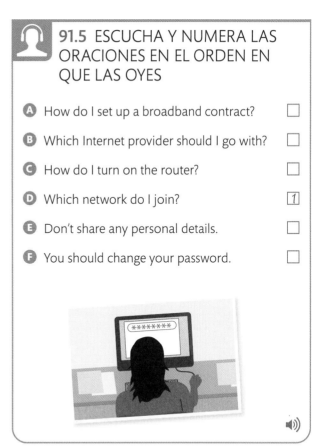

91.6 RESPONDE EN VOZ ALTA AL AUDIO, LLENANDO LOS ESPACIOS EN BLANCO CON LAS PALABRAS DEL PANEL

site   hot spot   menu   security

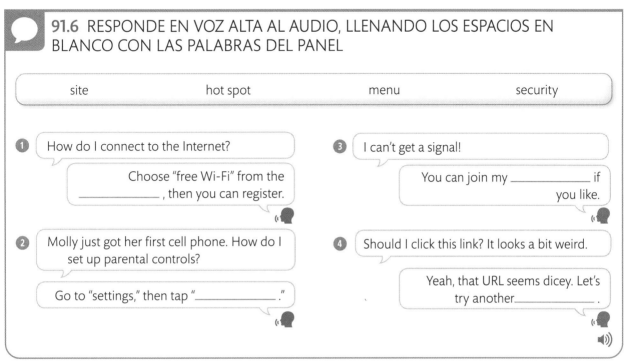

1. How do I connect to the Internet? — Choose "free Wi-Fi" from the _____ , then you can register.

2. Molly just got her first cell phone. How do I set up parental controls? — Go to "settings," then tap "_____."

3. I can't get a signal! — You can join my _____ if you like.

4. Should I click this link? It looks a bit weird. — Yeah, that URL seems dicey. Let's try another _____.

91.7 TAREAS COTIDIANAS

Hey, what's going on?

I'm setting up an online account for our energy bills.

I'm looking up some recipes for lunch.

I'm just tracking the grocery delivery.

91.8 MÁS EXPRESIONES

I'm booking a doctor's appointment.

I'm ordering more cat food.

I'm renewing my driver's license.

I'm canceling my gym membership.

I'm transferring some money.

91.9 TRABAJO Y ESTUDIOS

So what's on your agenda for today?

Let's see ... I need to check my emails ...

... catch up on the latest research ...

... watch the company live stream ...

... and sign up for that online training course.

How's it going?

Not too bad, thanks. I'm just uploading my essay ...

... then I have a webinar this afternoon.

91.10 DIVERTIRSE

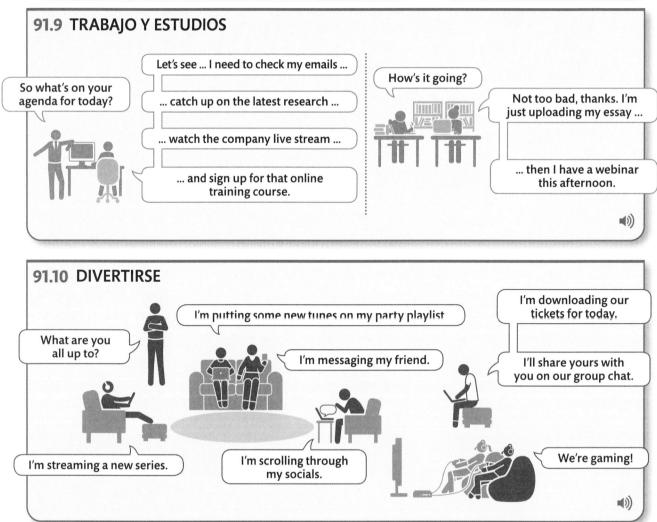

What are you all up to?

I'm putting some new tunes on my party playlist

I'm messaging my friend.

I'm downloading our tickets for today.

I'll share yours with you on our group chat.

I'm streaming a new series.

I'm scrolling through my socials.

We're gaming!

91.11 ESCUCHA Y NUMERA LAS IMÁGENES EN EL ORDEN EN QUE SE DESCRIBEN

A ☐
B ☐ 1
C ☐
D ☐
E ☐
F ☐

91.12 DI LAS ORACIONES EN VOZ ALTA, LLENANDO LOS ESPACIOS CON LAS PALABRAS DEL PANEL

webinar	booking	online	ordering
streaming	tracking	check	scrolling

1 I'm _____ a doctor's appointment.

2 I need to _____ my emails ...

3 I have a _____ this afternoon.

4 I'm _____ a new series.

5 ... and sign up for that _____ training course.

6 I'm _____ more cat food.

7 I'm _____ through my socials.

8 I'm just _____ the grocery delivery.

91.13 CONECTA LAS ORACIONES Y DILAS EN VOZ ALTA

I'm putting some new tunes → on my party playlist.

1 I'm downloading — our tickets for today.

2 I'll share yours with you — on our group chat.

3 I'm setting up an online account — ... then I have a webinar this afternoon.

4 I'm just uploading my essay ... — for our energy bills.

92 Problemas digitales

92.1 PROBLEMAS DE CONEXIÓN

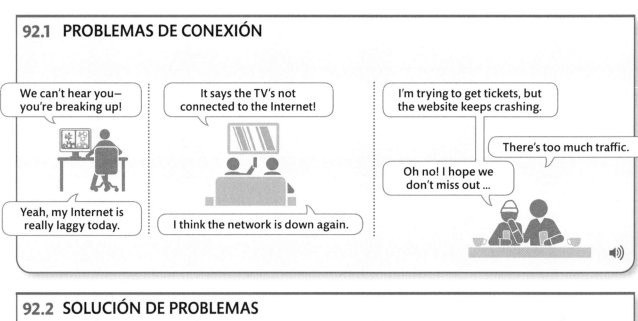

We can't hear you– you're breaking up!

Yeah, my Internet is really laggy today.

It says the TV's not connected to the Internet!

I think the network is down again.

I'm trying to get tickets, but the website keeps crashing.

There's too much traffic.

Oh no! I hope we don't miss out ...

92.2 SOLUCIÓN DE PROBLEMAS

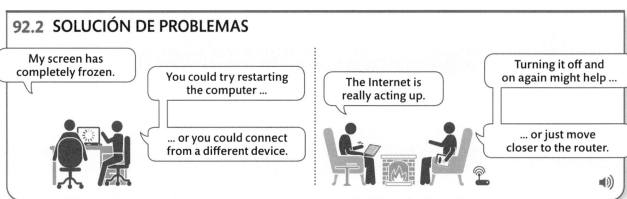

My screen has completely frozen.

You could try restarting the computer ...

... or you could connect from a different device.

The Internet is really acting up.

Turning it off and on again might help ...

... or just move closer to the router.

92.3 SEGURIDAD DIGITAL

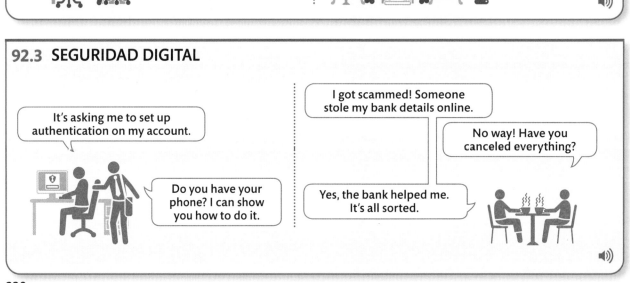

It's asking me to set up authentication on my account.

Do you have your phone? I can show you how to do it.

I got scammed! Someone stole my bank details online.

No way! Have you canceled everything?

Yes, the bank helped me. It's all sorted.

92.4 ESCUCHA A LA PERSONA A Y RESPONDE COMO LA PERSONA B

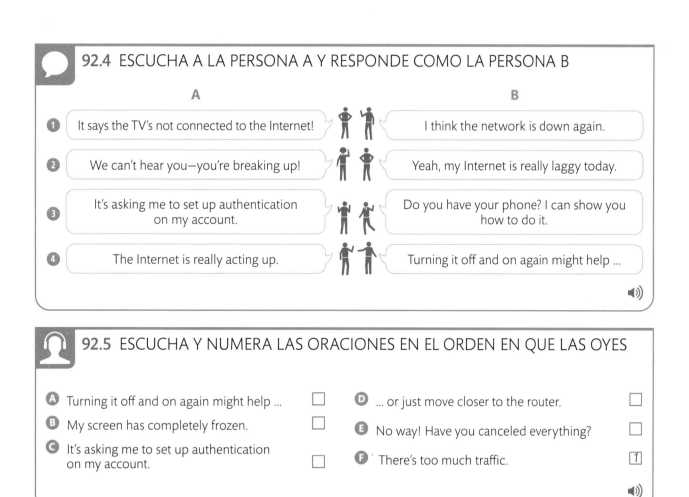

	A		B
1	It says the TV's not connected to the Internet!		I think the network is down again.
2	We can't hear you—you're breaking up!		Yeah, my Internet is really laggy today.
3	It's asking me to set up authentication on my account.		Do you have your phone? I can show you how to do it.
4	The Internet is really acting up.		Turning it off and on again might help ...

92.5 ESCUCHA Y NUMERA LAS ORACIONES EN EL ORDEN EN QUE LAS OYES

A Turning it off and on again might help ... ☐

B My screen has completely frozen. ☐

C It's asking me to set up authentication on my account. ☐

D ... or just move closer to the router. ☐

E No way! Have you canceled everything? ☐

F There's too much traffic. 1

92.6 CONECTA LAS ORACIONES Y DILAS EN VOZ ALTA

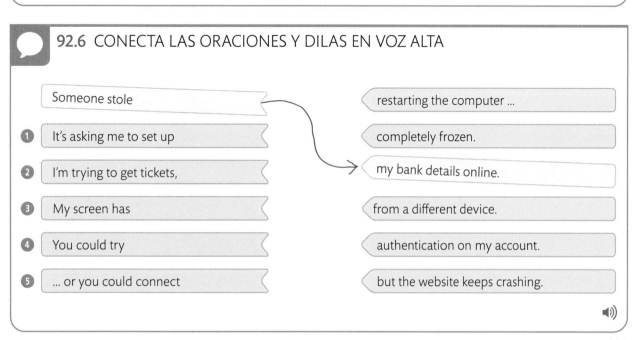

Someone stole → my bank details online.

1 It's asking me to set up — authentication on my account.

2 I'm trying to get tickets, — but the website keeps crashing.

3 My screen has — completely frozen.

4 You could try — restarting the computer ...

5 ... or you could connect — from a different device.

231

Correos electrónicos

93.1 ENVIAR Y RECIBIR

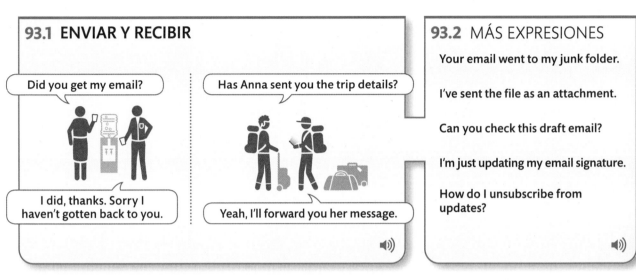

Did you get my email?

I did, thanks. Sorry I haven't gotten back to you.

Has Anna sent you the trip details?

Yeah, I'll forward you her message.

93.2 MÁS EXPRESIONES

Your email went to my junk folder.

I've sent the file as an attachment.

Can you check this draft email?

I'm just updating my email signature.

How do I unsubscribe from updates?

93.3 PROBLEMAS CON EL CORREO ELECTRÓNICO

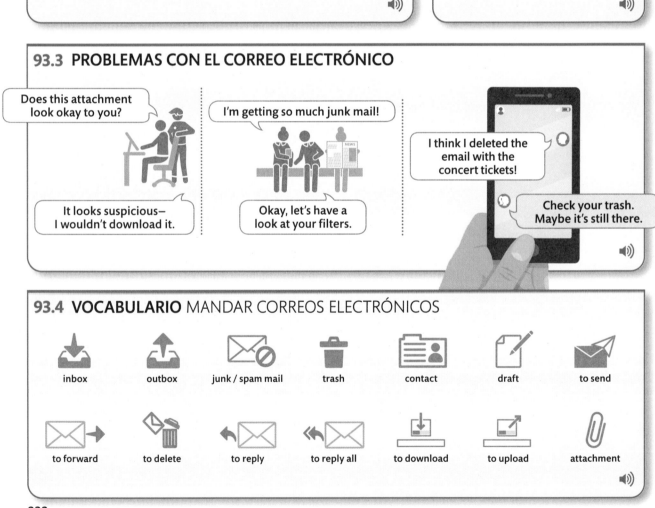

Does this attachment look okay to you?

It looks suspicious— I wouldn't download it.

I'm getting so much junk mail!

Okay, let's have a look at your filters.

I think I deleted the email with the concert tickets!

Check your trash. Maybe it's still there.

93.4 VOCABULARIO MANDAR CORREOS ELECTRÓNICOS

inbox

outbox

junk / spam mail

trash

contact

draft

to send

to forward

to delete

to reply

to reply all

to download

to upload

attachment

93.5 ESCUCHA A LA PERSONA A Y RESPONDE COMO LA PERSONA B

A		B
1 Did you get my email?		I did, thanks. Sorry I haven't gotten back to you.
2 Has Anna sent you the trip details?		Yeah, I'll forward you her message.
3 Does this attachment look okay to you?		It looks suspicious—I wouldn't download it.
4 I'm getting so much junk mail!		Okay, let's have a look at your filters.

93.6 RODEA CON UN CÍRCULO LO QUE OYES

1   **A**   **B**
2   **A**   **B**
3   **A**   **B**
4   **A**   **B**
5   **A**   **B**
6   **A**   **B**

93.7 RESPONDE EN VOZ ALTA AL AUDIO, LLENANDO LOS ESPACIOS EN BLANCO CON LAS PALABRAS DEL PANEL

filters	download	forward	trash

1 I think I deleted the email with the concert tickets!

Check your _____ . Maybe it's still there.

2 I'm getting so much junk mail!

Okay, let's have a look at your _____ .

3 Has Anna sent you the trip details?

Yeah, I'll _____ you her message.

4 Does this attachment look okay to you?

It looks suspicious—I wouldn't _____ it.

94 Mensajes y videollamadas

94.1 MENSAJES DE TEXTO

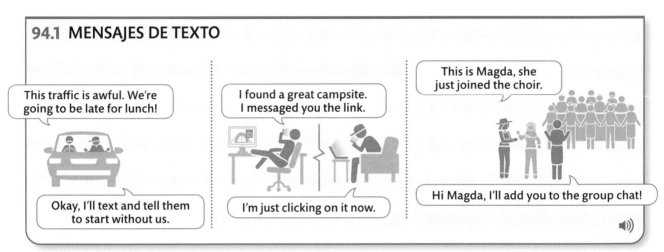

This traffic is awful. We're going to be late for lunch!

Okay, I'll text and tell them to start without us.

I found a great campsite. I messaged you the link.

I'm just clicking on it now.

This is Magda, she just joined the choir.

Hi Magda, I'll add you to the group chat!

94.2 LENGUAJE SMS

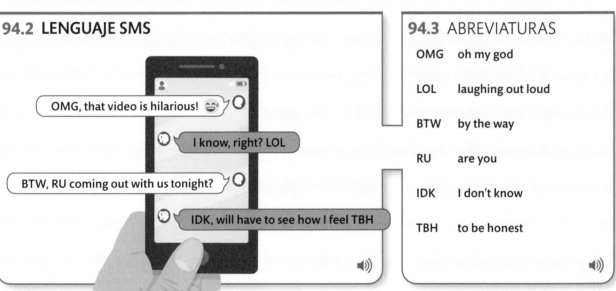

OMG, that video is hilarious! 😆

I know, right? LOL

BTW, RU coming out with us tonight?

IDK, will have to see how I feel TBH

94.3 ABREVIATURAS

OMG	oh my god
LOL	laughing out loud
BTW	by the way
RU	are you
IDK	I don't know
TBH	to be honest

94.4 VIDEOLLAMADAS

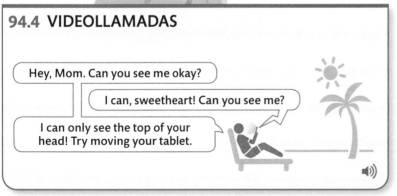

Hey, Mom. Can you see me okay?

I can, sweetheart! Can you see me?

I can only see the top of your head! Try moving your tablet.

🌐 DEBES SABER

En el inglés escrito informal que se utiliza en las aplicaciones de mensajería y en los mensajes de texto, es habitual omitir los signos de puntuación, sobre todo los puntos al final de los mensajes. También es posible ver abreviaturas en minúsculas (por ejemplo, **idk**) en lugar de en mayúsculas (por ejemplo, **IDK**).

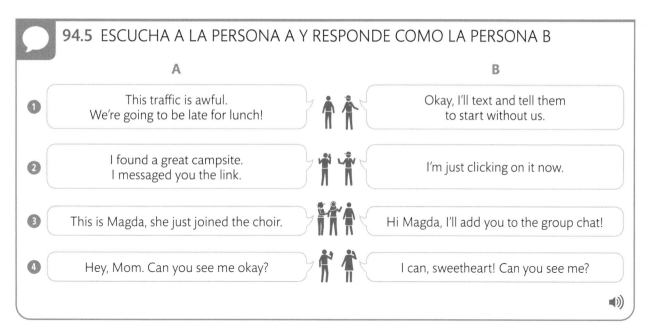

94.5 ESCUCHA A LA PERSONA A Y RESPONDE COMO LA PERSONA B

A		B
1 This traffic is awful. We're going to be late for lunch!		Okay, I'll text and tell them to start without us.
2 I found a great campsite. I messaged you the link.		I'm just clicking on it now.
3 This is Magda, she just joined the choir.		Hi Magda, I'll add you to the group chat!
4 Hey, Mom. Can you see me okay?		I can, sweetheart! Can you see me?

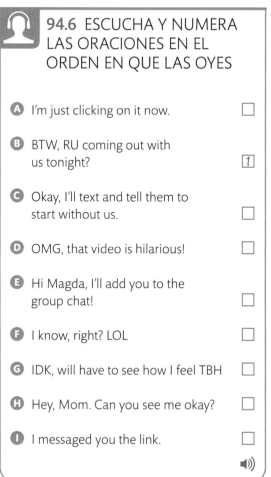

94.6 ESCUCHA Y NUMERA LAS ORACIONES EN EL ORDEN EN QUE LAS OYES

Ⓐ I'm just clicking on it now. ☐

Ⓑ BTW, RU coming out with us tonight? [1]

Ⓒ Okay, I'll text and tell them to start without us. ☐

Ⓓ OMG, that video is hilarious! ☐

Ⓔ Hi Magda, I'll add you to the group chat! ☐

Ⓕ I know, right? LOL ☐

Ⓖ IDK, will have to see how I feel TBH ☐

Ⓗ Hey, Mom. Can you see me okay? ☐

Ⓘ I messaged you the link. ☐

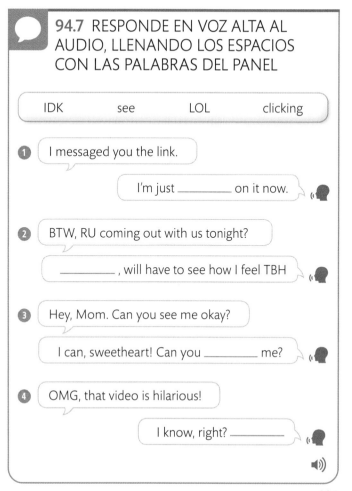

94.7 RESPONDE EN VOZ ALTA AL AUDIO, LLENANDO LOS ESPACIOS CON LAS PALABRAS DEL PANEL

IDK	see	LOL	clicking

1 I messaged you the link.

I'm just _____ on it now.

2 BTW, RU coming out with us tonight?

_____ , will have to see how I feel TBH

3 Hey, Mom. Can you see me okay?

I can, sweetheart! Can you _____ me?

4 OMG, that video is hilarious!

I know, right? _____

95 Redes sociales

95.1 USAR LAS REDES SOCIALES

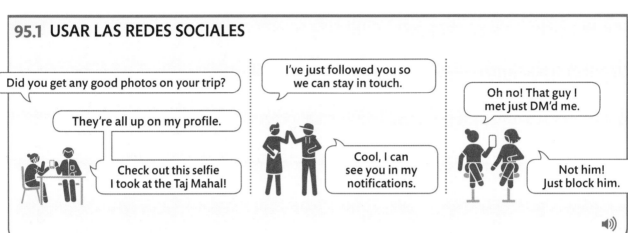

Did you get any good photos on your trip?

They're all up on my profile.

Check out this selfie I took at the Taj Mahal!

I've just followed you so we can stay in touch.

Cool, I can see you in my notifications.

Oh no! That guy I met just DM'd me.

Not him! Just block him.

95.2 CONTENIDOS VIRALES

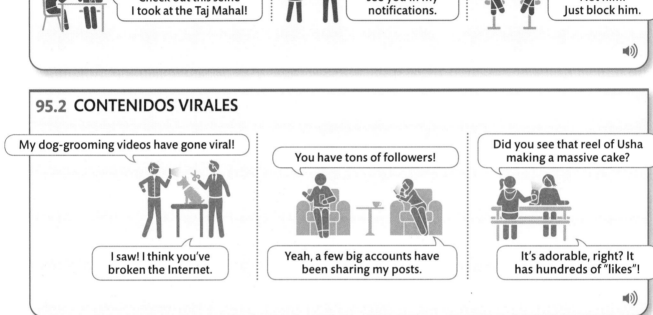

My dog-grooming videos have gone viral!

I saw! I think you've broken the Internet.

You have tons of followers!

Yeah, a few big accounts have been sharing my posts.

Did you see that reel of Usha making a massive cake?

It's adorable, right? It has hundreds of "likes"!

95.3 CREAR UN NEGOCIO

So we need to grow our social reach.

More video content would help.

Or how about a monthly podcast?

Maybe hook up with an influencer.

We could live stream the launch party.

95.4 MÁS EXPRESIONES

There are tons of comments on my post!

That's just a troll. I'm blocking them.

Click the follow button to get all our updates!

95.5 ESCUCHA A LA PERSONA A Y RESPONDE COMO LA PERSONA B

A		B
1	I've just followed you so we can stay in touch.	Cool, I can see you in my notifications.
2	Oh no! That guy I met just DM'd me.	Not him! Just block him.
3	Did you see that reel of Usha making a massive cake?	It's adorable, right? It has hundreds of "likes"!
4	You have tons of followers!	Yeah, a few big accounts have been sharing my posts.

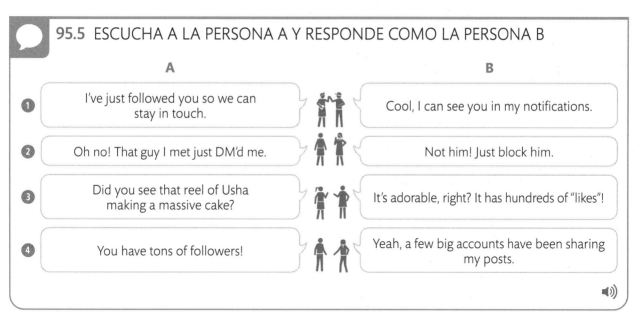

95.6 ESCUCHA EL AUDIO Y CONECTA LA RESPUESTA CORRECTA

Did you get any good photos on your trip?

Or how about a monthly podcast?

1 My dog-grooming videos have gone viral!

Not him! Just block him.

2 We could live stream the launch party.

I saw! I think you've broken the Internet.

3 Oh no! That guy I met just DM'd me.

They're all up on my profile.

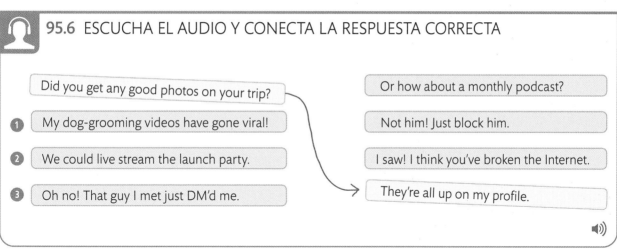

95.7 DI LAS ORACIONES EN VOZ ALTA, LLENANDO LOS ESPACIOS EN BLANCO CON LAS PALABRAS DEL PANEL

Internet	podcast	troll	profile	comments	content

1 Or how about a monthly _____ ?

2 That's just a _____ . I'm blocking them.

3 I saw! I think you've broken the _____ .

4 There are tons of _____ on my post!

5 They're all up on my _____ .

6 More video _____ would help.

96 Leer

96.1 HABLAR DE LIBROS

It's the best book I've read in ages.

I agree. I couldn't put it down!

Yeah, it had me on the edge of my seat!

The ending was a bit of a letdown.

I found it pretty rough going, actually.

🔊

🌐 **DEBES SABER**

Los modismos ingleses son muy comunes en las conversaciones cotidianas, y frases como **a bit of a letdown** y **on the edge of my seat** pueden ayudarte a que tu inglés hablado suene más natural. Estas expresiones idiomáticas no siempre tienen un sentido literal, así que tendrás que aprenderlas y practicarlas individualmente.

96.2 EN LA LIBRERÍA

Can you recommend a good vacation read?

Yes, this one is a real page-turner.

Can I help at all?

No, thanks. I'm just browsing.

I'm afraid that book's out of stock.

Okay, could you order it for me, please?

🔊

96.3 REVISTAS Y PERIÓDICOS

Want a flip through *Fashion Monthly*?

Yes, please, if you've finished with it.

Have you seen today's headlines?

No, what's been going on?

Did you renew our subscription to *World Weekly*?

Sorry, not yet—I'll do it now!

🔊

96.4 ESCUCHA A LA PERSONA A Y RESPONDE COMO LA PERSONA B

A   B

1. **A:** Have you seen today's headlines? 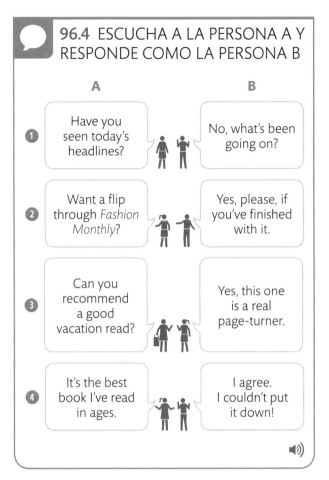 **B:** No, what's been going on?

2. **A:** Want a flip through *Fashion Monthly*? **B:** Yes, please, if you've finished with it.

3. **A:** Can you recommend a good vacation read? **B:** Yes, this one is a real page-turner.

4. **A:** It's the best book I've read in ages. **B:** I agree. I couldn't put it down!

96.5 ESCUCHA Y NUMERA LAS ORACIONES EN EL ORDEN EN QUE LAS OYES

A. The ending was a bit of a letdown. ☐

B. Okay, could you order it for me, please? ☐

C. Yeah, it had me on the edge of my seat! ☐

D. I found it pretty rough going, actually. ☐ 1

E. No, thanks. I'm just browsing. ☐

F. Sorry, not yet—I'll do it now! ☐

G. Did you renew our subscription to *World Weekly*? ☐

96.6 CONECTA LAS ORACIONES Y DILAS EN VOZ ALTA

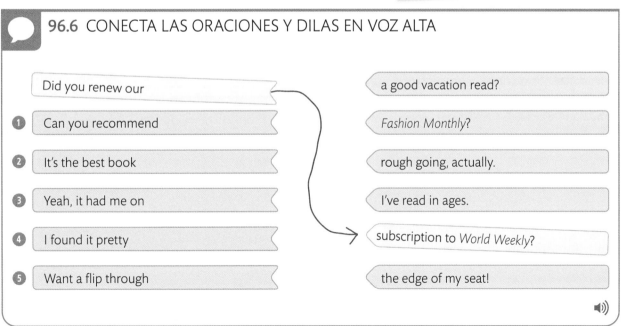

Did you renew our —————→ subscription to *World Weekly*?

1. Can you recommend —— a good vacation read?

2. It's the best book —— I've read in ages.

3. Yeah, it had me on —— the edge of my seat!

4. I found it pretty —— rough going, actually.

5. Want a flip through —— *Fashion Monthly*?

Respuestas

Puedes escuchar el audio de todas las respuestas marcadas con el símbolo . En las páginas 8 y 9 encontrarás más información sobre cómo acceder a todos los recursos de audio de este libro.

01

1.7
- (A) 2
- (B) 6
- (C) 7
- (D) 3
- (E) 8
- (F) 4
- (G) 1
- (H) 5

1.8
1. How do you **do**?
2. **Good** evening.
3. It's nice to **meet** you.
4. Good **afternoon**.
5. Hey, Jay, how's it **going**?
6. **Hey**, everyone!
7. How are you **doing**?
8. Long **time** no see!

02

2.6
1. This is my friend, Kit.
2. I'd like to introduce my friend, Kit.
3. I'd like you to meet my friend, Kit.
4. This is my partner, Kit.
5. I'd like to introduce my partner, Kit.
6. I'd like you to meet my partner, Kit.
7. This is my colleague, Kit.
8. I'd like to introduce my colleague, Kit.
9. I'd like you to meet my colleague, Kit.

2.7
1. Of course. I'm Samantha, but you can **call** me Sam.
2. It's a pleasure to **meet** you, Mr. Ali.
3. I don't think so. **Great** to meet you!
4. **How's it going**? I'm Joe.

04

4.4
- (A) 6
- (B) 4
- (C) 1
- (D) 8
- (E) 7
- (F) 2
- (G) 3
- (H) 5

4.5
1. Sorry, my English **isn't great.**
2. Sorry, I didn't **catch that.**
3. I'm not quite sure **what you mean.**
4. Sorry, I'm not **following you.**
5. Can you repeat **that more slowly, please?**

4.6
1. Sorry? Could you say that again, please?
2. Sorry? Could you repeat that more slowly, please?
3. Sorry? Could you explain that one more time, please?
4. Sorry? Could you talk me through that again, please?
5. Excuse me? Could you say that again, please?
6. Excuse me? Could you repeat that more slowly, please?
7. Excuse me? Could you explain that one more time, please?
8. Excuse me? Could you talk me through that again, please?
9. Pardon? Could you say that again, please?
10. Pardon? Could you repeat that more slowly, please?
11. Pardon? Could you explain that one more time, please?
12. Pardon? Could you talk me through that again, please?

05

5.5
1. Yes, I'm really **into** it right now!
2. I absolutely **love** them!
3. I've **always** loved it.
4. I'm a big **fan**!
5. Yeah, it's **pretty** good!
6. It's so my **thing**!
7. This soup is **great**, isn't it?
8. What do you **think**?

5.6
1. I'm not much of **a sushi fan.**
2. Skateboarding isn't really **my thing.**
3. No way! I can't **stand them.**
4. I couldn't think of **anything worse!**

5.12
- (A) 4
- (B) 3
- (C) 8
- (D) 1
- (E) 2
- (F) 5
- (G) 10
- (H) 7
- (I) 9
- (J) 6

5.13
1. I'd prefer tacos.
2. I'd rather have tacos.
3. I'd much rather have tacos.
4. I'd definitely go for tacos.
5. I'd prefer pizza.
6. I'd rather have pizza.
7. I'd much rather have pizza.
8. I'd definitely go for pizza.

06

6.5
1. Yeah, I know what you mean.
2. Yeah, I hear you.
3. Yeah, I couldn't agree more.
4. Yeah, I totally agree.
5. Absolutely, I know what you mean.
6. Absolutely, I hear you.
7. Absolutely, I couldn't agree more.
8. Absolutely, I totally agree.
9. Exactly, I know what you mean.
10. Exactly, I hear you.
11. Exactly, I couldn't agree more.
12. Exactly, I totally agree.

6.6
1. Absolutely, I couldn't **agree more.**
2. I don't think **so either.**
3. I know **what you mean.**
4. We might have to agree **to disagree on this!**
5. Sorry, I'm not **with you on this one.**

07

7.6 🔊
1. **Why** don't we bike to the park?
2. I **think** I'll give it a pass.
3. **Count** me in!
4. I know! **Let's** go swimming!
5. **Sure** thing!
6. I'm not that **interested**, to be honest.
7. **Sounds** good.
8. I don't really **feel** like it, sorry.

7.7 🔊
1. Is anyone going to Juan's party tomorrow?
2. Is anyone going to the beach tomorrow?
3. Is anyone going to the castle tomorrow?
4. How about hitting Juan's party tomorrow?
5. How about hitting the beach tomorrow?
6. How about hitting the castle tomorrow?
7. Are you up for Juan's party tomorrow?
8. Are you up for the beach tomorrow?
9. Are you up for the castle tomorrow?

08

8.4
A 2 E 6
B 8 F 5
C 1 G 3
D 7 H 4

8.5 🔊
1. Don't **mention** it.
2. Thank you so **much**!
3. My **pleasure**!
4. I can't thank you **enough**!
5. Thank you, I really **appreciate** it.

09

9.5
A 7 E 5
B 2 F 8
C 1 G 3
D 6 H 4

9.6 🔊
1. Thanks, I appreciate **you saying that.**
2. That's okay, **it was nothing.**
3. I'm really sorry **I forgot your birthday!**
4. Thank you, that **means a lot.**

10

10.4
A 4 E 6
B 1 F 8
C 7 G 3
D 5 H 2

10.5 🔊
1. Thank you **for your time.**
2. It was a pleasure **meeting you.**
3. Good talking **with you.**
4. Speak to **you soon.**
5. Bye! Have **a safe trip!**
6. Great to **catch up!**

10.6 🔊
1. It was a pleasure meeting you.
2. It was great meeting you.
3. It was good meeting you.
4. It was a pleasure to see you.
5. It was great to see you.
6. It was good to see you.
7. It was a pleasure talking with you.
8. It was great talking with you.
9. It was good talking with you.

12

12.4 🔊
1. Could we do Sunday instead?
2. Let's make it quarter after, just to be sure.
3. Friday works for me.
4. It's at 10.

12.6 🔊
1. Which day **suits** you for lunch this week?
2. Friday **works** for me.
3. Sunday is **good** with us!
4. Hey, are you free for a drink **on Tuesday**?
5. Sorry, we can't come over **next** Saturday.
6. Keep it **free**!
7. We've set the date for **May 31st** of next year!

13

13.6
A 4 E 5
B 1 F 6
C 3 G 8
D 2 H 7

13.7 🔊
1. It's really windy today, isn't it?
2. It's freezing today, isn't it?
3. It's boiling today, isn't it?
4. It's a little chilly today, isn't it?
5. It's lovely weather today, isn't it?
6. It's really windy out there!
7. It's freezing out there!
8. It's boiling out there!
9. It's a little chilly out there!
10. It's lovely weather out there!

15

15.4
A 5 D 2
B 1 E 4
C 6 F 3

15.6 🔊
1. Yes, I have a **brother and two stepsisters.**
2. I'm an **only child.**
3. I have two **younger sisters.**
4. We grew up **in Springfield.**

16

16.5
A 6 F 1
B 2 G 4
C 3 H 5
D 8 I 10
E 7 J 9

16.6 🔊
1. **Happy** birthday!
2. I hear **congratulations** are in order?
3. We're really **proud** of you!
4. All the **best** for your retirement.
5. Well **done**!
6. I'll **miss** you all!

17

17.3 🔊
1. I'm good! How are things with you?
2. I didn't know you were coming!
3. At a thrift store—for 10 dollars!
4. I'm an English teacher. How about you?

18

18.6 🔊
1. Interested in going for coffee this Saturday?
2. Interested in going for coffee next Friday?
3. Interested in going for coffee sometime?
4. Interested in going out this Saturday?
5. Interested in going out next Friday?
6. Interested in going out sometime?
7. I was wondering if you'd like to go for coffee this Saturday?
8. I was wondering if you'd like to go for coffee next Friday?
9. I was wondering if you'd like to go for coffee sometime?
10. I was wondering if you'd like to go out this Saturday?
11. I was wondering if you'd like to go out next Friday?
12. I was wondering if you'd like to go out sometime?

18.7 🔊
1. I was hoping **you'd ask me.**
2. You took **your time!**
3. That would be **really nice.**
4. I just like you **as a friend.**

18.12
Ⓐ 7		Ⓕ 6	
Ⓑ 1		Ⓖ 2	
Ⓒ 3		Ⓗ 10	
Ⓓ 4		Ⓘ 5	
Ⓔ 8		Ⓙ 9	

18.13 🔊
1. It was nice to **hang** out with you.
2. What kind of things are you **into**?
3. I'd really like to see you **again**.
4. I'd better **head** off. Early start tomorrow!
5. How long have you been **single**?
6. I'm just **booking** a ride.

19

19.4
Ⓐ 5		Ⓔ 2	
Ⓑ 1		Ⓕ 7	
Ⓒ 6		Ⓖ 4	
Ⓓ 3			

19.6 🔊
1. Anything you need, just **ask**.
2. Let me know if I can do **anything**.
3. I know things are **tough**, but we're here for you.
4. You've been a lot of **help**.
5. That's really **sweet**. I will!
6. I'm very **grateful**.
7. I know this hasn't been **easy**.
8. Thank you, I really **appreciate** it.

21

21.3
1. A
2. B
3. B
4. A
5. B
6. A

22

22.5
Ⓐ 3		Ⓓ 6	
Ⓑ 1		Ⓔ 2	
Ⓒ 4		Ⓕ 5	

22.6 🔊
1. Want to get curry **takeout** tonight?
2. Two burgers to **go**, please.
3. I'll **pick** it up on my way home.
4. Okay, I'll **order** it on the app.
5. We have no food. **Let's** get pizza!
6. Our fried chicken order still hasn't **arrived**.
7. Let me **check** what's happening.
8. Do you **want** fries with that?

23

23.6
Ⓐ 5		Ⓔ 6	
Ⓑ 3		Ⓕ 8	
Ⓒ 7		Ⓖ 2	
Ⓓ 1		Ⓗ 4	

23.7 🔊
1. Can I get a **beer**, please?
2. Do you serve **mocktails**?
3. A glass of **wine** for me, please!
4. What **cocktails** can you recommend?
5. What **soft drinks** are there?

24

24.7
Ⓐ 2		Ⓓ 6	
Ⓑ 3		Ⓔ 4	
Ⓒ 1		Ⓕ 5	

24.8 🔊
1. I'll bring you the **menu**.
2. I'll have the **steak**, please.
3. Could you bring us a **pitcher of water**, please?
4. I think I'll go for the **fish**.
5. I'll bring you the **black pepper**.
6. Could I have the **salad**?

24.13
1. A
2. B
3. B
4. A

24.14 🔊
1. Nothing **special**, to be honest.
2. No, I'll **get this**.
3. It's a bit too salty, **actually**.
4. **Really tasty**. How's yours?

24.15 🔊
1. This chicken is a bit too salty, actually.
2. This chicken is a bit too cold, actually.
3. This chicken is nothing special, actually.
4. This chicken is really tasty, actually.
5. This chicken is a bit too salty, to be honest.
6. This chicken is a bit too cold, to be honest.
7. This chicken is nothing special, to be honest.
8. This chicken is really tasty, to be honest.

25

25.5
Ⓐ 4 Ⓓ 5
Ⓑ 3 Ⓔ 6
Ⓒ 1 Ⓕ 2

25.7 🔊
① I'll start **weighing** the flour.
② **Chop** the butter into cubes.
③ **Preheat** the oven to 475°F (250°C).
④ Turn it down and **simmer** for 20 minutes.
⑤ I'm **roasting** a chicken for lunch.
⑥ **Mix** the ingredients together.
⑦ I've **baked** you a birthday cake!
⑧ Okay, I'll **set** the timer!

25.13
Ⓐ 4 Ⓔ 8
Ⓑ 5 Ⓕ 6
Ⓒ 1 Ⓖ 3
Ⓓ 2 Ⓗ 7

25.14 🔊
① I think I'll start **with a mushroom kebab.**
② I'd love **a bit of everything!**
③ I'm allergic **to shellfish.**
④ Should I make some **garlic bread to go with it?**
⑤ Thanks for **having us over.**
⑥ Something **smells good!**

25.15 🔊
① This is so delicious.
② This is really delicious.
③ This is absolutely delicious.
④ This is so amazing!
⑤ This is really amazing!
⑥ This is absolutely amazing!
⑦ This is so fantastic!
⑧ This is really fantastic!
⑨ This is absolutely fantastic!
⑩ This is so yummy.
⑪ This is really yummy.
⑫ This is absolutely yummy.

27

27.6
Ⓐ 5 Ⓓ 2
Ⓑ 1 Ⓔ 6
Ⓒ 3 Ⓕ 4

27.7 🔊
① The **3D glasses** made it so realistic!
② Which **screen** is it showing at?
③ Can we have **seats** at the back?
④ I wasn't **happy** about the ending.
⑤ Is there time to get **popcorn**?
⑥ How long is the **movie**?
⑦ Is this the **subtitled** screening?
⑧ Is the movie okay for **kids** under 10?

28

28.6
① A
② B
③ A
④ A
⑤ B
⑥ B

28.7 🔊
① I've booked seats **in the front row.**
② Is there **an intermission?**
③ Can I see **your tickets, please?**
④ Where is **the cloakroom?**

28.8 🔊
① Follow me. You're in the front row.
② Follow me. You're in the back row.
③ Follow me. You're in Box 5.
④ I've booked seats in the front row.
⑤ I've booked seats in the back row.
⑥ I've booked seats in Box 5.

29

29.5
Ⓐ 4 Ⓔ 1
Ⓑ 2 Ⓕ 7
Ⓒ 5 Ⓖ 3
Ⓓ 6 Ⓗ 8

29.6 🔊
① Here's **the lineup** for the whole weekend.
② I'll meet you back in **the main arena**.
③ No, we can just **turn up**.
④ 9 p.m., but the opening band has just **come on**.
⑤ What an amazing **performance**!

30

30.6
Ⓐ 3 Ⓔ 8
Ⓑ 5 Ⓕ 2
Ⓒ 1 Ⓖ 7
Ⓓ 4 Ⓗ 6

30.7 🔊
① Have you been to this yoga class before?
② Have you been to this Pilates class before?
③ Have you been to this fitness class before?
④ Have you been to this spin class before?
⑤ Have you been to this dance class before?

31

31.4 🔊
① Yes, we run them on Saturdays.
② Of course. What time would you like?
③ Over here!
④ No, I sprained my ankle last week!

31.6 🔊
① Wanna join us for a game of **badminton**?
② Are you coming to **ice hockey** practice?
③ Do you give **golf** lessons here?
④ I'd like to book a **tennis** lesson, please.
⑤ We run **soccer** practice on Mondays.

32

32.5
Ⓐ 6 Ⓓ 5
Ⓑ 1 Ⓔ 2
Ⓒ 4 Ⓕ 3

32.6 🔊
1 Any seats left for the golf tournament today?
2 Any seats left for the tennis final today?
3 Any seats left for track and field today?
4 Any seats left for the soccer game today?
5 Want to go to the golf tournament today?
6 Want to go to the tennis final today?
7 Want to go to track and field today?
8 Want to go to the soccer game today?

33.4
1 B
2 A
3 B
4 A
5 B

33.5 🔊
1 I'm giving **pottery** a try!
2 I've taken up **knitting** recently.
3 I only started learning **karate** a year ago.
4 I usually play **tennis** on weekends.
5 I've just started learning the **piano**.
6 I've been playing the **guitar** for six years.

33.6 🔊
1 I've been doing karate for two years.
2 I've been playing the guitar for two years.
3 I've been learning the piano for two years.
4 I've been playing tennis for two years.
5 I've been doing karate since I was 12.
6 I've been playing the guitar since I was 12.
7 I've been learning the piano since I was 12.
8 I've been playing tennis since I was 12.

35.6
1 A
2 A
3 A
4 B
5 A

35.7 🔊
1 Can I have a jar of honey, please?
2 Can I have a bunch of grapes, please?
3 Can I have a loaf of bread, please?
4 Can I have a punnet of strawberries, please?
5 Can I have a carton of eggs, please?
6 Could I have a jar of honey, please?
7 Could I have a bunch of grapes, please?
8 Could I have a loaf of bread, please?
9 Could I have a punnet of strawberries, please?
10 Could I have a carton of eggs, please?

36.2
A 3 D 6
B 5 E 2
C 1 F 4

36.3
1 B
2 A
3 B
4 B
5 B
6 A

36.9
A 3 D 5
B 6 E 4
C 1 F 2

36.10 🔊
1 Excuse me, where's the **frozen food** aisle?
2 Would you like to use the **self-checkout**?
3 Where can I find the **pet food**?
4 Do you have **baby products** here?
5 I can't find the **fruit** and **vegetables**.

37.5
A 2 D 3
B 1 E 6
C 4 F 5

37.6 🔊
1 Will it **survive** the winter?
2 When is the best time to plant these **seeds**?
3 How much **sunlight** do they need?
4 Does it need much **looking** after?
5 How often should I **feed** it?
6 How do I get rid of **weeds**?

37.7 🔊
1 We need some advice **on starting a vegetable garden.**
2 What's a good **compost to use?**
3 I don't really mind, but **my apartment doesn't get much light.**
4 What kind of houseplants **are you looking for?**
5 How do I **get rid of weeds?**

38.6
A 5 F 4
B 7 G 6
C 1 H 3
D 8 I 10
E 2 J 9

38.7 🔊
1 I'm looking for a **screwdriver**.
2 Where can I find a **hammer**?
3 Do you have any **drills**?
4 Who can I ask about **saws**?
5 What kind of **nails** do you sell?
6 Where are the **screws**?

38.8 🔊
1 What do I need for plastering walls?
2 What would you recommend for plastering walls?
3 What's best for plastering walls?
4 What do I need for tiling my bathroom?
5 What would you recommend for tiling my bathroom?
6 What's best for tiling my bathroom?
7 What do I need for filling a crack?
8 What would you recommend for filling a crack?
9 What's best for filling a crack?

39

39.4
Ⓐ 1 Ⓓ 2
Ⓑ 6 Ⓔ 4
Ⓒ 3 Ⓕ 5

39.6 🔊
❶ Do you have this sweater in a size 10, please?
❷ Do you have this jacket in a size 10, please?
❸ Do you have this suit in a size 10, please?
❹ Do you have this shirt in a size 10, please?
❺ Do you have this sweater in a larger size, please?
❻ Do you have this jacket in a larger size, please?
❼ Do you have this suit in a larger size, please?
❽ Do you have this shirt in a larger size, please?
❾ Do you have this sweater in the next size down, please?
❿ Do you have this jacket in the next size down, please?
⓫ Do you have this suit in the next size down, please?
⓬ Do you have this shirt in the next size down, please?

40

40.5 🔊
❶ The **boots** are too tight.
❷ Where can I return these **shoes**?
❸ This **dress** is too small.
❹ I have to return this, but I lost my **receipt**.
❺ The **pants** don't fit right.
❻ I need to return this **bag**.

41

41.6 🔊
❶ Can you do **Thursday at 3 p.m.?**
❷ Is Saturday afternoon **any good?**
❸ I just need **a quick trim.**
❹ Sorry, we're fully **booked on Thursday.**
❺ Can you come in **on Monday?**

41.7 🔊
❶ Can you fit me in on Monday?
❷ Can you fit me in on Tuesday afternoon?
❸ Can you fit me in on Wednesday morning?
❹ Can you fit me in on Thursday at 3 p.m.?
❺ Can you do Monday?
❻ Can you do Tuesday afternoon?
❼ Can you do Wednesday morning?
❽ Can you do Thursday at 3 p.m.?

41.11
Ⓐ 5 Ⓕ 7
Ⓑ 1 Ⓖ 2
Ⓒ 8 Ⓗ 6
Ⓓ 9 Ⓘ 3
Ⓔ 4

41.12 🔊
❶ I feel like a change, but I don't know what to **go for.**
❷ Just **my usual,** I think.
❸ I'll have some **gel** on it, please.
❹ What color would be **best** for me?
❺ Could you cut the bangs **a bit more?**
❻ I think a shorter style would really **suit you.**
❼ Leave it longer **on top,** please.

41.13 🔊
❶ What style would be best for me?
❷ What color would be best for me?
❸ What highlights would be best for me?
❹ What style would suit me?
❺ What color would suit me?
❻ What highlights would suit me?
❼ What style should I go for?
❽ What color should I go for?
❾ What highlights should I go for?

42

42.6
Ⓐ 3 Ⓓ 5
Ⓑ 1 Ⓔ 6
Ⓒ 2 Ⓕ 4

42.7 🔊
❶ How many would you **like?**
❷ Can you **put** it on the scale, please?
❸ How much does it **cost** to send this to Japan?
❹ I'm here to **pick up** a package.
❺ Can you **sign** for this, please?
❻ How soon will my package **arrive?**
❼ Can I **send** this letter to France?
❽ Sure. I've been **waiting** for it to arrive!

43

43.5
❶ A
❷ B
❸ A
❹ B

43.6 🔊
❶ I'd like to open a bank account, please.
❷ I'd like to withdraw $300 in cash, please.
❸ I'd like to open a savings account, please.
❹ I'd like to transfer money into my bank account, please.
❺ I'd like to deposit money into my savings account, please.

43.12 🔊
❶ You can transfer **your share later.**
❷ I've just ordered **our vacation money!**
❸ The ATM just **swallowed my card!**
❹ Should we split it **three ways?**
❺ Let me know **your bank details.**

44

44.5
Ⓐ 1 Ⓓ 2
Ⓑ 5 Ⓔ 3
Ⓒ 4 Ⓕ 6

44.6 🔊
❶ Do you run computer **courses** here?
❷ Do you have this as an **audiobook?**
❸ I need to renew these **books,** please.
❹ How do I join the **library?**
❺ Where is the children's **section?**
❻ Can I see your **newspaper** archive?

46

46.7
1. A
2. A
3. A
4. B

46.8 🔊
1. Is there a math club?
2. Is there a science club?
3. Is there a history club?
4. Is there an after-school club?
5. Is there an art club?

47

47.6
(A) 4 (D) 3
(B) 1 (E) 2
(C) 6 (F) 5

47.7 🔊
1. What are your entry **requirements**?
2. Sure, it's a two-year, **full-time** program.
3. I've just signed up for the French **class**.
4. The **teacher** is amazing!
5. The **website** also has lots of information.
6. What **qualifications** do I need?
7. Is there a chance to study **abroad**?
8. Students work once a week in a **salon**.

47.12
(A) 2 (D) 4
(B) 5 (E) 6
(C) 1 (F) 3

47.13 🔊
1. Do you know where the art school is?
2. Do you know where the humanities department is?
3. Do you know where the physics lecture is?
4. Do you know where the coffee shop is?
5. Can you tell me where the art school is?
6. Can you tell me where the humanities department is?
7. Can you tell me where the physics lecture is?
8. Can you tell me where the coffee shop is?
9. Any idea where the art school is?
10. Any idea where the humanities department is?
11. Any idea where the physics lecture is?
12. Any idea where the coffee shop is?

47.19
1. A
2. B
3. B
4. A

47.20 🔊
1. I'm finding it hard to **make friends**.
2. I'd **rather not**, actually.
3. Not **too bad**!
4. I'd be **up for that**!

47.21 🔊
1. How are you finding **your first week**?
2. I'm feeling **a bit homesick.**
3. I think I'll **pass.**
4. Sounds like **fun!**

48

48.5
(A) 2 (E) 6
(B) 4 (F) 1
(C) 3 (G) 7
(D) 5

48.6 🔊
1. Okay, let me get some **details** about you.
2. This **job** looks interesting ...
3. I'm looking for a **part-time** sales job.
4. What **hours** can you work?
5. Have you used this job search **website**?
6. Yes, could you email us your **resume**?
7. What **skills** do you have?
8. Is the job in the **window** still open?

49

49.5
1. A
2. B
3. B

49.6 🔊
1. I really want to apply for **this job.**
2. I just need to fill in **my personal details and it'll be ready.**
3. Don't forget to send **your cover letter, too!**
4. Have you finished **your application yet?**

50

50.5 🔊
1. I'm used to working under pressure.
2. I'm a quick learner.
3. I enjoy solving problems.
4. I'm really eager to use my planning skills.

50.6 🔊
1. What can you bring to our **company**?
2. What **salary** are you expecting?
3. What's the **notice** period in your current job?
4. How soon could you **start**?
5. I'm used to **working** under pressure.
6. I'm good with **customers**.

50.7 🔊
1. I have the experience you're looking for.
2. I have the skills you're looking for.
3. I have the qualifications you're looking for.
4. I have the enthusiasm you're looking for.
5. I have the strengths you're looking for.

51

51.7
(A) 3 (E) 2
(B) 1 (F) 4
(C) 5 (G) 6
(D) 7

51.8 🔊
1. Your first **break** is at 12:30.
2. And always wear your **hard hat**!
3. It's great to have you on the **team**.
4. I've set up your **email** account.
5. Want to grab some **lunch**?
6. How's your **morning** been?
7. Do you have **everything** you need?
8. Can you type in a **password**?

52

52.5
1 A
2 A
3 B
4 A

52.6 🔊
1 It's in half an hour. **How about** yours?
2 Not again! Okay, **let's call** the supervisor.
3 I'm **scheduled for** the morning shift.
4 Thanks. I'll **put it in** my calendar.

53

53.4
A 3   E 8
B 1   F 6
C 4   G 5
D 2   H 7

53.5 🔊
1 Now let's turn to **the subject of ...**
2 The focus of **my presentation is ...**
3 Last, **I'd like to finish by saying ...**
4 Does anyone have **anything to add?**
5 Now I'd like to **talk about ...**
6 First, **I'd like to begin by saying ...**

53.6 🔊
1 Today, I'd like to talk about ...
2 First, I'd like to talk about ...
3 Now I'd like to talk about ...
4 Last, I'd like to talk about ...
5 Finally, I'd like to talk about ...
6 Today, I'm going to talk about ...
7 First, I'm going to talk about ...
8 Now I'm going to talk about ...
9 Last, I'm going to talk about ...
10 Finally, I'm going to talk about ...

54

54.5 🔊
1 Can I jump in? **I totally agree.**
2 If I can just add ... **It will be a slow process.**
3 So that's the situation. **Let's hear your thoughts.**

4 Just to clarify ... **Which changes exactly?**
5 May I go first? **For me, these changes are important.**

54.7 🔊
1 Let's hear from James on this **point**.
2 I think we're all here, so let's get **started**.
3 If you **ask** me, it's a nonstarter.
4 I see where you're **coming** from, so ...
5 Can I **jump** in? I totally agree.
6 Just to **clarify** ... Which changes exactly?
7 Let's go around the table and see where we all **stand**.

54.11
A 5   E 7
B 4   F 2
C 1   G 6
D 8   H 3

54.12 🔊
1 You, too. Let's stay **in touch**.
2 That's right. Sorry, I didn't catch **your name**.
3 Me, too. Let's **follow up** in the office.

55

55.6
A 6   E 3
B 5   F 7
C 4   G 2
D 1

55.7 🔊
1 Sorry for interrupting, **please keep going.**
2 Should we schedule **another meeting?**
3 My connection **keeps dropping.**
4 Would you like to **speak first?**
5 Can you enlarge it **on your screen?**
6 Great! I'll run through **the key points**.

57

57.7 🔊
1 We'd need to **put in a new kitchen.**
2 I want a property **close to the subway.**
3 I really like **the layout.**
4 I think **it's too small for us.**

57.8 🔊
1 We'd like a house with a yard.
2 We'd like an apartment with a yard.
3 We'd like a property with a yard.
4 We'd like a house close to the subway.
5 We'd like an apartment close to the subway.
6 We'd like a property close to the subway.
7 We'd like a house near a school.
8 We'd like an apartment near a school.
9 We'd like a property near a school.

57.13
A 3   D 5
B 1   E 2
C 6   F 4

57.14 🔊
1 How much is the **rent**?
2 Are **utility bills** included?
3 Can I put this **picture** up?
4 The **washing machine** is leaking.
5 Are **pets** allowed?
6 As soon as you've signed the **rental agreement**!

57.15 🔊
1 Can I have a **roommate**?
2 One year, with an option to **renew**.
3 Are utility **bills** included?
4 Do you need a **deposit**?
5 Do I **pay** the rent monthly?
6 What **references** do you need?

58

58.5
A 1   D 5
B 3   E 6
C 4   F 2

58.6 🔊
1 Is everything packed and **ready**?
2 Hope **the move** goes well!
3 Do you have any spare **boxes**?
4 I've told everyone our **moving** date.
5 We have to move out by the **weekend**.
6 I've **packed** up the bedroom.
7 Let's **load** the moving van!
8 We can **unpack** in the morning.

58.7 🔊
1 Hope the move **goes well!**
2 Let's load **the moving van!**
3 Where do you want us **to start?**
4 I've packed up **the bedroom.**
5 I'm here to pick up **the keys to my house.**

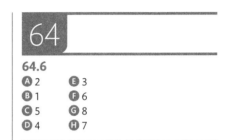

59.7
Ⓐ 3   Ⓔ 8
Ⓑ 4   Ⓕ 6
Ⓒ 1   Ⓖ 2
Ⓓ 7   Ⓗ 5

59.8 🔊
1 Are you free for drinks later?
2 Are you free for lunch later?
3 Are you free for coffee later?
4 Are you free for drinks tomorrow?
5 Are you free for lunch tomorrow?
6 Are you free for coffee tomorrow?
7 Are you free for drinks on Sunday?
8 Are you free for lunch on Sunday?
9 Are you free for coffee on Sunday?

60.5
1 A
2 B
3 B
4 A

60.6 🔊
1 Whose turn is it to empty **the dishwasher?**
2 I've cleaned the counters **and the oven.**
3 Great job! The kitchen **was in a bad state.**
4 Phew! That was **a major spring-clean!**

61.5
Ⓐ 7   Ⓕ 9
Ⓑ 6   Ⓖ 4
Ⓒ 1   Ⓗ 5
Ⓓ 3   Ⓘ 8
Ⓔ 2

61.6 🔊
1 Could you give us a quote for fixing our fence?
2 Could you give us a quote for hanging some shelves?
3 Could you give us a quote for laying a carpet?
4 Could you give us a quote for painting our kitchen walls?
5 Are you able to give us a quote for fixing our fence?
6 Are you able to give us a quote for hanging some shelves?
7 Are you able to give us a quote for laying a carpet?
8 Are you able to give us a quote for painting our kitchen walls?

62.7
Ⓐ 1   Ⓓ 5
Ⓑ 4   Ⓔ 3
Ⓒ 2   Ⓕ 6

62.8 🔊
1 Is she good **with children?**
2 I think he has **a broken leg.**
3 She's lost weight **and stopped eating.**
4 Hi, I'd like to **adopt a cat.**
5 We have to get him microchipped **and book his vaccinations!**

63.6
Ⓐ 4   Ⓔ 8
Ⓑ 5   Ⓕ 2
Ⓒ 7   Ⓖ 3
Ⓓ 1   Ⓗ 6

63.7 🔊
1 The power has **gone off.**
2 The power is **back on!**
3 The faucet has been **dripping** for days.
4 When was the furnace last **serviced?**

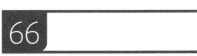

64.6
Ⓐ 2   Ⓔ 3
Ⓑ 1   Ⓕ 6
Ⓒ 5   Ⓖ 8
Ⓓ 4   Ⓗ 7

64.7 🔊
1 Should we play **the next level?**
2 Can you turn on **the subtitles?**
3 Is the console **plugged in?**
4 What should we **watch tonight?**

66.5 🔊
1 We're almost there—it's the next stop.
2 Yes, via the railway station.
3 Yes, they're right at the back.
4 Yup, just log on to our network.

66.6 🔊
1 Excuse me, does this bus go to the library?
2 Excuse me, are we nearly at the library?
3 Excuse me, is this the right stop for the library?
4 Excuse me, does this bus go to the town center?
5 Excuse me, are we nearly at the town center?
6 Excuse me, is this the right stop for the town center?
7 Excuse me, does this bus go to the shopping center?
8 Excuse me, are we nearly at the shopping center?
9 Excuse me, is this the right stop for the shopping center?

67.7
Ⓐ 6   Ⓓ 1
Ⓑ 4   Ⓔ 2
Ⓒ 3   Ⓕ 5

67.8 🔊
1. Can I reserve a **seat**?
2. What time is the next Nashville **service**?
3. There's a really long **line** for tickets!
4. Does this train **stop** at Birmingham?
5. Let's wait in the **waiting** area.
6. Hello. Can we **book** two round-trip tickets to Tampa, please?
7. Do I **tap** in at the turnstile?

67.13
Ⓐ 3
Ⓑ 1
Ⓒ 4
Ⓓ 5
Ⓔ 2

67.14 🔊
1. Excuse me, how do I get to Tampa?
2. Excuse me, how many stops is it to Tampa?
3. Excuse me, how much is a round-trip ticket to Tampa?
4. Excuse me, how much is a one-way ticket to Tampa?
5. Excuse me, how do I get to Atlanta?
6. Excuse me, how many stops is it to Atlanta?
7. Excuse me, how much is a round-trip ticket to Atlanta?
8. Excuse me, how much is a one-way ticket to Atlanta?

68

68.4 🔊
1. What **time** is boarding?
2. Can I change to a window **seat**?
3. What's the gate **number**?
4. How long is the **delay**?
5. Any chance I can **upgrade**?
6. What time does the **gate** close?
7. Place your bag in the **bin**, please!
8. Where is the **check-in** desk?

68.9
Ⓐ 6   Ⓓ 3
Ⓑ 1   Ⓔ 4
Ⓒ 5   Ⓕ 2

68.10
Ⓐ 3   Ⓓ 1
Ⓑ 4   Ⓔ 6
Ⓒ 5   Ⓕ 2

68.11 🔊
1. I'll put our stuff **in the overhead bin.**
2. Please switch your digital devices **to "airplane" mode.**
3. We'll shortly be passing through **the cabin with snacks and drinks.**
4. Your tray tables **should be securely fastened.**
5. Make sure your seat **is in the upright position.**

68.14
1. B
2. A
3. B
4. A

68.16 🔊
1. Where do we meet our **taxi**?
2. I can't see our **suitcases** anywhere!
3. It's carousel 3. I'll grab a **cart**.
4. Yes, I need to exchange some **Euros**.
5. I'm here to pick up a rental **car**.

69

69.6 🔊
1. For getting around town, mainly.
2. You just need to download the app!
3. There are bike docks all over town!
4. The brakes are loose.

69.7
Ⓐ 6   Ⓓ 1
Ⓑ 5   Ⓔ 4
Ⓒ 3   Ⓕ 2

69.8 🔊
1. What type of **bike** do you want?
2. The **battery** needs charging.
3. The front **tire** is flat.
4. Would you like a **test ride**?
5. I need a bike to get to and from **work**.
6. There are bike **docks** all over town!
7. You just need to download the **app**!
8. The **brakes** are loose.

70

70.5
Ⓐ 7   Ⓔ 6
Ⓑ 4   Ⓕ 3
Ⓒ 1   Ⓖ 2
Ⓓ 8   Ⓗ 5

70.6 🔊
1. Hello. Can I **book** a taxi from the airport?
2. How soon will the **cab** be here?
3. Can you **drop** me here, please?
4. I'm traveling with my service **dog**.
5. I left my laptop in one of your **taxis**.
6. Can you take me to this **address**?
7. How **long** will it take to get there?
8. Can I **pay** with contactless?

71

71.6
1. A
2. A
3. B
4. A

71.7 🔊
1. The windshield is **cracked.**
2. The steering wheel is **jammed.**
3. The tire keeps **going flat.**
4. The oil needs **to be changed.**

73

73.4
Ⓐ 2   Ⓓ 4
Ⓑ 3   Ⓔ 6
Ⓒ 1   Ⓕ 5

73.5 🔊
1. Do I need **a visa?**
2. Can I bring my **guide dog?**
3. Is it suitable **for young children?**
4. What's your **cancelation policy?**

73.6 🔊
1 Is this cruise all-inclusive?
2 Is this beach vacation all-inclusive?
3 Is this city break all-inclusive?
4 Is this safari all-inclusive?
5 Is this cruise adults only?
6 Is this beach vacation adults only?
7 Is this city break adults only?
8 Is this safari adults only?
9 Is this cruise suitable for young children?
10 Is this beach vacation suitable for young children?
11 Is this city break suitable for young children?
12 Is this safari suitable for young children?

74

74.4
1 A
2 A
3 A
4 B
5 A
6 B

74.10
A 4   D 2
B 1   E 5
C 6   F 3

74.11 🔊
1 I'd like **a 7 a.m. wake-up call.**
2 The room **is too hot.**
3 The shower **is leaking.**
4 The Wi-Fi password **is wrong.**
5 I'd like a hair dryer **brought to my room.**

74.12 🔊
1 Could I have a hair dryer sent up, please?
2 Could I have some fresh towels sent up, please?
3 Could I have a club sandwich sent up, please?
4 Could I have two extra pillows sent up, please?
5 Could I have a hair dryer brought to my room, please?
6 Could I have some fresh towels brought to my room, please?

7 Could I have a club sandwich brought to my room, please?
8 Could I have two extra pillows brought to my room, please?

74.16 🔊
1 Did you enjoy **your stay?**
2 Yes, and help yourselves **to the buffet.**
3 Here's your bill **if you'd like to check it.**
4 Is it possible to **stay an extra night?**
5 Can I get **your room number?**

74.17 🔊
1 Could I have some more **coffee?**
2 Are you paying by **card?**
3 Could you call me a **cab,** please?
4 The **bed** was a little hard.
5 Can I leave my **luggage** here?

74.18 🔊
1 Can I see your **passport,** please?
2 What time is **checkout?**
3 We'd like a room with **queen beds,** please.
4 The **room** was a bit noisy.
5 Dinner was **delicious.**
6 Do you have a **king** bed available?
7 The **restaurant** serves dinner until 10 p.m.
8 Your room is on the second **floor.**

75

75.5
1 B
2 B
3 A
4 A

75.7 🔊
1 Want to get off **at the next stop?**
2 Quick! **Take a picture!**
3 Is there **wheelchair access?**
4 What are **your opening times?**
5 How much is **the entrance fee?**

76

76.5
A 3   E 6
B 1   F 5
C 2   G 4
D 7   H 8

76.6 🔊
1 Can we pitch our tent over in that field?
2 Can we set up camp over in that field?
3 Can we park our camper over in that field?
4 Can we pitch our tent near the shower block?
5 Can we set up camp near the shower block?
6 Can we park our camper near the shower block?
7 Can we pitch our tent across from the trailers?
8 Can we set up camp across from the trailers?
9 Can we park our camper across from the trailers?

77

77.4
A 5   E 1
B 8   F 2
C 7   G 6
D 4   H 3

77.5 🔊
1 Can we hire a **paddleboard** here?
2 How much is a **sun lounger** for the day?
3 Where can we buy a **beach ball?**
4 Can we hire a **paddleboat** for the day?
5 Do you do **surfing** lessons?

77.6 🔊
1 Can we hire **a paddleboat here?**
2 Is it safe **to swim today?**
3 Yes, but you must **stay between the flags.**
4 Do you do **surfing lessons?**

78.4
Ⓐ 4 Ⓓ 2
Ⓑ 1 Ⓔ 3
Ⓒ 6 Ⓕ 5

78.5 ◀))
❶ Excuse me, do you know **the way** to the bus station?
❷ Can you tell me how to **get to** the museum?
❸ Yes, **go straight** ahead and it's on your left.
❹ Take the **first right** after the library.
❺ No, you need to **go past** the church ...
❻ ... then **cross** the road ...
❼ It's just **next to** the hospital.

78.6 ◀))
❶ Excuse me, do you know the way to the church?
❷ Excuse me, can you tell me how to get to the church?
❸ Excuse me, do you know the way to the museum?
❹ Excuse me, can you tell me how to get to the museum?
❺ Excuse me, do you know the way to the bus station?
❻ Excuse me, can you tell me how to get to the bus station?
❼ Excuse me, do you know the way to the bank?
❽ Excuse me, can you tell me how to get to the bank?

79.6
Ⓐ 2 Ⓕ 8
Ⓑ 5 Ⓖ 3
Ⓒ 1 Ⓗ 7
Ⓓ 6 Ⓘ 4
Ⓔ 9

79.7 ◀))
❶ The train is canceled **due to lack of available train crew.**
❷ Yeah, I won't make the beach. **I have a stomach bug!**
❸ Look at the board. **Our train has been canceled!**
❹ Your insurance should cover you **if you get a doctor's note.**

81.4
Ⓐ 6 Ⓓ 3
Ⓑ 2 Ⓔ 4
Ⓒ 1 Ⓕ 5

81.6 ◀))
❶ I have a really sore throat.
❷ I have a really bad headache.
❸ I have a really itchy rash.
❹ I have a really sore ear.
❺ I have a really itchy eye.

81.10 ◀))
❶ Yes, I'm taking antibiotics.
❷ How often should I take it?
❸ For about a week.
❹ Yes, I also have a runny nose.
❺ Hmm ... it looks like an allergy.

81.11
Ⓐ 8 Ⓕ 9
Ⓑ 5 Ⓖ 6
Ⓒ 1 Ⓗ 2
Ⓓ 7 Ⓘ 4
Ⓔ 3

81.12 ◀))
❶ I have a really sore **eye.**
❷ I also have a runny **nose.**
❸ My **hand** really hurts.
❹ I have an itchy rash on my **foot.**
❺ My **ear** is killing me.

82.6 ◀))
❶ I need to see the primary care **nurse.**
❷ Hi there, I'd like to book an appointment with **Doctor** Cole.
❸ Can I **reschedule** my appointment?
❹ Can I book an **appointment** for my daughter?
❺ Do you have **anything** sooner?
❻ When's the next **available** slot?
❼ If you need an urgent appointment, we'll place you on the **triage** list ...
❽ I think I might have an **eye** infection.

82.7 ◀))
❶ I'd like to book an appointment with the doctor.
❷ I'd like to reschedule an appointment with the doctor.
❸ I'd like to book a checkup with the doctor.
❹ I'd like to cancel an appointment with the doctor.
❺ I'd like to book an appointment with the dentist.
❻ I'd like to reschedule an appointment with the dentist.
❼ I'd like to book a checkup with the dentist.
❽ I'd like to cancel an appointment with the dentist.
❾ I'd like to book an appointment for my daughter.
❿ I'd like to reschedule an appointment for my daughter.
⓫ I'd like to book a checkup for my daughter.
⓬ I'd like to cancel an appointment for my daughter.

83.7
Ⓐ 3 Ⓔ 4
Ⓑ 1 Ⓕ 7
Ⓒ 8 Ⓖ 6
Ⓓ 5 Ⓗ 2

83.8 ◀))
① I've had a bad cough for a week **and it's getting worse.**
② I've been **vomiting all night.**
③ I'm due for **a checkup.**
④ I've been under **the weather.**

84

84.5 ◀))
① I need a **doctor immediately.**
② I burned my hand on the **stove. It's really painful.**
③ I'll grab **some tissues.**
④ My husband has **severe chest pains.**
⑤ He's having **a seizure.**

84.6
① B
② A
③ A
④ B

84.7 ◀))
① It looks like she may need **stitches.**
② Hold this cold pack over the **swelling.**
③ My husband has severe chest **pains.**
④ That's a nasty **scrape.**

85

85.3
Ⓐ 4
Ⓑ 3
Ⓒ 5
Ⓓ 2
Ⓔ 1

85.4 ◀))
① I need to see someone as soon as **possible.**
② We have a **medical** emergency.
③ How soon will I be seen by a **doctor?**
④ I have a **checkup** with the nurse at 4:30.
⑤ Do I need to have **surgery?**
⑥ I'm going to need to **examine** you.

85.10
Ⓐ 7   Ⓔ 2
Ⓑ 8   Ⓕ 3
Ⓒ 6   Ⓖ 1
Ⓓ 4   Ⓗ 5

85.11 ◀))
① I'll just take your blood **pressure** first.
② Still a bit **groggy.**
③ Don't worry. We'll have you up and **about** in no time.
④ I'll just check your **temperature** and pulse …
⑤ You may feel lightheaded as the **anesthetic** takes effect.
⑥ How long will I be **under** for?
⑦ Now count **backward** from 5 …
⑧ There were no **complications.**

86

86.6
Ⓐ 1   Ⓓ 2
Ⓑ 6   Ⓔ 3
Ⓒ 4   Ⓕ 5

86.7
Ⓐ 6   Ⓕ 10
Ⓑ 2   Ⓖ 9
Ⓒ 1   Ⓗ 4
Ⓓ 7   Ⓘ 3
Ⓔ 8   Ⓙ 5

86.8 ◀))
① I brush my teeth **twice a day.**
② I need to see **the hygienist.**
③ I think my crown **has come loose.**
④ Can I have **my teeth whitened?**
⑤ My son's first teeth **are coming through.**

87

87.7 ◀))
① I've been feeling a bit low this week.
② I've been feeling very low this week.
③ I've been feeling really low this week.
④ I've been feeling a bit anxious this week.
⑤ I've been feeling very anxious this week.
⑥ I've been feeling really anxious this week.
⑦ I've been feeling a bit depressed this week.
⑧ I've been feeling very depressed this week.
⑨ I've been feeling really depressed this week.
⑩ I've been feeling a bit up and down this week.
⑪ I've been feeling very up and down this week.
⑫ I've been feeling really up and down this week.

87.8 ◀))
① How is this **affecting** you?
② These sessions are really **helping** me.
③ I'm finding it hard to **cope.**
④ Your feelings are **valid.**
⑤ How did that make you **feel?**
⑥ That's a real **trigger** for me.
⑦ Can we **explore** this more?
⑧ I'm doing **better** this week.

89

89.8
Ⓐ 4   Ⓔ 7
Ⓑ 1   Ⓕ 6
Ⓒ 8   Ⓖ 5
Ⓓ 3   Ⓗ 2

89.9 ◀))
① We'll need to check our system **and get back to you.**
② Is there anything else **I can help you with?**
③ He knows where **to reach me.**
④ Hello, I wonder **if you can help me …**
⑤ Thank you so much **for calling.**

90

90.7 ◀))
① Sorry, I can't **talk** now.
② I can't remember my **PIN.**
③ I'll **message** you back.
④ I'll put you on **speaker.**
⑤ My phone has **died.**
⑥ I've been **locked** out.
⑦ My **screen** has frozen.

90.8 🔊
1 Hello? You're **breaking** up—the signal is terrible.
2 Sounds perfect. **See** you then!
3 Good, thank you. I'm just **checking** in about tonight.
4 Okay. We can **fix** it for you.

91

91.5
A 5   D 1
B 2   E 4
C 6   F 3

91.6 🔊
1 Choose "free Wi-Fi" from the **menu**, then you can register.
2 Go to "settings," then tap "**security**".
3 You can join my **hot spot** if you like.
4 Yeah, that URL seems dicey. Let's try another **site**.

91.11
A 6   D 3
B 1   E 2
C 4   F 5

91.12 🔊
1 I'm **booking** a doctor's appointment.
2 I need to **check** my emails …
3 I have a **webinar** this afternoon.
4 I'm **streaming** a new series.
5 … and sign up for that **online** training course.
6 I'm **ordering** more cat food.
7 I'm **scrolling** through my socials.
8 I'm just **tracking** the grocery delivery.

91.13 🔊
1 I'm downloading **our tickets for today.**
2 I'll share yours with you **on our group chat.**
3 I'm setting up an online account **for our energy bills.**
4 I'm just uploading my essay … **then I have a webinar this afternoon.**

92

92.5
A 6   D 3
B 5   E 4
C 2   F 1

92.6 🔊
1 It's asking me to set up **authentication on my account.**
2 I'm trying to get tickets, **but the website keeps crashing.**
3 My screen has **completely frozen.**
4 You could try **restarting the computer …**
5 … or you could connect **from a different device.**

93

93.6
1 A
2 A
3 B
4 B
5 A
6 B

93.7 🔊
1 Check your **trash**. Maybe it's still there.
2 Okay, let's have a look at your **filters**.
3 Yeah, I'll **forward** you her message.
4 It looks suspicious—I wouldn't **download** it.

94

94.6
A 7   F 8
B 1   G 6
C 5   H 2
D 3   I 4
E 9

94.7 🔊
1 I'm just **clicking** on it now.
2 **IDK**, will have to see how I feel TBH
3 I can, sweetheart! Can you **see** me?
4 I know, right? **LOL**

95

95.6 🔊
1 I saw! I think you've broken the Internet.
2 Or how about a monthly podcast?
3 Not him! Just block him.

95.7 🔊
1 Or how about a monthly **podcast**?
2 That's just a **troll**. I'm blocking them.
3 I saw! I think you've broken the **Internet**.
4 There are tons of **comments** on my post!
5 They're all up on my **profile**.
6 More video **content** would help.

96

96.5
A 7   E 6
B 2   F 4
C 5   G 3
D 1

96.6 🔊
1 Can you recommend **a good vacation read?**
2 It's the best book **I've read in ages.**
3 Yeah, it had me on **the edge of my seat!**
4 I found it pretty **rough going, actually.**
5 Want a flip through *Fashion Monthly*?

Índice

Los temas principales se indican en **negrita**.

Agradecimientos

Los editores quieren dar las gracias a las siguientes personas:
Sophie Adam y Elizabeth Blakemore por su asistencia editorial; Amy Child, Mark Lloyd y
Collette Sadler por su asistencia en diseño; Jane Ewart por el apoyo a la gestión del proyecto;
Sonia Charbonnier por las fuentes tipográficas; Oliver Drake por la corrección de los textos
ingleses; Elizabeth Wise por el índice; Christine Stroyan por la gestión de las grabaciones de
audio, e ID Audio por la grabación y la producción del audio.

Todas las imágenes son copyright de DK.
Para información adicional, por favor visita **www.dkimages.com**.